Pilgrimage of Love

AMERICAN ACADEMY OF RELIGION

REFLECTION AND THEORY IN THE STUDY OF RELIGION SERIES

SERIES EDITOR
James Wetzel, Colgate University

A Publication Series of
The American Academy of Religion
and
Oxford University Press

NEWMAN AND GADAMER
Toward a Hermeneutics of Religious Knowledge
Thomas K. Carr

GOD, PHILOSOPHY AND ACADEMIC CULTURE
A Discussion between Scholars in the AAR and APA
Edited by William J. Wainwright

LIVING WORDS
Studies in Dialogues about Religion
Terence J. Martin

LIKE AND UNLIKE GOD
Religious Imaginations in Modern and Contemporary Fiction
John Neary

BEYOND THE NECESSARY GOD
Trinitarian Faith and Philosophy in the Thought of Eberhard Jüngel
Paul DeHart

LESSING'S PHILOSOPHY OF RELIGION AND THE GERMAN ENLIGHTENMENT
Toshimasa Yasukata

AMERICAN PRAGMATISM
A Religious Genealogy
M. Gail Hamner

OPTING FOR THE MARGINS
Postmodernity and Liberation in Christian Theology
Edited by Joerg Rieger

MAKING MAGIC
Religion, Magic, and Science in the Modern World
Randall Styers

THE METAPHYSICS OF DANTE'S *COMEDY*
Christian Moevs

PILGRIMAGE OF LOVE
Moltmann on the Trinity and Christian Life
Joy Ann McDougall

Pilgrimage of Love

Moltmann on the Trinity and Christian Life

JOY ANN McDOUGALL

OXFORD
UNIVERSITY PRESS

2005

OXFORD

UNIVERSITY PRESS

Oxford University Press, Inc., publishes works that further
Oxford University's objective of excellence
in research, scholarship, and education.

Oxford New York
Auckland Cape Town Dar es Salaam Hong Kong Karachi
Kuala Lumpur Madrid Melbourne Mexico City Nairobi
New Delhi Shanghai Taipei Toronto

With offices in
Argentina Austria Brazil Chile Czech Republic France Greece
Guatemala Hungary Italy Japan Poland Portugal Singapore
South Korea Switzerland Thailand Turkey Ukraine Vietnam

Published by Oxford University Press, Inc.
198 Madison Avenue, New York, New York 10016

www.oup.com

Oxford is a registered trademark of Oxford University Press

Library of Congress Cataloging-in-Publication Data
McDougall, Joy Ann.
Pilgrimage of Love : Moltmann on the Trinity and Christian Life /
Joy Ann McDougall.
    p. cm.—(Reflection and theory in the study of religion)
Includes bibliographical references and index.
ISBN-13 978-0-19-517705-3

1. Moltmann, Jürgen. 2. Trinity—History of doctrines—20th century. 3. Christian
life. 4. Theology, Doctrinal—History—20th century. I. Title. II. Series.
BT111.3.M33 2005
231'.044'092—dc22   2004021552

Printed in the United States of America
on acid-free paper

*For my parents, Seena and John McDougall,
and in memory of Hans W. Frei*

Preface

This book began as a dissertation that was completed several years ago at the Divinity School of the University of Chicago. Since that time this project has seen several new additions and been through significant reconstruction. Throughout this arduous process I owe my heartfelt thanks to those colleagues, friends, and family who have accompanied me along the way.

Let me express my deep appreciation first to Bernard McGinn and David Tracy for their collaborative directorship of my dissertation and their ecumenical spirit in reaching across the confessional and the historical boundaries of their disciplines to support my research in contemporary Protestant theology. I owe a special word of gratitude to Bernie for nominating this project to the American Academy of Religion Series at Oxford University Press and for his unfailing support during the revision of the original manuscript. Here, too, my thanks go to Kim Connor and Jim Wetzel, the editors of the AAR series, for their enthusiastic recommendation of this project for the Reflection and Theory in the Study of Religion Series, and to my editor Cynthia Read at Oxford University Press for her careful shepherding of a first-time author through the twists and turns of the publishing process. Special thanks go as well to my research assistant, Gina Weiser, not only for her meticulous copyediting of the final manuscript but also for her artistry in refining its prose.

I owe much gratitude to Jürgen Moltmann for inspiring this project during his unforgettable final teaching semester in Tübingen in 1992, and then for supporting my research during the academic year of 1994–95, a year that was made possible through a dissertation grant from the Deutscher Akademischer Austauschdienst. Jürgen's critical reading of my work over the past few years has no doubt improved its quality. Moreover, his repeated encouragement not to follow his theology but rather to critically engage and openly disagree with it has rung in my ears throughout the revision process. I thank him for inviting me into the open fellowship of the Spirit about which he passionately writes.

With any pilgrimage in life, one discovers only at its end the many persons who have helped you find your way. So was the case with this project. Gazing back, I owe a personal thank you to David Kelsey, who first sparked my interest in the doctrine of the Trinity and in Moltmann's theology at Yale Divinity School many years ago. As my intellectual pilgrimage took me elsewhere— first to the University of Chicago and then to the Candler School of Theology at Emory University—others readily stepped in along the way. Here I wish to thank most especially Kathryn Tanner for her selfless support of my work. For many years now, Kathryn's critical precision, her no-nonsense work ethic, and her gentle spirit have taught me what the vocation of the theologian and sisterhood in Christ are all about. I owe her more than she knows. So, too, my thanks go to my colleague Mark Jordan, who helped me through several fits and starts to take the slab of stone that this dissertation once was and to carve it into a sculpture with my own "voice" finally etched in it. A long list of friends and colleagues also encouraged this project through spirited theological conversations, careful readings of its chapters, and personal support. In particular, many thanks to Sigrid Brandt, Amy Carr, Rebecca Chopp, Hilda Koster, Armin Kutscher, Mark McIntosh, Joanne McGuire, Jan Pranger, Don Saliers, and Bruce and Ruth Woll. Finally, I give thanks to Arnfridur Gudmundsdottir for her feminist sisterhood as we each set forth on our own theological pilgrimage in Chicago. Thank you, Addy, for always being there as my family, especially when you too found yourself a long way from your home.

This work is dedicated to my parents, Seena and John McDougall, whose manifold expressions of love over the years have made my theological work possible. Among so many other gifts, they gave me the freedom to pursue my own path wherever it might lead me. This book is also dedicated to the memory of my first theological teacher, Hans W. Frei, who trusted in my vocation years before I could believe in it myself. Although there is much in this present work that I suspect he would disagree with, I know that his hermeneutical sensibilities, his distrust of system-building, and his passion for theological truth infuse this work.

Last but not least, my thanks go to my husband, Steffen Lösel, for accompanying this book's pilgrimage from the beginning to its end. As our shared love for theology took us from place to place, he knows better than anyone the personal costs of pursuing a common academic vocation. For taking the risk to venture with me into this far country, I give thanks. For his im/patience, his wit, and his wisdom, I give thanks. In our life together he embodies the true love about which this work speaks.

Contents

Foreword by Jürgen Moltmann, xi

1. Introduction: The Return of the Trinitarian God of Love, 3

2. The Dialectic of Crucified and Creative Love in Moltmann's Early Theology, 29

3. The Relational Ontology of Love in the *Messianic Theology,* 59

4. A Social Trinitarian Theology of the Human Person, 101

5. The Human Pilgrimage in the Messianic Life of Faith, 121

6. Conclusion: Toward a Contemporary Trinitarian Theology of Love, 153

   Notes, 165

   Bibliography, 193

   Index, 201

Foreword

I read this work on the development of my doctrine of the Trinity with great pleasure and growing interest. Joy Ann McDougall's knowledgeable perspective helped me to recognize, as it were from the outside, those paths, right or wrong, which my thoughts have traveled from the theology of *The Crucified God* in 1972 to the doctrine of the Trinity in 1980. There is a Latin adage: "Etiam libelli habent sua fata." How much more do ideas have their own destiny! It is exciting to see, how they continue to work in other minds, in other contexts, and in other times. I consider it to be a wonderful gift that ideas that once influenced me now come back to me in such a wise and empathetic manner in this book. Here I do not rethink the misunderstandings or controversies that I once occasioned. Rather, I can simply delight in the author's independent "thinking with" and "thinking beyond" my own work.

At the same time it is difficult to write this foreword. Not because I find it difficult to praise this study and to recommend it wholeheartedly to all who want to participate in the contemporary theological discussion on the new trinitarian thinking. On the contrary: I could not name anything better right now! No, what is difficult is to restrict myself to writing simply a foreword, rather than entering into a comprehensive discussion of the author's critical concerns, and her projected creative projects of further work. I will try, however, not to let this foreword get out of hand and turn into a reply. It shall remain an inviting foreword, which does not tempt the author to an epilogue.

The first thing we owe to this work is that it demonstrates my

path from the theology of the cross in *The Crucified God* of 1972 to the doctrine
of the Trinity in *The Trinity and the Kingdom of God* in 1980. Theologically
speaking this period was the most interesting for me. When I wrote the theology of the cross, I wanted to express something that had been stirring within
me for a long time: How can one speak about God in Germany "after Auschwitz"? I discovered my own answer in the question: How can Christians speak
about God after Golgotha? I did not in any way know where this new beginning
after the *Theology of Hope* in 1964 would lead me. When I wrote the doctrine
of the Trinity in 1980, however, I had the five volumes of the *Messianic Theology*
already in view, even if not yet fully in my mind. Joy Ann McDougall points
out correctly how the reversal of the soteriological question into the theological
question signified the first step into the trinitarian mystery of God: What does
Christ's death on the cross mean not only for the salvation of the godforsaken
world, but first of all for the very self of God? Is God indifferent vis-à-vis the
death of the Son of God, or does the God, whom Jesus called "Abba, dear
Father," suffer the death of the beloved child? At the time it prompted a ve-
hement debate over the fact that I rejected the philosophical and theological
axiom of the impassibility of God, and replaced it with the passion of God in
the twofold sense of the word.

The second point this work correctly emphasizes is the social doctrine of
the Trinity, which I introduced into the new trinitarian debate in 1980. Everything that we think and say enters into conversation, and, often enough, into
controversy with others. Our contributions are always one-sided in order to
correct other one-sided perspectives. You can see this easily when you isolate
such one-sided positions from their context. For my part, I found it necessary
to correct the one-sidedness of the Western modalism that was represented in
the doctrine of the Trinity from Augustine to Schleiermacher, and, in my own
time, in the doctrines of Karl Barth and Karl Rahner. For this reason, I posited
a social doctrine of the Trinity, as it had been set forth by Orthodox theology
in the East over and against a psychological doctrine of the Trinity, which saw
in the mental triad of the individual subject, the understanding, and the will
an image of Father, Son, and Spirit. While my opponents derived the "threefold
identity" of God from the unity of God, I went from the threeness of the
persons to the "threefold unity" of God, by understanding the unity as a perichoretic "community." In my view, the oft repeated charge of "tritheism" derives from Islam and is directed against the Christian faith as such. Within
trinitarian thinking, however, it makes no sense. If one wishes to overcome
both the one-sidedness of the psychological and the social doctrines of the
Trinity, one needs to combine both ways dialectically: from threeness to unity
and from unity to threeness. Such a dialectical combination in the doctrine of
the Trinity may sound somewhat speculative, but it has significant consequences for the theological anthropology of the *imago trinitatis*. In this way not
only the social character but also the self-relatedness of the human person is

emphasized. This is the path that McDougall chooses, and I am happy to follow her on it.

Last but not least, McDougall demonstrates that through the recovery of pneumatology in *The Spirit of Life* in 1991 the expanse of the Trinity widened once more for me. While the Western tradition treated the Holy Spirit as the bond of love (*vinculum amoris*) between Father and Son, and thus as a neutral power and not as a divine person, the independent personhood of the Spirit within the Trinity and in Christian life became significant to me. After the Western Church rescinded the *filioque* clause in the Nicene Creed, the Holy Spirit no longer needs to be relegated to the third place. McDougall identifies a "red thread" that runs through my publications, namely, the understanding of love in the Trinity and in every person's life of faith that is guided by God the Holy Spirit. Out of the concept of dialectical love she develops the concept of creative and God-corresponding love in order to develop a "trinitarian theology of love." Up to now I had not seen this "red thread" in my own thinking. However, I now see this in a new way, and I welcome it.

I want to respond to two critical observations, which I have heard already from other sides. The first refers to my style, my methodology, and my hermeneutic. I am not betraying any secrets, when I admit that, before writing each book, each chapter, and each presentation I construct a graphic diagram of the concepts, the lines of thought, the connections, and the equivalents, in order to gain clarity. As the old saying goes: "Think first, then speak." Once I have a clear schema, I gladly give myself over to the passion of presentation, in order to write in an inviting and stimulating fashion. I like to use poetic expressions instead of logical deductions, because I am not only writing for academic colleagues and doctoral students, but for all interested readers, theologians or not. For this reason I avoid forcing readers into logical or even ideological agreement. Rather, I appeal to their imaginations and their independent spirits. This has resulted in various criticisms from academic colleagues, who, in their search for my method, have failed to recognize its underlying scheme. By and large, however, this has made my books accessible for a wider audience. I attempted to give an account of this "hermeneutic of hope" in my book, *Experiences of Theological Thinking: Paths and Forms of Christian Theology*, chapter 2.

A second criticism is that many miss in my books concrete ethical suggestions and directions for the life of faith. This criticism is misplaced in two respects: (1) For whom and where shall I become "concrete?" For those who believe and act in America or in Korea, in Africa or in Europe? The situations are so different that local Christians would experience suggestions and directions from a German professor as patronizing, and would be forced to reject them. Instead I have tried to speak so as to stimulate the readers to imagine what is necessary in their situation. This goal is reflected productively in many dissertations in Africa, Indonesia, and Korea. (2) In my own ecclesial and political situation in Germany, I have commented quite often and concretely on many questions of everyday life, especially because I have not found many ethicists who have arrived at concrete decisions. Whoever leafs through the comprehensive *Research Bibliography* by James Wakefield will find a large number of such "concrete" statements, beginning with a Theological Declaration on Human Rights, to comments on the right to work, the right to resistance, the social function of ownership, nuclear disarmament, the debate on abortion, and questions on medical ethics and so forth. I have discussed at length the social disabling of "disabled" persons and called upon the churches to give them room to live in our congregations. I have discussed the evils of racism, sexism, and capitalism, and have contributed in my 1975 book, *The Church in the Power of the Spirit*, to the German church-reform-movement of those years. Indeed, I did not write a theological ethic, because I wanted to be concrete, rather than ascending to those metalevels at which most ethical proposals are located. Whatever is concrete has a specific location, a specific time, and is directed toward a specific community. Such proposals cannot be presented on a metalevel of ethical reflection.

In her conclusion, McDougall calls for a "robust doctrine of sin." I find that very courageous and hope that she will succeed. When I searched for a "theology after Auschwitz" in 1972, I followed the path of Christ's passion and his descent into hell into such depths of evil that the concepts of sin, guilt, and godlessness were struck out of my hands. Auschwitz and the death-camps of Treblinka and Maidanek: you do not understand such experiences with God, and you do not understand without God, as Elie Wiesel once said. One does not even want to understand it, because one does not want to offer any explanation. Is it sin? Is it blasphemy? Can we grasp this reality with moral and traditional theological concepts? I do not know. We will have to learn from those who have suffered it. The will to total destruction might well be the depths of evil, because it wants to plunge creation and God into nothingness. Faced with the destructive nothingness, trinitarian God-talk needs to turn once more into a theology of the cross, which itself leads into a world of resurrection. I do not want to anticipate the author, however, but rather only hint at why such a robust doctrine of sin was not possible for me thus far. Furthermore, my personal remarks shall indicate how stimulating and exciting it has been and will remain for me to read this book. I pass it on with great thankfulness. It will make its own way.

Tübingen, the first of August, 2004   Jürgen Moltmann

Pilgrimage of Love

I

Introduction

The Return of the Trinitarian God of Love

Thus it is that in this question we are occupied with about the trinity and about knowing God, the only thing we really have to see is what true love is; well in fact, simply what *love* is.
—Augustine, *De Trinitate*, 8.5.10

What constitutes the distinctively Christian understanding of God? If we take the scriptures and ecumenical creeds as a reliable witness of the consensus reached among the earliest Christian communities, this question might appear to be easily answered: "God is love" and "God is Trinity." Indeed, in the early church these two truths of the Christian faith were intrinsic to one another. The doctrine of the Trinity symbolized the divine economy of love—the history of God's creative, redeeming, and sanctifying presence as the Father, the Son, and the Holy Spirit. It provided believers with what Nicholas Lash calls the "'summary grammar'" for their profession of faith in the God who is love.[1]

Today the contemporary Christian might well become perplexed by the idea that the doctrine of the Trinity holds the key to divine love. While Christian communities regularly invoke the doctrine in their creeds and in liturgical practices such as baptism and doxologies, for many believers the meaning of the Trinity appears remote from their experiences of God's redeeming and sanctifying love. In 1943 Anglican theologian Leonard Hodgson first drew attention to this widening breach between trinitarian doctrine and the everyday practices of the Christian faith. "How many laymen," he challenged, "would not rather regard it as an unintelligible metaphysical doctrine which orthodoxy requires them to profess, but which has no direct relevance to their life or their prayers?"[2] A generation later Karl Rahner confirmed Hodgson's suspicions when he commented wryly on the widespread apathy of contemporary believers toward the doctrine: "Despite their orthodox confession of the Trinity, Christians are, in their practical life, almost mere 'monotheists.' . . . should the doctrine of the Trinity have to be dropped as false, the major part of religious literature could well remain virtually unchanged."[3]

Until quite recently the eclipse of the Trinity in popular piety was well matched by its displacement in academic theology.[4] Systematic theologians, whose province has been the conceptual clarification of trinitarian belief, had come to regard the doctrine as abstruse and impractical speculation, lacking in sufficient philosophical and biblical warrants in support of a modern defense. Although many theologians continue to rehearse doctrinal formulas about the Trinity, their operative concept of God is often a thinly disguised modalism or christomonism. They either translate trinitarian belief into a threefold pattern of human experiences of the one God or reduce it to a focus on Jesus Christ as the definitive self-revelation of God; in neither case do theologians venture further to explore the relationships that obtain among Father, Son, and Holy Spirit.[5]

Having lost its secure moorings within the doctrine of God, the Trinity has simultaneously drifted to the margins of theological discussions over divine love. Many contemporary theologians explicate the Christian belief in a God who is love without reference to the trinitarian symbol of faith. They interpret the divine attribute of love *theistically*—as a personal relation, an attitude, or an act that can be predicated of the one God.[6] Let us look briefly at two illustrations of such theistic approaches to divine love.

In his recent book *The Model of Love: A Study of Philosophical Theology*, Dutch Reformed theologian Vincent Brümmer investigates the nature of divine love as the key to God's relationship to humankind and its various implications for the Christian concept of God.[7] Although Brümmer contends that his model of love is in close dialogue with both the Christian scriptures and tradition, the doctrine of the Trinity receives only passing historical reference in his work.[8] Even more curiously, Brümmer distinguishes his model of love from the Western tradition's "attitudinal" model on the grounds that his purports to be a truly personal and "relational" model. In staking his claim, however, Brümmer disregards the fact that the doctrine of the Trinity had been the original locus in Christian theology for predicating such personal and relational attributes of God.[9]

Sallie McFague's highly influential book *Models of God: Theology for an Ecological, Nuclear Age* offers another instructive example of a nontrinitarian approach to divine love.[10] Although McFague moves a step closer than Brümmer to formulating a trinitarian doctrine, her threefold "model" of divine love as "mother" (*agape*), "lover" (*eros*), and "friend" (*philia*) is only nominally trinitarian. Her doctrine of God is more adequately described as neo-modalist, since her three metaphors represent the threefold transcendent and yet immanent relationship of the one God who is love to the world. For that matter, McFague does not stake any ontological claims about the trinitarian essence of divine love itself.[11] She argues for a purely "functional" trinitarianism on the pragmatic grounds that her trinity of metaphors (chosen from among the many names of God) will help unseat the ethically dubious, reigning metaphors of Father, Son, and Spirit.[12] In the end there is nothing absolutely necessary about these three being one.

McFague's and Brümmer's models of divine love illustrate well a phenomenon that has become common among many contemporary theologies: the divorce of their account of the attributes of God from the doctrine of the Trinity, the particular historical self-revelation of God as Father, Son, and Spirit. Although both authors claim a fully relational model of divine love, they situate this relationality between God and humankind and reject that it has any ontological basis in the trinitarian relations of the Godhead. As a result, the symbol of the Trinity becomes superfluous to their constructive theological proposals about the nature and relationship between divine and human loves.

Jürgen Moltmann and the Contemporary Revival of Trinitarian Theology

During the past thirty years the tide that I have sketched here appears to be turning, as a dramatic explosion of interest in the doctrine of the Trinity has appeared on the theological horizon. This renaissance of trinitarian theology has rapidly crossed confessional and continental borders and sparked new ecumenical debates among the European, North American, and once-called third-world contexts. Theologians across the spectrum—from postliberal narrativists and process thinkers to feminists and other liberationists—have all claimed a stake in this new trinitarian debate, framing widely divergent theological programs in terms of either a retrieval or a reconstruction of the classical trinitarian heritage.[13]

Spurring on this trinitarian revival is a growing disenchantment with the Christian doctrine of God to which "modern theism" gave birth.[14] Trinitarian theologians today are challenging the widely accepted Enlightenment verdict that the Trinity is a *speculative* truth that is beyond the pale of religious experience, and that, as such, the doctrine represents a secondary, if not altogether expendable, appendage to the monotheistic core of Christian faith.[15] They seek to reclaim the doctrine's original function in the biblical witness and the liturgical life of the church as the symbol of the central events of Christian revelation: Jesus' crucifixion and resurrection and the sending of the gift of the Spirit of love. As Catherine LaCugna describes in more poetic terms, trinitarian theologians seek to return the doctrine from the " 'far country' " of "speculative disquisition upon the interior dynamics of trinitarian life."[16] In *God for Us: The Trinity and the Christian Life*, LaCugna argues forthrightly that the Trinity must be revitalized as a soteriological doctrine: "[It] summarizes what it means to participate in the life of God through Jesus Christ in the Spirit. The mystery of God is revealed in Christ and the Spirit as the mystery of love, the mystery of persons in communion who embrace death, sin, and all forms of alienation for the sake of life."[17] For LaCugna along with a company of other theologians, neither the story of human salvation nor the God of love proclaimed in that narrative can be spoken of apart from the doctrinal symbol of the Trinity.

Many contemporary theologians strive not only to restore the epistemological foundations of trinitarian belief but also to revitalize the doctrine's influence on Christian praxis. Certainly there are wide disagreements about what such trinitarian praxis might entail, and even whether one should speak in terms of trinitarian-shaped practices.[18] Some theologians situate the practical relevance of the doctrine in the sphere of personal ethics, while others envisage it as the basis for a theology of culture.[19] Some interpret trinitarian praxis as a charge to social action, while still others appeal to the doctrine in order to sound the trumpet for ecclesial reform.[20] Yet amid this diversity, contemporary trinitarian theologians concur that the doctrine should have wide-ranging normative implications for the human person, interpersonal relations, and the social structures and institutions that join human beings together in community. As Elisabeth Johnson argues, the symbol of the Trinity "functions": "[It] . . . powerfully molds the corporate identity of the Christian community, highlights its values and directs its praxis."[21]

During the last thirty years no theologian has played a more pivotal role in revitalizing trinitarian doctrine and its implications for Christian praxis than German Reformed theologian Jürgen Moltmann. In his early work *The Crucified God* (1972), Moltmann traced the ills of modern Christian theology specifically to the eclipse of its trinitarian understanding of God.[22] He decried the dispassionate and distant God of modern theism as both incommensurate with the identity of the trinitarian God revealed in the cross-event and irrelevant to the challenges of protest and secular atheism. In *The Trinity and the Kingdom* (1981), Moltmann deepened his earlier critique by contending that the modern demise of the doctrine had sprung forth from flawed developments within Western trinitarian thought. He challenged that the Western doctrine suffered from a latent monarchianism that subordinated the distinct personhood of Father, Son, and Spirit to the absolute monarchy of the one God. Furthermore, he charged that this Western "monotheistic monarchianism" has had disastrous consequences for the Christian life of faith; it has provided a theological justification for structures of domination and subordination in the familial, political, and ecclesial realms of human existence.[23]

In the midseventies Moltmann moved beyond this wide-ranging critique to reconstruction of the doctrine. Following good Reformation tradition, he pursued the doctrine's roots beyond the dogmatic formulations of the early church *ad fontes*—in search of the distinctive God of love witnessed to in the scriptures. His intent was to complete one of the unfinished tasks of the Reformation: to revise "the church's doctrine of the Trinity on the basis of the Bible."[24] Moltmann sought not only a doctrine that corresponded more adequately to the biblical witness but also a "concrete doctrine" and "practical theory" that would reunite the doctrine of the Trinity with the experience and practices of contemporary believers.[25]

In *The Trinity and the Kingdom*, the first volume of his six-volume *Messianic Theology*, Moltmann set this ambitious theological program into motion. He proposed a social reconstruction of the doctrine in which he reformulated the trinitarian kingdom in communal terms as fellowship or *koinonia*. For Moltmann, this fellowship of reciprocal indwelling relationships among the Father, Son, and Holy Spirit represents the consummate expression of divine love. This fellowship of love, he argued further, is open and inviting to all of creation and to humankind in particular, who is uniquely destined to be the Trinity's counterpart in fellowship.

The practical significance of Moltmann's social trinitarian program rests on his bold claim that trinitarian fellowship not only describes divine community but also prescribes the nature of true human community. "True human fellowship," Moltmann contends, "is to correspond to the triune God and be his image on earth. True human fellowship will participate in the inner life of the triune God."[26] In the ensuing volumes of his *Messianic Theology*, Moltmann sought to make good on these claims by developing a theology of creation, christology, pneumatology, and eschatology that elucidates how human beings participate in the divine fellowship and are transfigured into a visible image of this fellowship on earth.[27] When viewed in its entirety, Moltmann's *Messianic Theology* is the story of this coming kingdom of fellowship. Its successive volumes trace the intertwined pilgrimages of the Father, the Son, and the Holy Spirit into the world and of human beings' journeying toward perfect fellowship with the Trinity and one another.

Today Moltmann's social trinitarian theology is virtually unparalleled in its impact on the ecumenical and international discussion about the Christian concept of God.[28] In particular, his provocative trinitarian interpretation of the "suffering God" and his relational ontology of the Trinity have both had a positive reception and spawned a new generation of trinitarian proposals.[29] Champions of Moltmann's theology point to its prophetic and kaleidoscopic vision: prophetic in exposing and denouncing various idolatries of the modern church and society, and kaleidoscopic in bringing ever-new trinitarian concepts into sight that illuminate the fellowship of the divine life and its liberating possibilities for the life of faith.

This positive reception notwithstanding, Moltmann's social trinitarian the-

ology has also been the lightning rod for much critical discussion. Two lines
of inquiry dominate the contemporary debate over his constructive trinitarian
proposals. The first focuses on Moltmann's relational ontology of the Trinity
and its implications for God's relationship to the created order and, most particularly, for the notions of divine and human freedom. To return to my earlier
example, Sallie McFague challenges Moltmann's trinitarian theology on both
epistemological and moral grounds. On the one hand, she objects to Moltmann's claims to knowledge about the nature of trinitarian life, on the grounds
that such claims exceed the limits of human experience and the scriptural
witness. On the other, she contends that Moltmann's desire to protect God
from any dependency on the world led him to propose an immanent Trinity
that dangerously separates and distances God from the world. In her judgment,
this trinitarian move results in "a picture of the divine nature as self-absorbed
and narcissistic" and, even more, pits divine freedom against that of human
creation.[30]

Curiously enough, British Reformed theologian Alan Torrance criticizes
Moltmann's trinitarian ontology on essentially the opposite grounds. In his
book *Persons in Communion*, Torrance argues that Moltmann ties the Trinity
too closely to the course of human history and, in so doing, compromises the
transcendence and sovereignty of the triune God over creation. At the same
time that Moltmann immanentalizes the trinitarian life, Torrance worries that
his Reformed colleague elevates and overestimates the individual's role in salvation. In particular, Torrance contends that there are "Pelagian tendencies" in
Moltmann's descriptions of doxology. In Torrance's words, the believer's "doxological participation in the transcendent triune life" appears more as a task
to be achieved rather than "an event of grace."[31]

The second constellation of criticisms concerns Moltmann's provocative
proposals for putting the trinitarian doctrine into Christian practice. Here, too,
critics part ways over whether Moltmann's theology promises too much or
delivers too little. For example, in his book *These Three Are One: The Practice
of Trinitarian Theology*, David Cunningham commends Moltmann for turning
the contemporary theological discussion about the Trinity to political and social
concerns. Nonetheless, he charges that Moltmann falls short of realizing his
ultimate goal of creating a practical and concrete trinitarian theology. Here
Cunningham criticizes the "high level of abstraction" in Moltmann's proposals
and asserts that he "offers few concrete suggestions" for how his ideas translate
into practice.[32]

While Cunningham looks for more concrete ideas from Moltmann, others
wish for far less. Several contemporary theologians accuse Moltmann of overfreighting trinitarian doctrine by taking concepts usually reserved for the trinitarian realm and applying them too readily to human beings' relationships
and social structures. For example, Catholic theologian Werner Jeanrond agrees
with Moltmann that divine love should lay the cornerstone for Christian ethics,

but he questions whether human community can or even should be asked to correspond to the divine communion of love as Moltmann proposes. Jeanrond presses Moltmann on whether he does not "confuse levels of theological language" by substituting "our symbolic representations of God's loving relationship" for the critical reflection needed to develop "strategies for Christian praxis in the world."[33]

Anglo-American theologian Karen Kilby's criticisms of Moltmann's social trinitarian program travel along similar lines but are even more trenchant. In her recent article, "Perichoresis and Projection: Problems with Social Doctrines of the Trinity," Kilby raises a series of significant methodological objections about the contemporary enthusiasm for social doctrines of the Trinity.[34] Moltmann serves as her chief exemplar for showing how social trinitarians import highly anthropomorphic language for the divine life, and then reverse the direction of their social analogies and propose them as norms for human relationships. At this point, Kilby charges, Moltmann's social doctrine of the Trinity creates a vicious hermeneutical circle in which the author does little to clarify the divine life but projects onto it his preferred political ideals and ethical agenda for human society.

With this wide-ranging debate as our backdrop, this study engages Moltmann's social trinitarian theology with the dual aim of evaluating its theological contributions and at the same time advancing a constructive agenda for its further development. Guiding this inquiry is what I take to be Moltmann's twofold wager on behalf of his social reconstruction of the doctrine. First, his social doctrine gives rise to a distinctive model of the divine life as fellowship, a model that corresponds to the economy of the Father, the Son, and the Holy Spirit's creative, redeeming, and sanctifying agency. Second, this model of trinitarian fellowship provides the foundation of a "theological doctrine of freedom" in the Christian life.[35] Put another way, I will be examining the "constative" and "commissive" force of Moltmann's proposed reconstruction of the doctrine, asking first what it discloses about the God who is love, and second what specific kinds of human action, relationships, and forms of life it commends to those who profess trinitarian belief.[36]

In investigating Moltmann's works I pursue both a hermeneutical and a systematic-theological agenda. On the hermeneutical side, I seek an answer to one of the most vexing issues in reading Moltmann's extensive body of work, namely, how to understand the ongoing evolution within his trinitarian theology. What are its driving theological impulses, its methodological convictions, and its practical concerns? What continuities exist between his early trilogy and his mature *Messianic Theology*, and wherein lie the genuine disjunctions in Moltmann's work?

In terms of my systematic-theological agenda, I seek to resolve a different kind of puzzle in Moltmann's work, namely, what is the doctrinal logic that links his doctrine of the Trinity to his claims about Christian praxis? Over and against those critics who find Moltmann's theology thoroughly unsystematic at this point, I shall argue that there is a coherent, if also underdeveloped, theological strategy that links his doctrine of the Trinity to his vision of the Christian life—what I construe as a "social trinitarian analogy of fellowship."[37] By this term, I refer to how Moltmann's personal and relational ontology of trinitarian fellowship functions as a divine archetype or what I view as an elastic rule of faith for right relationships in the personal, ecclesial, and political spheres of the Christian life. In support of this interpretation, I seek to demonstrate in the chapters ahead how the notion of trinitarian fellowship provides the key to the author's social trinitarian vision of God, his theological anthropology, and his understanding of the process of redemption. In sum, I argue that the concept of trinitarian fellowship is more than a recurring rhetorical figure in Moltmann's diverse works. Trinitarian fellowship is actually the structuring theological principle that unifies his *Messianic Theology*.

An Introduction to Moltmann's Trinitarian Approach

Before introducing my methods of analysis for this project, let us orient ourselves first to Moltmann's theological method. This is by no means a straightforward matter especially since Moltmann has been remarkably reticent throughout his career in commenting on methodological questions. Rather than prefacing his books with a prolegomena or even a chapter on theological method, most of Moltmann's books plunge the reader directly into the midst of a theological debate. This means that he considers methodological questions in retrospect and often only in response to critical discussions of his work. Nowhere is this more evident than in his *Messianic Theology*, where Moltmann waits until the sixth and final volume of his series to reflect upon his methodology in any detail. In the preface to this last volume, entitled an "afterword instead of a foreword," Moltmann candidly admits that he did not set his theological method in advance: "For me, theology was, and still is, an adventure of ideas. It is an open inviting path. Right down to the present day, it has continued to fascinate my mental and spiritual curiosity. My methods therefore grew up as I came to have a perception of the objects of theological thought. *The road emerged only as I walked it.*"[38]

Given the many winding turns on Moltmann's theological path, there is simply no single methodological foundation to unearth beneath all his works. Let me suggest, instead, three leitmotifs of Moltmann's trinitarian theology that can serve as our entrée into his work: its biblical-narrative structure, its soteriological approach in an eschatological key, and its doxological-political paradigm of Christian praxis.[39] Although Moltmann has changed his theological course many times over the years, these three leitmotifs have been his mainstays throughout. They form the backbone of his methodological commitments and crystallize his theology's highest aims.

In what follows I introduce each of these three themes as signposts that can alert us to the most significant trajectories in Moltmann's theological career. Along the way, I will also flag for the reader both the interpretative issues and the theological criticisms of Moltmann's trinitarian theology that I will be addressing throughout this study. This will set the stage for my more detailed discussions of these issues in the chapters ahead.

A Biblical Foundation and Narrative Structure

Ever since his first major publication, *Theology of Hope*, Moltmann has unwaveringly turned to the biblical witness as the chief source and *norma normans* for his theology. Moltmann's commitment to a biblical theology reflects, of course, the Reformation tenet *sola scriptura* but also his more direct debts to the theology of Karl Barth (via Moltmann's teachers, Hans Joachim Iwand, Ernst Wolf, and Otto Weber) and the regnant biblical scholars of his day, that of Gerhard von Rad, Ernst Zimmerli, and Ernst Käsemann. Moltmann became acquainted with this latter group of Old and New Testament scholars during his studies and his early teaching career. They drew his attention to the biblical patterns of history and apocalyptic, messianic hope, and the kingdom of God, all of which figure prominently in the *Theology of Hope* and form the messianic horizon of his mature theology.[40]

The relationship between Moltmann's trinitarian theology and Barth's is complex and contentious, and it will merit ongoing investigation as this study unfolds. With regard to the biblical foundation of his trinitarian theology, however, Moltmann follows his Reformed predecessor's initial lead in defending the Trinity's "biblical root" in scripture.[41] Like Barth, Moltmann does not attempt to locate the Trinity directly in the Bible (for instance, by appealing to certain proof-texts such as the New Testament's triadic formulas) but rather contends that the doctrine is a true and necessary interpretation of the New Testament witness. If we are to make sense of the New Testament narratives, argues Moltmann, we must speak of God in terms of Father, Son, and Holy Spirit.

Where Moltmann parts ways with Barth is over the latter's identification of the Trinity's biblical root in terms of lordship or divine sovereignty. Moltmann criticizes Barth's rooting of the doctrine in the notion of lordship as a reflection of modernity's distorted view of freedom as absolute autonomy rather than a valid interpretation of the kingdom of God made manifest in Christ and witnessed to in the scriptures.[42] As we will see in the chapters to come, this disagreement over the nature of the divine kingdom proves decisive for the respective forms of their doctrines of the Trinity, as well as for their theologies of love and freedom.

Initially Moltmann's trinitarian hermeneutics of the scriptures were quite limited. In *The Crucified God*, for example, his main resources for the doctrine are the passion narrative from the Gospel of Mark and Paul's theology of the cross. At this early stage Moltmann defines his material norm for the doctrine squarely in terms of the cross-event: "The content of the doctrine of the Trinity is the real cross of Christ himself. The form of the crucified Christ is the Trinity."[43] While Moltmann never veers away from the cross-event as the core of his doctrine, he sets it within an expanded narrative framework in his mature trinitarian theology.[44] In *The Trinity and the Kingdom*, for example, he traces a history of Christ that stretches from the Son's sending into the world to his exaltation. There Moltmann relies especially on the Johannine corpus and the other synoptic Gospels to fill in the contours of the relationships among the divine persons. In the latter volumes of his *Messianic Theology*, Moltmann complements this history of Christ with a history of the Spirit in an effort to balance the christocentrism of his Western theology with the rich pneumatological traditions that he has discovered in Eastern Orthodox trinitarian theology and other sources.

We will dig more deeply into the biblical foundation of Moltmann's theology as we explore the actual development of his doctrine in chapters 2 and 3. Noteworthy at this point is simply the author's guiding hermeneutical principle, namely, to preserve the particularity of the scriptural witness and to resist subsuming this dynamic history beneath a general speculative concept. As John O'Donnell rightly comments, Moltmann's basic theological impulse is "to let the biblical revelation create its own ontology."[45] To serve this aim, Moltmann develops what I term a "biblical-narrative approach" to the doctrine.[46] By this I mean that he isolates different narratives within the biblical text, each of which traces the Father's, the Son's, and the Spirit's actions and relationships toward one another and humankind. He then draws these various plotlines together into a composite narrative account—what he terms the trinitarian history of God.

The outlines of this biblical-narrative approach to the doctrine first emerge in Moltmann's response to a volume of critical essays about *The Crucified God*. Here he argues that the biblical witness does not yield a doctrine of the Trinity that can be fixed in static terms or be subsumed into a metaphysical formula. To do justice to the fullness of God's dynamic involvement with the world, a doctrine would have to have "changing vectors" that correspond to the various "historical experiences" of the Trinity.[47] Over the course of writing his *Messianic Theology*, Moltmann eventually sketches four such "forms of the Trinity" that represent in an abbreviated form these changing vectors or "*movements*" within this trinitarian history.[48] These four forms of the Trinity—the monarchial, historical, eucharistic, and doxological—differ from one another in terms of which aspect of the trinitarian history they portray and which of the divine persons appear as the primary agents in their narratives. In the monarchial Trinity, for example, all the action proceeds from the Father who begets the Son and the Spirit and sends them forth in the creation of the world. In contrast, the focal point of the doxological Trinity is the Spirit's and the Son's joint action in glorifying the Father and drawing all things into union with God.

Like the biblical narrative itself, Moltmann's narrative approach to the doctrine resists tidy schematization. Over the course of his career he adds new narrative patterns to his theology as he develops different doctrines and new aspects of the Trinity's history with the world. Only when viewed together do these separate narratives depict the entire economy of creation, salvation, and glorification. Since Moltmann never distills from this complex trinitarian history of God a single concept of divine love, one of our interpretative tasks in the chapters ahead will be to examine each of these biblical-narrative patterns in order to view the different facets of his understanding of divine love. Only after we traverse this entire trinitarian history will we be able to synthesize the author's vision of divine love and to evaluate how well his biblical-narrative approach fares in reconstructing the doctrine of the Trinity.

A Soteriological Doctrine in an Eschatological Key

Our second motif of Moltmann's trinitarian theology has already been present in the preceding discussion, namely, the doctrine's link to soteriology. In all his writings Moltmann stresses that the doctrine of the Trinity must be viewed *pro nobis*, that is, as an account of God's identity that arises in response to God's salvific and reconciling action on behalf of humankind. In *The Crucified God* Moltmann sets himself this strict "economic" measure for his trinitarian theology by arguing that we cannot speak of God apart from God's relationship to us but only as God is *"for us in the history of Christ which reaches us in our history."*[49] Eventually Moltmann will relax the strictures of this statement, defending the possibility of doxological statements that celebrate and give thanks for God in God's self. Nonetheless, he continues to tie all his chief claims about God's trinitarian nature to specific events in salvation history.

While many theologians anchor their trinitarian theology in the economy of salvation, what distinguishes Moltmann's approach is his bold starting point at the cross-event. Originally it was the theodicy question that drew Moltmann to develop such a trinitarian theology of the cross. Along with others of the post–World War II generation in Germany, Moltmann approached the cross-event as a way of confronting the radical evil and the collective despair and suffering of his generation.[50] He grew increasingly restless with classical interpretations of a theology of the cross as God's dialectical revelation in hiddenness and the justification of the unrighteous sinner. Recalling Bonhoeffer's cry that "only a suffering God can help,"[51] Moltmann wrestled with the nature of God's presence at the cross. "Instead of asking just *what God means for us human beings* in the cross of Christ," he explains in *The Crucified God*, "I asked too *what this human cross of Christ means for God.*"[52] For Moltmann, the cross eventually came to symbolize God's identification with human suffering—an act of divine solidarity that not only accomplishes human salvation but also has ontological implications for the Trinity. This radical notion precipitated a revolution in Moltmann's thinking about God. It was the first major step toward reformulating the doctrine of the Trinity and the catalog of classical attributes for God.

If the cross-event provided the original impetus for Moltmann's trinitarian theology, the resurrection-event proves just as critical to his eventual reformation of the doctrine. In his first groundbreaking work, *Theology of Hope*, and more recently in *The Coming God*, Moltmann depicts the resurrection in bold eschatological terms as the inbreaking of a new future—the coming rule of God. He describes the resurrection not as a closed event in the past but as a divine promise and an anticipated hope of new creation that lies in the coming future. The resurrection does not simply fulfill world-immanent possibilities; it is a *novum*, "a new possibility altogether for the world, for existence and for history."[53]

The impact of this eschatological interpretation of the resurrection reverberates throughout Moltmann's theology. Eschatology is no longer a topic reserved for the final pages of his dogmatics. It becomes, as he describes it, "the medium of Christian faith as such, the key in which everything in it is set, the glow that suffuses everything here in the dawn of an unexpected new day."[54] Such statements are more than metaphorical exuberance on Moltmann's part. In his *Messianic Theology*, Moltmann reformulates each of the classical doctrines from creation to the church and the sacraments in terms of their eschatological goal of fellowship with the Trinity. This means that Moltmann transcribes his entire trinitarian history of God into an eschatological key, such that this divine history becomes "open" for the transformation and redemption of the world.[55]

The Holy Spirit occupies a pivotal role within this eschatological framework. The Spirit is no longer the poor relation in the economy of salvation, subordinated to the salvific exchange of the Father and Son at the cross, but gains her own distinctive work of salvation. She represents the creative love of God that bears the promise of new creation to fruition. She draws and transforms individuals, the church, and indeed all of human history into participating ever more deeply in the fellowship of the Trinity.

In the next chapter we will analyze in further detail Moltmann's early interpretations of the cross- and resurrection-events, since they provide the fulcrum upon which balances his entire trinitarian history of God. At this point let us pause to observe one methodological consequence of the author's soteriological approach, namely, that it obviates the classical division between *theologia*, speech about the eternal and ineffable being of God, and *oikonomia*, speech about the economy of redemption. In Moltmann's trinitarian theology, *theologia* and *oikonomia* become one unified story of divine love and human liberation. Moltmann demonstrates this link between the trinitarian God of love and his creative, redemptive, and sanctifying works in the world in statements such as this one: "The history of salvation is the history of the eternally living, triune God who draws us into and includes us in his eternal triune life with all the fulness of its relationships. . . . *God loves the world with the very same love which he is in himself.*"[56] Here as elsewhere throughout his writings, Moltmann emphasizes that the trinitarian God of love is none other than the God who enters the world, becomes open to the vicissitudes of its history, and reconciles the world into the divine fellowship.

By lacing *theologia* and *oikonomia* together in this manner, Moltmann seeks a via media between the theocentric approach to the doctrine characteristic of Karl Barth and the anthropocentric one of Friedrich Schleiermacher. On the one hand, Moltmann moves beyond Barth's exclusive focus on the self-revealing agency of the trinitarian Godhead (*theologia*), which eclipses, if not eliminates, the role that human experience plays in mediating divine revelation. On the other, Moltmann reaches beyond Schleiermacher's exclusive focus on humankind's experience of God's threefold relation to the world (*oikonomia*), which did not admit claims about the nature of the triune God in and of itself.[57] As I shall argue in the chapters ahead, Moltmann reunites the revelation of the triune God with human experiences of divine love by developing a distinctive social trinitarian anthropology and a robust theology of grace. Through the sanctifying activity of the Holy Spirit, human beings partake of the fellowship of the Trinity and gain the capacity to mirror, albeit in finite and fragile ways, the trinitarian life in their own expressions of human freedom and love.

If Moltmann's soteriological approach to the doctrine seeks to overcome this classic methodological impasse, it also brings a host of theological challenges in its tow. The most frequently heard criticism of Moltmann's doctrine is that his passion-laden portrayals of the immanent Trinity reveal a speculative tendency in his work that ultimately betrays his biblical hermeneutical commitments.[58] To others, such speculation about the divine life proves symptomatic of the author's dangerous blurring of the divine and created orders that sacrifices the alterity and hiddenness of God.[59] Still others object to Moltmann's soteriological approach to trinitarian theology on sheerly ethical grounds. To some of his political and liberationist colleagues, for example, his appeals to the immanent Trinity suggest a divine consolation (or, even worse, compensation) for the evils of the world. By resolving human suffering in the realm of the immanent Trinity, Moltmann appears to smooth over how radical suffering actually interrupts human history and to sidestep the concrete social action needed to defeat such created evils.

Moltmann's eschatological approach to trinitarian theology is no less controversial. His repeated claim that the Trinity is "open" for the transformation of the world raises the unavoidable question of whether the Trinity itself is in process and awaits the fulfillment of human history to reach its own consummation. If this is indeed what Moltmann means, then his eschatological approach throws into question classical claims to divine omnipotence and omniscience. Furthermore, it suggests that the world is necessary to God's being, a claim that jeopardizes the gratuity of God's creating, redeeming, and sanctifying activities on behalf of humankind.

To resolve these questions of both interpretation and theological critique, we will need to analyze carefully in the chapters ahead both the ontological and the praxiological claims that Moltmann makes on behalf of his soteriological approach. As I noted earlier, Moltmann significantly revises his trinitarian history of God as he draws on a larger repertoire of resources from scripture and church theological traditions in his later works. Along the way he refines how he sees the relationship of this trinitarian economy to the eternal life of God. All these developments affect, in turn, Moltmann's claims about the nature of trinitarian love, as well as about the capacities of the individual and the community of faith for enjoying God's gift of fellowship and freedom in the Christian life.

The Praxis of Trinitarian Faith: A Political and Doxological Doctrine

The third leitmotif concerns Moltmann's efforts to revitalize the praxis of trinitarian faith in the contemporary world. As I noted at the outset of this introduction, Moltmann is hardly alone in this concern. There is a growing chorus of contemporary theologians anxious to put the doctrine of the Trinity to good works. In my view, what distinguishes Moltmann's proposal is his holistic understanding of trinitarian praxis. That is to say, Moltmann interprets trinitarian praxis at once in sociopolitical and doxological terms. On the one hand, the doctrine offers the interpretative key to the various forms of human agency and social relations that constitute our everyday lives and collective existence. On the other hand, it invites humankind not only toward action in the world but also toward contemplation and worship of the glory of God. In classical terminology, we might say that trinitarian praxis joins the Christian life of action, a *vita activa*, with that of contemplation, a *vita contemplativa*.[60]

From the very beginnings of his career, Moltmann has been committed to discerning the practical implications of theological beliefs and awakening the church to its political-ethical responsibilities. Moltmann was schooled in this by his personal biography, particularly by his experiences on the war front as a youth and the three years that he spent thereafter as a prisoner of war in England. Years later Moltmann would recall that his personal despair and the collective guilt of his people over the meaningless suffering of his generation were always at the root of his theological concerns.[61]

As a theological student back in Germany, Moltmann was convinced even more of the church's political responsibilities. Here his influences came from different quarters—his theology teachers (many of whom had been members of the Confessing Church movement), his wife, Elisabeth, whose family had also been involved in the resistance movement, and his own study of the writings of Dietrich Bonhoeffer and the dialectical theology movement. His five years serving as a pastor also left their mark. In Moltmann's words, it left him with an abiding concern for the practical—"not so much with what is always right, but more with the word which is addressed to us in the here and now . . . not so much with pure theory but with a practical theory."[62]

In his first major book, *Theology of Hope*, Moltmann's social and political agenda was still quite rudimentary. There he blended the messianic neo-Marxism of Ernst Bloch with the Old and New Testament accounts of divine promise into an impassioned rhetoric of revolutionary change. He exhorted the church to come forth and become an "exodus church" in modern society.[63] Its mission was to awaken hope in the resurrection promises of the gospel and to become an agent of eschatological unrest and social change. This exodus church was to keep society on the move toward the inbreaking kingdom of God in the world.

In the late 1960s Moltmann sharpened the political agenda of his theology. As public discussion erupted in postwar Germany over the Christian churches' silence in the face of the horrors of Auschwitz, Moltmann and a close friend, Catholic theologian Johann-Baptist Metz, broke their silence. Together they formulated a new "political theology," in which they urged their fellow theologians "to talk about God with a face turned to the world."[64] At the time this meant first and foremost addressing theology to the political realm, which they judged to be the governing force in modern society. In Moltmann's words, they sought "to raise the political consciousness of theology itself. . . . Political theology designates the field, the milieu, the environment and the medium in which Christian theology should be articulated today."[65]

Despite criticisms to the contrary, neither Metz nor Moltmann sought to reduce theology to politics or to use theology to legitimate a certain political order. Rather, they developed a "political hermeneutic of the gospel" that interpreted its message in terms of political and economic liberation from concrete situations of human suffering.[66] In retrospect, Moltmann admitted that there was a large dose of romanticism in his early political theology. He still needed to define more clearly what he meant by the term "political" and to specify what forms of social life and political structures corresponded to the coming kingdom of God.[67]

In *The Crucified God* a couple of these missing pieces fell into place. Most important, Moltmann discovered a norm for his political theology in the theology of the cross. The theology of the cross came to serve as both a critical and a constructive principle. Drawing on the critical theory of the Frankfurt school, he first used the theology of the cross to expose the idolatry that he saw in the apathetic and moralistic God of modern theism. Moltmann identified a dangerous correlation between Christianity's assimilation into a bourgeois political religion and what he called the emerging "vicious circles of death" in modern society: its poverty, racial and cultural alienation, industrial pollution, political oppression, and senselessness.[68]

In light of this idolatry critique, Moltmann transformed his political theology of the cross into a theology of liberation that sought to break free from these vicious circles of death. He challenged the church to exercise its discipleship in concrete solidarity with the victims of the world. "Christian life," he began to describe at that early time, "is a form of practice which consists in following the crucified Christ, and it changes both man himself and the circumstances in which he lives. To this extent, a theology of the cross is a practical theory."[69]

The early seventies saw crucial developments not just on the political side of Moltmann's practical agenda. As he became more involved in political theology, Moltmann became increasingly concerned that Christian faith could be mistaken for a form of social activism. If theology becomes too closely identified with any single political agenda, it could easily devolve into a "political moralism" or "social pietism."[70] To counter this danger in his writings, Moltmann developed a "theology of play," in which he focused on God's delight in creation and the creature's joyful response and praise of God's goodness. He anchored this theological aesthetics in a tenet from the Calvinist Westminster Catechism that the ultimate purpose of life is "to glorify God and enjoy him forever."[71] Theology, he argued, should not only give thanks and praise to God in response to God's gracious deeds but also adore God for God's sake.

Moltmann's intent in creating a theology of play was neither frivolous nor casual. He especially did not wish this invitation to celebration to detract from his political theology's call to social transformation. On the contrary, he envisioned the two dimensions of the Christian life working hand in hand. The believer, who first experiences the joy of faith and a foretaste of the coming kingdom, begins to experiment with the kingdom's liberating possibilities and to put them into praxis. Just as justification and sanctification come into being together, Moltmann argues that so, too, liberating and joyful faith must become active in works of love.

With the publication of *The Trinity and the Kingdom*, these two streams of Moltmann's political and aesthetic theology flowed together to form what I describe as his doxological-political paradigm for the Christian life of faith. On the political side, Moltmann sees his social doctrine not just as a remedy for the modern eclipse of the doctrine of the Trinity but also as a salve for society's worst social and political ills.[72] In essence trinitarian fellowship provided Moltmann with his long-desired theological norm for right human relationships and social and political structures that correspond to the kingdom.

This constitutes, however, only half of Moltmann's vision of trinitarian praxis. He argues just as fervently for a "doxological theology," a worshipful contemplation of the triune God that includes meditation, adoration, and praise.[73] Moltmann signals the growing importance of doxological theology to his theological program in the opening pages of *The Trinity and the Kingdom*, where he warns against theology succumbing to the "pragmatism" of modernity by measuring the truth of Christian doctrines strictly in terms of what they achieve. Such a notion of the "practical," Moltmann argues, can only impoverish the life of faith: "Christian love is not merely a motivation, and Christian faith is more than the point from which action takes its bearings. Being a Christian is also characterized by gratitude, joy, praise and adoration. Faith lives in meditation and prayer as well as in practice."[74]

Moltmann anchors his doxological theology initially in soteriology. It is a joyful response to God's self-revelation and gracious goodness in the economy of salvation. Ultimately, however, doxological theology moves beyond thanksgiving over God's works to sheer wonder and glorification of God for God's own sake. In doxology the believer has a perception of God that is born out of love and even participation in the divine life: "Here we know only in so far as we love. Here we know in order to participate. Then to know God means to participate in the fulness of divine life."[75]

Moltmann's doxological theology will prove critical to our study in two respects. First, Moltmann cultivates as doxology quite different Christian practices than those of social or political action with which his social trinitarian theology is often narrowly identified. These doxological practices are as diverse as keeping the Sabbath, personal prayer, and communal worship. Although these practices differ from the political, they are not a diversion from them. Rather, Moltmann insists that the doxological and political work together in the life of faith. They both "lead men and women into the history of God"[76] and toward its eschatological goal of participation in the divine communion of love. Chapter 5 will test the strength of this tie that binds the doxological to the political, as I explore how the love of God and the love of neighbor relate to one another in the life of faith. At that point we can evaluate how well Moltmann succeeds in drawing the doxological and political dimensions of the Christian life into a symphonic unity with one another.

Doxological theology is for a second reason critical to this study. It is the theological genre in which Moltmann speaks of human knowledge of the immanent Trinity and God's eternal relations. In doxology the Trinity opens its divine fellowship to the believer, who experiences, in turn, a foretaste of the eternal life. At this point doxological theology becomes truly messianic theology: it anticipates the ultimate goal of new creation—our participation in and eternal enjoyment of God's fellowship.

Here, too, significant theological questions arise for our project ahead. First, what is the nature of the human being's doxological participation in the divine fellowship, and how is it mediated through Christ and the Holy Spirit? Second, what knowledge of the immanent Trinity does the believer receive in doxology, and how does this knowledge relate to that gained through the trinitarian economy? Addressing these questions will help us resolve one of the critical debates surrounding Moltmann's doxological theology, namely, whether it gives way to unwarranted theological speculation about the immanent trinitarian life.

To conclude this introduction to Moltmann's methodology, two final observations are in order that help illuminate our constructive theological project ahead. The first concerns how Moltmann relates theory to praxis, orthodoxy to orthopraxy in his theology. In many ways Moltmann's position on this question resembles closely that of liberation theologians' "turn to praxis."[77] By this I mean simply that he agrees with liberationists who contend that theology's foundation and its aim is emancipatory praxis on behalf of the marginalized and oppressed. Moltmann announces this kind of praxiological commitment in his theology in the opening pages of *The Trinity and the Kingdom*: "The practical act which is necessary in today's misery is the liberation of the oppressed. Theology is hence the critical reflection about this essential practice in light of the gospel. It does not merely aim to understand the world differently, it aims to transform it."[78]

Moltmann parts ways with liberationists at the point, however, in which they insist that praxis precedes theory and becomes its exclusive criterion for truth. In *Experiences in Theology*, the last volume of his *Messianic Theology*, Moltmann clarifies his differences with liberation theologians on this issue. He likens privileging praxis in this way to a monastic or a pietistic theology that mandates certain spiritual practices or experiences as its prerequisite. Once a certain form of social engagement becomes the sine qua non for doing Christian theology, then, Moltmann warns, theology threatens to become "a kind of social pietism of virtuous thinking." Furthermore, he continues, if theory always follows praxis as its second step, then Christian theology cannot defend itself from the charge of ideology. "[It] gives rise to the suspicion that the Christian faith is . . . only being pressed into service so that a presupposed socio-political option may be imbued with Christian engagement."[79]

In his own work, Moltmann presumes a hermeneutical circle between theory and praxis: there is neither a theory that does not rely on certain experiences nor praxis that does not involve some prior theoretical interests and commitments. Given this hermeneutical circle, Moltmann argues that theory and praxis should relate to one another dialectically.[80] The ultimate criterion for Christian praxis, he states further, can only be "Christ crucified," who calls the believer into solidarity with the marginalized and the outcast, and into conflict with those in power: "Who is the criterion of this praxis of justice? It is Christ, who is present, hidden, in the poor, the sick and the children (Matthew 25)."[81]

Although Moltmann's brief remarks about the relationship between theory and praxis leave many questions still unanswered, they do clear away a couple of misapprehensions about how orthodoxy and orthopraxy relate in his theology. First, his remarks alert us to the fact that both an idealist interpretation of Moltmann's method, in which doctrines dictate Christian praxis in a top-down fashion, and a pragmatist one, in which praxis dictates the truth of theological doctrines, miss their mark. Instead, I propose that Moltmann's theological method can best be described by what Rebecca Chopp defines as "critical praxis correlation."[82] By this I mean that Moltmann roots his theology in the practical activity of the community of faith, but he critically reformulates such praxis in light of theological principles. Moltmann assumes a dynamic and critical relationship between his theological norms and praxiological goals, one in which neither trinitarian orthodoxy nor orthopraxy has the final say.

Moltmann's reservations about liberationist methodology are also illuminating because they mirror criticisms that are often heard against his own theology, namely, that his social trinitarian doctrine is window dressing for a predetermined social and political agenda. Just as he warns that a certain sociological analysis can render Christian faith superfluous in liberation theology, so some of Moltmann's critics charge that a certain political and social ideology dictates his own social trinitarian theology.[83] Although being aware of this danger hardly immunizes Moltmann's theology against a similar ideology critique, nonetheless, his cautionary remarks are helpful. They reveal a theological criterion that we can use to evaluate his proposals for Christian praxis in our project, namely, how well it comports with the message and ministry of the crucified Christ.

The second methodological observation takes us in fully another direction—to the role that the passions and the imagination play in Moltmann's trinitarian theology. Moltmann appeals to human beings' passions and aesthetic sensibilities throughout his works, but they play an especially pivotal role in the believer's doxological encounter with God. Here Moltmann describes how the believer perceives the creative and suffering love of God, which in turn becomes a speculum for seeing her own passions anew. In Moltmann's words, the individual encounters "the living God" and "learns to know himself in the mirror of God's love, suffering and joy."[84] Further, Moltmann argues that this doxological encounter of divine and human passions fits poorly within modern paradigms of knowledge, in which knowledge either is reduced to "narcissistic" self-knowledge or becomes "operational" and a matter of appropriation and possession.[85] Doxology corresponds better to the Greeks' and the ancient church's notion of "knowing in wonder."[86] Here worship and praise awaken a passionate thirsting after God and an imagination for the creative possibilities of the coming kingdom.

For Moltmann, awakening this kind of passionate knowledge of God and the self is theology's highest aim and ultimate task. "Theology," he exhorts his readers in *Experiences in Theology*, "comes into being wherever men and women come to the knowledge of God and, in the praxis of their lives, their happiness and their suffering, perceive God's presence with all their senses. It is to this that systematic theology should, last and first, make its contribution."[87] Moltmann goes on to insist that becoming a true theologian requires first of all one's own passionate engagement with God—a baring of one's soul that includes both suffering and delight in God's presence. Out of this passionate and doxological encounter springs forth the theologian's "intellectual love for God" and a "pleasure in wisdom," which Moltmann ventures to call "a passion for the kingdom" or a "theo-fantasy."[88] Here the theologian's imagination is infused with passion and delight at the prospect of the coming kingdom and seeks to ignite this same spiritual imagination in others.

With a few notable exceptions, most interpreters of Moltmann's works ignore the author's remarks about theology awakening the believer's affections and imagination.[89] There are many reasons for this neglect. Moltmann suggests that many dismiss his doxological claims as "fanciful" and as an excuse to evade the rigors of systematic theology.[90] As we will see throughout this study, there is more than some truth to the criticism that Moltmann's theology lacks a certain "logical rigor."[91] Yet, I would add to this the more troubling reason that these spiritual and affective dimensions of doctrine have largely disappeared from the modern theological imagination. Contemporary academic discourse no longer expects that systematic theology will also always be a spiritual theology that can ignite the passions and transform the soul.

How might we counter this tendency in order to take seriously Moltmann's claims about the role of the passions and imagination in trinitarian theology? Earlier I borrowed Paul Ricouer's language of a twofold wager to interpret Moltmann's claims on behalf of his social doctrine of the Trinity, namely, that it gives rise to liberating thought and emancipatory action. To this twofold wager let me now add a third dimension, namely, that Moltmann's symbol of the Trinity will spark the believer's passions and her spiritual imagination. In other words, we will also be searching for the prophetic potential of Moltmann's trinitarian theology for awakening its readers' passions for the kingdom and sparking creative possibilities for its consummation.

Tracing the Pilgrimage of Love: A Method of Procedure

Bearing Moltmann's theological approach in mind, I turn now to my method of procedure for analyzing his trinitarian theology. For a variety of reasons, presenting a judicious reading of Moltmann's trinitarian theology is not an easy task. Surely every interpreter of Moltmann's thought finds herself challenged by the sheer magnitude of his published writings.[92] As I intimated earlier, Moltmann's trinitarian publications extend over a span of more than thirty years, during which time his interpretation of the doctrine has undergone significant and ongoing revision. Most notably, after the original German publication of *The Trinity and the Kingdom*, in 1980, he refined his constructive proposal for a social doctrine of the Trinity several times in ongoing conversation with critics, new dialogue partners, and emerging theological issues.[93]

Charting a course through this evolving theology is complicated further by the *contextual* character of Moltmann's writings. By contextual I do not just mean Moltmann's particular sociopolitical and cultural location as a "first world" European male theologian.[94] Rather, I refer specifically to the fact that Moltmann has always self-consciously engaged in public theology, that is, in formulating a theology that addresses itself to the pressing issues of church and society within his contemporary context. In this regard he stands firmly in the tradition of dialectical theology and the Confessing Church movement and insists on the theologian's responsibility to respond to the particular *kairos* of his own time.[95]

Moltmann's commitment to such a public theology was evident already in his first major trilogy. At the time he described his trilogy's contextual character with these words: "I wanted to achieve something specific in the respective intellectual, theological and political situation. They are written from their time for their time and therefore are to be understood as theology in the context of contemporary life. *They have therefore been correctly characterized as more pastoral and prophetic than professorial and systematic.*"[96] During the 1960s and 1970s Moltmann adopted an even more explicitly contextual approach as many of his writings took the form of dialogues with Marxists, as well as with Jewish, Orthodox, and so-called third world liberation theologians. Eventually Moltmann distanced himself from writing this kind of contextual theology to devote his efforts to certain long-term doctrinal issues. His theology did not exit, however, from the public arena. A steady stream of new social and political issues, from feminism to ecology and most recently to globalization, continues to inform his new theological directions.

The significance of Moltmann's public theology is that it requires that each work be carefully interpreted with its specific context and dialogue partners in view. Although there are lines of continuity among his works, no work can be singled out, for example, in which he finalizes his doctrine of the Trinity and puts it to rest. Rather, each of his books qualifies and complements another in its theological perspective; therefore, each must be read as if in an ongoing dialogue with the others.

The interpretive challenges presented by Moltmann's public theology are certainly magnified by his refusal to lay a single methodological foundation for his theology. As I have already argued, this is no mere oversight on Moltmann's part. It can be attributed to a certain degree to his effort to match his theological genre to its divine subject, namely, the coming kingdom of God. Given the eschatological nature of God, Moltmann reasons, Christian theology can hardly take the form of apodictic dogmas or unchanging truth claims. It must be subject to ongoing reformation in light of the inbreaking reality of the trinitarian kingdom.

This eschatological proviso both chastens and inspires the theologian. On the one hand, it chastens her for the illusion of being able to create a comprehensive and timeless dogmatic system. "The divine promise and the awakened hope," Moltmann writes, "teach every theology that it must remain fragmentary and unfinished, because it is the thinking about God of men and women who are on the way and, being still travelers, have not yet arrived home."[97] Yet, it exhorts the theologian not to be determined by the realities of the here and now but rather to be inspired by the creative possibilities of the kingdom to come and to remain open to their ongoing revision.

Set in this eschatological key, Moltmann's trinitarian theology has a distinctive theological style and form that I describe as both promissory and provisional. As he explains in *The Spirit of Life*, he creates theological images and symbols that invoke readers' imagination for the coming kingdom and elicit their passions for its fellowship and freedom:

> The metaphors for experiences of God in history have to be flexible, so that they invite us to voyage into the future and encourage us to seek the kingdom of God. The true symbols of transcendence impel us to transcend. This applies to theological conceptions and terms too. If they are related to "the wandering people of God," this eschatology relativizes them. They become signposts, and search images for God's future.[98]

His ever-shifting metaphors and concepts for God are not intended to capture and preserve divine truth. They are "signposts" that point beyond themselves and exhort his readers to venture forth in pursuit of the kingdom. At the same time that trinitarian symbols give rise to eschatological hope, they are also evanescent. Moltmann's is a finite and fragmentary vision of God that subjects itself to ongoing reformation.

In this light one can best understand why Moltmann refuses to define his *Messianic Theology* either as a systematic theology or as a dogmatics. He describes his major work instead as "systematic contributions to theology" so as to avoid the false impression that he is attempting a "total system" or a "universal doctrine."[99] As he explains elsewhere, his contributions are meant as "proposals" for open and public debate in the wider church; they are intentionally experimental, provocative, and subject to continual revision. For this reason, Moltmann enjoins his readers to enter into spirited dialogue with his theological proposals, to "seek agreement or dissent, but not repetition," and in so doing to journey toward deeper insight into the coming kingdom of God.[100]

Given Moltmann's self-understanding of the theological task and the distinctive genre of his writings, the question arises all the more urgently of how best to read his trinitarian theology. In this study we will take our cues from Moltmann's trinitarian theology itself and not attempt to impress a conceptual framework on his writings that would be alien to the dynamic and eschatological character of the trinitarian history that he seeks to articulate. Instead, I will adopt a hermeneutic in accordance with the fundamental assumption of his trinitarian theology, namely, that the divine love is disclosed *narratively*, that is, through the trinitarian history of creation, salvation, and consummation. This means that we, too, will adopt a version of this narrative approach by tracing the evolving patterns in Moltmann's writings with which he describes the relationships among Father, Son, and Spirit. Since Moltmann significantly expands his presentation of the trinitarian history of God over the course of his writings, we will need to proceed in a roughly chronological fashion through his major writings to discover the emerging aspects of his notion of trinitarian love. This will enable us not only to see how Moltmann builds layer upon layer his narrative framework for the doctrine but also to disclose the crucial doctrinal links that join his various theological claims.

The title of this work, *Pilgrimage of Love*, is intended as a guiding metaphor for our study. It stems from process theologian Daniel Day Williams, who in his work *The Spirit and the Forms of Love* describes divine love as a reality that emerges in and over time. For Williams, the true and full meaning of love will only be disclosed at the end of all time: "*Agape* indeed bears an assurance for every future. . . . But what love may do and will do, what creative and redemptive work lies ahead, can only be known partially in the history of love until the 'end.' "[101] Now significant differences exist between Moltmann's trinitarian notion of divine love and that of a process theologian such as Williams.[102] Notwithstanding these, this metaphor lends itself well to Moltmann's theology. "Pilgrimage of love" calls to mind that Moltmann's trinitarian theology narrates the story of God *pro nobis*—of the seeking and gathering love of God who links God's very destiny to the creation and salvation of humankind. For this reason, tracing the trinitarian pilgrimage of love in Moltmann's theology entails following the kenotic descent of the God who is love into the world and the cosmic ascent of his creation into the loving communion of God.

This metaphor of "the pilgrimage of love" also alerts the reader to the fact that this trinitarian history has not yet drawn to a close. It is an eschatological concept whose full meaning will not be known until the end of time. Given this eschatological proviso, Moltmann's trinitarian theology finds itself on a pilgrimage in which it is subject to revision in light of the inbreaking messianic kingdom of God. Its images are "related to 'the wandering people of God' " and point always beyond themselves toward the consummation of the kingdom of fellowship.[103]

In light of the foregoing introduction to Moltmann's trinitarian theology and to my own method of procedure, let me offer a brief map of the pilgrimage ahead. In chapters 2 and 3, I analyze the developments in Moltmann's trinitarian doctrine from his early writings through his mature *Messianic Theology*. Chapter 2 focuses on the emergence of Moltmann's trinitarian theology in the companion volumes of the *Theology of Hope* and *The Crucified God*. Here I analyze Moltmann's "dialectical christology" and how it gives rise to the author's initial dialectical concept of trinitarian love as crucified and creative love.

Chapter 3 traces the evolution from Moltmann's early trinitarian theology of the cross to his social reconstruction of trinitarian doctrine in *The Trinity and the Kingdom*. Here we will see how Moltmann's earlier cross-centered account of the trinitarian history of God unfolds into an eschatological narrative that stretches from the sending of the Son and the Spirit from the Father in creation to the consummation of creation in fellowship with God in the eschaton. I will also set forth two competing models of divine love that first emerge in *The Trinity and the Kingdom*: a protological concept of divine passion as the ecstatic self-communication of the good and an eschatological concept of *koinonia*, or the fellowship of Father, Son, and Spirit. Here our task will be to clarify the relationship between these two concepts of trinitarian love and to demonstrate how they advance beyond Moltmann's earlier dialectical concept of divine love.

In chapters 4 and 5, I turn my attention to elucidating and evaluating the praxiological implications of Moltmann's social trinitarian theology of love. If chapters 2 and 3 proceed from the economy of salvation to the trinitarian nature of God's being as love, chapters 4 and 5 move in the opposite direction: from Moltmann's doctrine of the Trinity to its implications for the creation, salvation, and glorification of human beings. Chapter 4 lays the cornerstone for Moltmann's vision of the life of faith by investigating the author's messianic and social trinitarian reconstruction of an *imago Dei* anthropology. Here we discover how Moltmann reinterprets the notion of *imago Dei* as a twofold analogy of relations: the individual's relationship to God the Father as *imago Christi*, and a social or interpersonal analogy of relations, an *imago Trinitatis*, that appears among human beings.

Chapter 5 investigates how Moltmann's social trinitarian theology guides the way of salvation and the life of discipleship. The first part of the chapter analyzes what I term Moltmann's "trinitarian pattern of salvation": the eschatological process through which the human being is adopted into the trinitarian life and transfigured into its very image. Here I focus especially on the differentiated and interdependent roles that Christ and the Holy Spirit play in accomplishing the work of salvation. The second half of the chapter demonstrates how trinitarian fellowship functions as a divine archetype for determining the nature of right relationships in human life. Here I argue that this analogy to trinitarian fellowship serves as an elastic rule of faith rather than a narrow prescriptive program for the Christian life. After looking at several examples of such lived trinitarian fellowship, the chapter concludes with an assessment of the liberating dimensions of Moltmann's praxis of trinitarian fellowship, as well as a constructive proposal for its further development.

2

The Dialectic of Crucified and Creative Love in Moltmann's Early Theology

This chapter examines Moltmann's concept of God and his interpretation of divine love in his early theology, spanning the period from the publication of his first two major constructive works, *Theology of Hope* (1964) and *The Crucified God* (1972), until the publication of *The Church in the Power of the Spirit* (1975). The middle to late 1970s mark a "natural break" in Moltmann's theological development, since at that point he began to shift from his thematic and highly contextual approach to theology and start the systematic development of his mature theology.[1] Although Moltmann did not lay out a full-fledged doctrine of the Trinity in these earliest writings, they presage his mature trinitarian theology in several key aspects. Here we discover key interpretations of scripture, motifs drawn from the Western theological tradition, and analyses of contemporary culture, all of which recur in a more nuanced form in the *Messianic Theology*. A central aim of this chapter will be to identify these theological resources in Moltmann's early writings to clarify both the biblical and the conceptual origins of his later trinitarian theology.[2]

Moltmann's early writings are significant to this study, however, not simply because they prefigure his mature trinitarian theology. They contain a distinct concept of divine love that will provide us with a foil to the author's social trinitarian concept of love in his later works. The doctrinal key to this early concept of divine love lies in Moltmann's "*dialectical* Christology,"[3] a doctrinal framework that undergirds both *Theology of Hope* and *The Crucified God*. Like much of German Protestant theology written in the immediate wake of Karl Barth's *Church Dogmatics*, Moltmann's early theology can be broadly categorized as christocentric: the cross and resurrection are the core of divine revelation that informs all other loci of classical theological reflection.[4] What distinguishes Moltmann's christocentrism is how he interprets the cross- and resurrection-events in terms of a "radical historical dialectic of sharp contradictions,"[5] for example, in terms of absence and presence, suffering and hope, hell and bliss. This radical dialectic is open-ended, insofar as history continues to swing back and forth between the eschatological promise of new creation (already anticipated in the resurrection) and the cruciform character of present reality. This open dialectic structures all of world history, lending it dynamic movement toward consummation in the eschatological kingdom of God.

The second major aim of this chapter is to trace how this cross-resurrection dialectic emerges in Moltmann's early writings and, more specifically, to see how it authorizes his earliest trinitarian concept of God and concept of divine love. Identifying Moltmann's concept of divine love proves a difficult task in these early writings, largely due to the wholly unsystematic character of the author's early reflections about the doctrine of God. His discussions on the nature of divine love are scattered throughout his writings and are encapsulated within other thematic complexes. To a certain degree the unsystematic character of Moltmann's reflections on God can be attributed to the contextual character of these writings; these are situational works, responding to particular theological developments, as well as cultural and intellectual currents of his day.

Moltmann, however, also practices an unusual methodology in his early trilogy of works—a method that he describes as "the whole of theology in one focal point."[6] He isolates one aspect of Christian revelation in each work and uses it as his lens through which to view the whole compass of theological doctrines. Moltmann interpreter Douglas Meeks offers the most helpful reading of how this methodology structures Moltmann's early trilogy. He suggests that Moltmann's focal point shifts from Easter and the theme of eschatology in *Theology of Hope*, to Good Friday and the theology of the cross in *The Crucified God*, and finally to Pentecost and pneumatology and ecclesiology in *The Church in the Power of the Spirit*.[7] In this early trilogy of works, the logic of these particular biblical events (and their narrative renderings) prevails over any overarching doctrinal schema.

Building on Meeks's interpretative strategy, I pay particular attention in this chapter to those biblical interpretations that drive Moltmann's theological agenda in this early period. In terms of our larger project, these early biblical interpretations secure the cornerstone for his distinctive biblical-narrative approach to trinitarian theology that I introduced in the previous chapter. Moreover, these biblical interpretations offer a first opportunity to respond to critics' queries about Moltmann's indebtedness to various philosophical frameworks for his model of divine being and its agency in history.

Theology of Hope as Prolegomena to a Doctrine of God

Theology as Eschatology: A New Theological Program

When Moltmann's first major work, *Theology of Hope*, burst onto the German theological scene in 1964, it galvanized public attention to a degree unrivaled since the publication of Barth's commentary on Romans in the early 1920s. *Theology of Hope* went through six editions within the first three years and received an enormous critical reception within the ecumenical and international theological communities.[8] The critical success of *Theology of Hope* can be traced certainly to the fact that it spoke to the spirit of the age. With the rapid economic recovery and technological and industrial achievements of the 1950s, a spirit of optimism had certainly swept over Germany. German society was captivated by a sense of creative expectancy with regard to future technological or material advances, and there was an accompanying hope for a gradual humanization of political, religious, and economic structures of society.[9] As Moltmann explained later, "The theme of hope, of a new dawn, was as it were in the air in 1964."[10]

Although Moltmann's *Theology of Hope* echoes this cultural spirit of hope, a distinctive theological agenda drives the work. Moltmann's aim was to provide a detailed study of the Christian understanding of eschatological hope as his contribution to a much broader theological debate over the nature of Christian revelation and its relationship to history. This debate had been simmering among Protestant theologians since the turn of the twentieth century with the so-called rediscovery of the future-eschatological character of biblical theology, and in particular the centrality of primitive Christian apocalypticism to the New Testament. In the 1920s the dialectical theology movement in Germany made the first attempt to return this radical biblical eschatology and its apocalyptic language to the contemporary theological scene. Dialectical theologians, such as Barth, Bultmann, and Gogarten, all used this biblical eschatology as a tool of prophetic critique against the optimism of Protestant liberalism in the aftermath of World War I.

In the late fifties and sixties, a group of young German theologians reignited this pre–World War II debate over biblical eschatology, revelation, and history. Moltmann belongs to this loosely defined "school of hope," which found itself at odds with the dominant theological schools that had emerged from the dialectical theological movement. The "school of hope" questioned whether Barth, Bultmann, and Gogarten—as well as their successors—had not done away with the historical character of biblical eschatology.[11] Of special concern to Moltmann were the damaging social and political consequences that these dehistoricized models of eschatology held for contemporary Christianity. For example, he attributed the Protestant church's marginalization in debates over the reconstruction of post–World War II German society in large part to theology's failure to link its biblical eschatological vision to concrete history. While theologians awaited a transhistorical kingdom of God, Moltmann charged, secular humanist philosophies were co-opting Christianity's messianic vision and transforming it into an immanent vision of a utopian atheist world. As Moltmann observed dryly at the time, "A Christian faith in God without hope for the future of the world has called forth a secular hope for the future of the world without faith in God."[12]

Against this historical backdrop, Moltmann's *Theology of Hope* seeks to regain Christianity's revolutionary sociopolitical potential. It calls for a resurrection of Christian messianic hope through a total reorientation of theology in an eschatological key. In words reminiscent of Barth's Romans commentary, Moltmann announces his revolutionary eschatological program in the opening pages of *Theology of Hope*: "From first to last, and not merely in the epilogue, Christianity is eschatology, is hope, forward looking and forward moving, and therefore also revolutionizing and transforming the present. The eschatological is not one element *of* Christianity, but it is the medium of Christian faith as such, the key in which everything in it is set."[13] Moltmann's rhetoric here recalls that of the dialectical theologians, who sought to revitalize the biblical apocalyptic perspective for contemporary theology. And yet, at the same time he also challenges directly his predecessors' views of revelation as distortions of the biblical account.[14]

In particular, Moltmann criticizes both Barth's model of God's eternal self-revelation and Bultmann's model of revelation as the disclosure of authentic selfhood on the grounds that they both treat the eschaton as if it were a transhistorical phenomenon, that is, as a transcendental limit between time and eternity. These transcendental eschatologies reduce divine revelation into an "epiphany of the eternal present"[15] and, in turn, negate any meaningful experience of God in history. In *Theology of Hope* Moltmann seeks to reverse this transcendental turn in eschatology by recovering the genuinely historical character of biblical eschatology. In so doing, he aims to reclaim Christian theology's hope for the future of this world and the theologian's role as prophet and social critic in the public square.

The Biblical God of Hope

As I stated earlier, certain biblical hermeneutical keys appear in Moltmann's early work, keys which the author develops more fully in his *Messianic Theology*. In *Theology of Hope* the biblical hermeneutical key is Moltmann's model of revelation as a divine word of promise in both the Old and New Testaments. The author builds his exegetical case for this model of divine revelation as promise by drawing on recent scholarship by historians of religion and Old Testament theologians, in particular that of Walter Zimmerli and Gerhard von

Rad.[16] Following their exegetical lead, Moltmann treats the Exodus experience as the paradigm for divine revelation in the history of Israel. Here God "reveals himself in the form of promise and in the history that is marked by promise."[17] Put differently, not only does the God of Exodus promise to act in human history, but God's being comes to be known through his faithfulness to these promises. Moltmann describes God's unveiling in his eschatological promises this way: "His name is a wayfaring name, a name of promise that discloses a new future, a name whose truth is experienced in history inasmuch as his promise discloses its future possibilities."[18]

Central to Moltmann's view of biblical revelation is the dialectical character of these divine promises in history; these divine promises contradict present reality and point forward to its yet unrealized future.[19] As a dialectical word of promise, divine revelation not only happens in history but also introduces creative possibilities into that history. For example, the revelation by the God of Exodus of a new future instilled a messianic hope in Israel that became the source of radical transformation of its present reality.[20] Here the promissory Word of God not only portends the future but also creates it.

If the Exodus event is Moltmann's interpretive key to God's revelation in the history of Israel, the resurrection of the crucified Christ is the focal point of messianic hope in *Theology of Hope*. The author presents the resurrection as the continuation rather than either the fulfillment or the abrogation of Old Testament promises. The resurrection is itself an open promise that signifies definitively, if only proleptically, an end to death's dominion. In Moltmann's formulation, "the resurrection has set in motion an eschatologically determined process of history, whose goal is the annihilation of death in the victory of the life of the resurrection."[21]

Moltmann's interpretation of the resurrection as a cosmic victory over evil and death follows quite traditional lines. Distinctive, however, is his insistence on the unrealized nature of this promissory-event. The resurrection is not a completed event of the historical past, an event to be simply remembered in faith by the Christian community. It is an eschatological event that has its full reality still ahead of it. In the author's words, the resurrection is a *"promissio inquieta"* that produces an ongoing dynamic in history until it "finds rest in the resurrection of the dead and a totality of new being."[22] For this reason Christian faith in the resurrection, like the Hebrew faith in the God of Exodus, is thoroughly messianic: a faith in God's promises for an as yet outstanding future.

Both in *Theology of Hope* and even more so in *The Crucified God*, Moltmann interprets the cross- and resurrection-events as a dialectic of identity in contradiction. He describes these events in highly dualistic terms as "death and life, nothing and everything, godlessness and the divinity of God."[23] In *Theology of Hope* the resurrection provides the symbolic key to the nature of divine presence; it reveals God as the source of new life: "the God who creates life and new being out of nothing."[24] The cross, meanwhile, appears as a cipher for all the negativities of human history and for divine absence.

Although Moltmann portrays the resurrection promise of new creation in harsh contradiction to the crucified character of present reality, this harsh dialectic is neither a reason to resign oneself to an already determined history nor a reason to seek solace in a spiritualized eschatological realm. On the contrary, the resurrection represents a divine protest against all the negativities and sufferings of the world.[25] As the inbreaking of the divine promise of new life into the midst of history, the resurrection provides the creative impetus for human action—impetus for those who hold resurrection hope in Christ to engage in action to realize this divine promise in this world.

God as the Power of the Future: The Biblical God in a Modern Key

As I argued previously, one of Moltmann's major aims in *Theology of Hope* is to reinvigorate a realist dimension to Christian faith in the world by interpreting biblical revelation as a concrete historical hope for God's coming eschaton. For this biblical God of hope to be truly conceivable within the modern world, Moltmann needed a philosophy of history that could provide an alternative to the modern paradigm of history as a closed causal nexus, a history fully determined by a materialist and mechanistic set of causes. The neo-Marxist philosophy of hope of Ernst Bloch served this function in Moltmann's early work. Bloch's philosophy offered a view of human history analogous to the biblical one in understanding history as fundamentally open to creative possibility and change from the future.[26]

Although Moltmann has been criticized for his overdependence on this atheist philosophy in *Theology of Hope*, his reception of Bloch's ideas was always a critical one.[27] He highlights the affinities between his biblical theological perspective and Bloch's messianic humanism, all the while modifying the latter's philosophical system for his own theological ends. Both Moltmann and Bloch see the biblical symbol of the messianic God and the coming kingdom of God as a medium of hope in history and a catalyst for transformation in human society.[28] For Bloch, however, humankind's faith in the transcendent God of biblical religion remains a highly ambiguous phenomenon. Although religious faith instills revolutionary hope for change in history, it also always creates deceptive hopes for a future beyond history. For this reason Bloch aims ultimately to demythologize biblical religion into a revolutionary form of humanism, one that places its hope fully in the immanent possibilities of humankind and in nature. On this point Moltmann parts ways with Bloch's critical theory of religion. He rejected its ultimate goal, what he described as an "immanent transcending without transcendence,"[29] on the grounds that such an immanent possibility could never overcome the real negativities of suffering and death in history. Despite this fundamental disagreement, Moltmann continues to use Bloch's critical theory of religion as an idolatry critique against those forms of Christian faith that curtail human freedom and agency in the world.

Despite their ultimately divergent views on the sociocritical function of religion in society, Bloch's philosophical system proved absolutely vital to *Theology of Hope*. It offers Moltmann an ontological framework with which he could describe meaningfully God's eschatological engagement in human history. In his major work *Philosophy of Hope*, Bloch had developed an eschatology of being itself—what he termed "an ontology of the not-yet-being and of possibility in the world process."[30] In contrast to the modern view of history as a closed system of determined possibilities, history becomes, in Bloch's utopian framework, a radically open process; here the future takes ontological priority over past and present reality as the source of all genuine novelty in history.

In *Theology of Hope* Moltmann critically adapts this Blochian notion of the "power of the future" into a theological paradigm for God's "mode of being" (*Seinsweise*) in history. He uses Bloch's utopian notion to describe how the biblical God of promise acts in human history as a source of its creative possibility: "As this power of the future, God reaches into the present. As creator of new possibilities he liberates the present from the shackles of the past and from the anxious insistence on the status quo."[31] Framed in this Blochian ontology, the God of hope appears neither as a transcendental reality outside of history nor as a subjective reality immunized from the course of human history. Rather, the God of hope is present in world history as an inbreaking eschatological reality—a coming reality that injects new possibilities into history from its anticipated end.[32]

Moltmann received much criticism for translating biblical eschatology into Bloch's idiom. Many read into Moltmann's notion of God as "the power of the future" the all-too-familiar strains of a German Idealist concept of God, in which God's being is identified with the process of the world's becoming. As a result, Moltmann's *Theology of Hope* was criticized both for compromising the decisive character of divine revelation in the death and resurrection of Christ and for sacrificing divine sovereignty to the vicissitudes of world history.[33] In several significant essays published subsequently to *Theology of Hope*, Moltmann responded to these criticisms and clarified in biblical terms what he means by God's mode of being as "future."[34] He distances his model of revelation explicitly from the philosophical frameworks of both German Idealism and process metaphysics, by invoking a key distinction between the philosophical understanding of future as *futurum* and the biblical concept of *adventus*. If one speaks of future as "*futurum*," he explains, one refers to that which "emerges from the eternal process of becoming and begetting of being. It is the actualization of the primordial potential."[35] In other words, *futurum* is the result of the immanent processes of history and can be predicted or extrapolated from history itself. When one speaks of the future of God as *"adventus,"* however, one refers to the coming of the biblical God into history from its eschatological end. In this case God's future can be announced or anticipated in history but cannot be simply extrapolated from history's progress.

Moltmann's proposal is that we need to consider God's mode of being in this latter sense of *adventus,* that is, as the advent of new creative possibilities into history. As the source of new life, the God of hope introduces productive contradictions into history, which liberates humanity both from its determinism to the past and from its "utopia of the *status quo.*"[36] This God of hope is a life-giving force, the principle of creative transformation in history, and the ultimate source of freedom in history.

Theology of Hope *as Prolegomena to a Doctrine of God*

Although *Theology of Hope* clarifies much about God's mode of being in history as eschatological promise, the nature of the God of hope and of his coming eschatological kingdom remains quite opaque. Moltmann discusses the being of God only indirectly in this first major work within the context of his eschatological model of revelation.[37] Here the only clues to God's being come via descriptions of God's creative activity in history. But even when Moltmann describes the God of hope's paradigmatic activity, for example, as *"creatio ex nihilo, justificatio impii,* and *resurrectio mortuorum,"*[38] he actually only describes divine agency quite formally—as a principle of contradiction that liberates humankind from past or present structures of evil, suffering, and death. In short, beyond the statement that God is an eschatological source of new life, the positive affirmations that can be made about the God of hope are slim.

We also gain little direct insight from Moltmann's first major work into his understanding of divine love. In fact, the book altogether downplays the theme of Christian love except to treat love as the fruit of active faith in the God of hope.[39] This is no mere oversight on Moltmann's part but can be attributed to the author's exclusive focus at the time on the theme of Christian hope. During this earliest phase of his theological development, Moltmann views hope as the quintessential problem of modern theology, whereas love was that of the Middle Ages and faith that of the Reformation.[40]

What does emerge clearly in *Theology of Hope* is Moltmann's distinctive model of biblical revelation—his prolegomena to his early concept of God. To conclude, let us note this model's three key features. First, Moltmann emphasizes that the biblical God is a God who reveals himself *historically.* Over and against the Hellenistic God who is utterly transcendent to history, the biblical God comes to be known solely through his promissory acts or events in history. God's identity emerges through his faithfulness to these divine promises in history, and in this way, the stage of world history becomes constitutive to discerning God's self-identity.[41]

Second, biblical revelation is an *eschatological* promissory-event; it tells of a coming God, the power of the future, and his still outstanding messianic kingdom. Although the ground of Christian revelation lies in the past (in Jesus' resurrection from the dead), its ultimate significance lies in the future—in the yet unrealized promise of new creation. In this way Christian faith is suspended between past and future, "memory and hope."[42] Related to this eschatological aspect of divine revelation is its third key feature: its *dialectical* character. For Moltmann, divine revelation is always a promise that contradicts past and present reality and, in so doing, instills hope in history for a different future. This eschatological dialectic of revelation in history has a christological foundation: it is rooted in the absolute contradiction between the cross-event as symbol of all the negativities of created reality and the resurrection-event as God's definitive promise for a new creation.

These three dimensions of biblical revelation—the historical, the eschatological, and the dialectical—all bear epistemological significance for Moltmann's doctrine of God and the task of Christian theology as a whole. This model of biblical revelation prescribes, first of all, that all human speech about God is highly provisional and subject to constant critical revision in light of the inbreaking eschatological reality of God. Put differently, divine revelation is neither an unveiling of what is already completed in the past nor simply a continuation of that which is already immanent within world history. Revelation is the advent of genuine novelty into history and, therefore, renders all speech about God provisional. In this light, Christian theology remains itself incomplete and a wayfaring enterprise. In Moltmann's words, "Christian theology is, therefore, even in its very language, according to ancient terminology, *theologia viae*, but not as yet *theologia patriae*. That is, it is still the theory of historical action, and not as yet the theory of *theoria Dei*, the vision of God."[43]

The dialectical nature of divine revelation also signifies that all knowledge of God is dynamic and self-involving. Knowledge of the God of hope provokes an ongoing creative transformation of existing reality. The experienced contradiction between future hope and existing reality introduces creative new possibilities into history, and in so doing "call[s] forth practical movement and change."[44] In this way the universal eschatological horizon of divine revelation activates the vocation of individuals, as well as the church, to be concretely engaged in realizing the kingdom of God on earth.

The Trinitarian Theology of the Cross

Theological and Political Considerations in Moltmann's Turn to the Cross

In the period following the publication of the *Theology of Hope*, Moltmann gradually shifted his focus to the other side of his dialectical christology, namely, to the cross-event. By the publication of *The Crucified God* in 1972, the cross clearly had become the author's new hermeneutic lens through which to investigate all other doctrines of Christian faith. Moltmann speaks now in the same programmatic terms about the theology of the cross that he previously had about eschatology: "The death of Jesus on the cross is the *centre* of all Christian theology. It is not the only theme of theology, but it is in effect the entry to its problems and answers on earth."[45]

Initially many of Moltmann's contemporaries saw his turn to a radical theology of the cross as a retreat from his revolutionary program for an eschatological theology. From the first, however, the author explains his new tack as complementary to that of *Theology of Hope* and emphasizes the continuity between his two works in their common dialectical christological vision: "The theology of the cross is none other than the reverse side of the Christian theology of hope. . . . *Theology of Hope* began with the *resurrection* of the crucified Christ, and I am now turning to look at the *cross* of the risen Christ."[46] If we discovered the positive side of the dialectic with God as the source of creative possibilities in *Theology of Hope*, we discover the negative side of this historical dialectic—God's presence in suffering and death—in *The Crucified God*.

As is true of most developments in Moltmann's theology, both theological and political considerations contributed to his turn to the theology of the cross in the late sixties. One key theological stimulus came from the numerous critical responses that Moltmann had received to *Theology of Hope*.[47] Although criticisms of the book were quite varied, many were concerned that Moltmann's description of God in Blochian terms as the power of the future was too one-sided, especially with regard to its stress on God's messianic activity on behalf of humankind. Such a radical eschatological perspective threatened to uncouple Christian hope in the coming kingdom of God from the salvation that was already accomplished in Jesus Christ. Although Moltmann disagreed with those who rejected his radical biblical eschatology per se, he did concede that he needed to clarify the relationship between God's futurity and his salvific activity in Christ.[48] *The Crucified God* responded to this theological challenge, as Moltmann sought to demonstrate how resurrection hope in the God of the future was anchored historically in God's revelation in the cross-event.

A variety of secular impulses also impacted Moltmann's christological thinking in the late sixties. The turn of political events—in particular, the collapse of "socialism with a human face" with the march of Warsaw Pact troops on Prague in 1968, the assassination of Dr. Martin Luther King and the crisis it signaled for the black civil rights movement in the United States (to which Moltmann was witness during his year at Duke University in 1967–68), the international student protest movement, and the war in Vietnam—all contributed to the sobering direction that Moltmann's theology took in this period. These political events not only tempered the optimism of *Theology of Hope* but also precipitated his turn to the cross as the Christian symbol of "hope and resistance"[49] in the midst of a cultural milieu of forsakenness and desolation.

Another critical factor in Moltmann's theological development during this period was his active engagement in Marxist-Christian dialogue. In these dialogues he was explicitly challenged to distinguish his Christian identity from his commitments to certain socialist and political goals. This challenge from the socialist Left coupled with the gradual retreat of the German Protestant church into traditionalist forms of theology and social apathy led to the trenchant critique with which *The Crucified God* opens. Moltmann charges both the church and theology of becoming caught in a dual crisis of "relevance" and of "identity": "The more theology and the church attempt to become relevant to the problems of the present day, the more deeply they are drawn into the crisis of their own Christian identity. The more they attempt to assert their identity in traditional dogmas, rights and moral notions, the more irrelevant and unbelievable they become."[50] The author sought the remedy for this twofold crisis in the return to the theology of the cross. On the one hand, the theology of the cross provides a robust theological basis for Christian engagement in society; on the other, it provides a critical principle for claiming Christianity's nonidentity and independence from any particular social program or institution.[51]

These diverse theological and political strands of Moltmann's thinking in the late sixties coalesced around what surely becomes the driving concern of *The Crucified God*: the question of theodicy or divine righteousness in the face of radical evil and meaningless suffering in history. According to Moltmann's personal recollections, the theodicy question had been at the root of his reflections about God since the war.[52] But it was the rising protest atheism of the late sixties, as well as the emerging discussion among Jewish theologians on the possibility of any "theology after Auschwitz," that finally drove the theodicy issue to the top of Moltmann's theological agenda. As the voices of religious alienation—those of Camus, Dostoyevsky, and Horkheimer—protesting against the triumph of evil and suffering grew louder in the wider culture, Moltmann's proposal for an eschatological faith in a God of hope began to founder. Although the God of hope might prove liberating to those who have the historical freedom to bring about transformation in society, such a God offers little comfort to history's innumerable victims who appear to have been forsaken by God to their fate. Such a God appears altogether too remote from the concrete suffering of the contemporary world to elicit true faith.

In *The Crucified God*, Moltmann seeks a more profound soteriological response to the theodicy question through a critical retrieval of the Reformers' theology of the cross. He revises sharply his dialectical christology of the *Theology of Hope*, so that the crucifixion now becomes the focal point of God's identification with the acute suffering and injustices of human history. Here at the cross God reveals his true being as more than eschatological hope; God reveals God's self as "the event of suffering, liberating love"[53] that mediates forgiveness to the godless sinners and hope to the innocent godforsaken ones of human history. In what follows I will examine in detail Moltmann's interpretation of the cross as this revelation of divine suffering, since it provides the springboard for the author's initial trinitarian concept of God and for his early concept of divine love in *The Crucified God*.

The Soteriological Significance of the Cross of the Risen Christ

Moltmann interprets the cross-event by way of a complex exegesis of the passion narrative in the Gospel of Mark, to which he contributes key insights drawn from Pauline theology. He begins with a historical interpretation of Jesus' death, his "historical trial," and then doubles back to offer a corresponding theological interpretation of this death as a divine act, which he terms as "the eschatological trial of Jesus Christ."[54] Although Moltmann's ultimate interpretation of the cross is the theological one, he proceeds first historically to demonstrate the identity between the historical figure of Jesus and the risen Christ, and, even more, to show the faithfulness of God who reveals God's self to be the same in these two events. In *The Crucified God*, Moltmann presents a multilayered interpretation of Jesus' historical trial as that of the "rebel," the "blasphemer," and the "godforsaken" one.[55] For our purposes, only the third and last interpretation of the crucifixion is directly relevant, since it provides the foundation for the author's interpretation of the cross as a trinitarian event of love.

Moltmann's interpretation of Jesus' death as that of the "godforsaken" rests primarily on the Gospel of Mark's account of Jesus' death as a death of profound despair and abandonment by God. Moltmann's chief biblical cue is the cry of dereliction ascribed to Jesus in Mark 15:34, which hearkens back to Psalm 22:2: "My God, why hast thou forsaken me?" Moltmann interprets this cry as springing forth from the rupture that has occurred in the fellowship between Jesus and God the Father. As intimate as Jesus' fellowship with God was throughout his ministry, so, too, writes Moltmann, is now his abandonment by God absolute in his death: "The torment in his torments was this abandonment by God."[56]

Moltmann's reading of Jesus' dereliction cry in terms of divine abandonment reveals the author's guiding soteriological interest in the question of divine righteousness in light of innocent suffering. Essentially Jesus repeats the modern atheist's protest against a providential God given the terrible injustices of human history. In Jesus' dying cry, we hear the righteous person's cry against a God who appears to have broken faith with his beloved creation:

> Jesus is not calling for the compassion of God upon his own person,
> but for the revelation of the righteousness of the God who promised

"not to forsake the work of his hands." Abandoned by God, the righteous man sees God's deity itself at stake, for he himself is the faithfulness and honour of God in the world. . . . In the words "My God, why hast thou forsaken me?" Jesus is putting at stake not only his personal existence, but his theological existence, his whole proclamation of God. . . . *In the death of Jesus the deity of his God and Father is at stake.*[57]

On Moltmann's reading of the cross-event, Jesus is subject at his death to the darkest depths of divine abandonment, as well as the accompanying atheistic doubts. The crucifixion puts to trial not only Jesus' messiahship and the kingdom that he proclaimed but also the very existence of the God whom he proclaimed.

While this experience of "godforsakenness" captures the deepest human dimension of the cross, Moltmann stresses that from this perspective alone Jesus' death bears no salvific significance; absolutely nothing distinguishes Jesus' cross from all the other "crosses in the history of human suffering."[58] Solely from the vantage point of the resurrection does the cross-event obtain its unique salvific significance. The resurrection sheds light retroactively on the cross-event, so that Jesus ultimately becomes visible in his divine sending— as "the *incarnation* of the coming God in our flesh and in his death on the cross."[59] In the resurrection-event we come to know retroactively not only that the human Jesus became subject to divine godforsakenness but that God himself did.

From this resurrection-faith perspective Moltmann elucidates two related ways in which the cross-event proves salvific for humankind. First, the death of the crucified Christ is an act of divine solidarity or kenotic identification with the depths of evil and suffering of the human situation. At the cross we discover a God who so utterly identifies with the human situation as to become one with it. Jesus' cry of dereliction reveals that God in God's self submits to the most painful contradiction of human existence—divine abandonment. In Moltmann's words, "The abandonment on the cross which separates the Son from the Father is something which takes place within God himself; it is *statis* within God—God against God."[60] At the cross this contradiction causes a division or separation within God's being—between Father and Son, a separation that in the resurrection is healed in the reunion of the two. If we bracket for a moment the profound ontological implications of treating the cross-event as a rupture in God's very being, what is soteriologically relevant here is that through Christ's suffering of godforsakenness, God opens divine fellowship to all who suffer in the world. Since God willingly undertakes the death of absolute divine abandonment in God's self, God spares humanity of it.

God overcomes suffering and evil not only through this act of solidarity with us but also in taking this action for us. Here Moltmann interprets Jesus' death as an act of "personal representation" for humankind, but not as an expiatory sacrifice " 'for our sins.' "[61] Rather, it is a historical mediation of liberation, or, better said, a proleptic anticipation of resurrection for us. In the cross-event an eschatological qualification has occurred in human history that enables humankind to participate in the new life and future promise of eternal life of the resurrection. In Moltmann's formulation: "The cross of Christ modifies the resurrection of Christ under the conditions of the suffering of the world so that it changes from being a purely future event to being an event of liberating love."[62] In this way Moltmann secures the historical knot more tightly between the salvation accomplished in the cross-event and the eschatological hope of the resurrection than he had previously in *Theology of Hope*.

This victory over death does not fully exhaust the meaning of God's act for us on the cross. Following the dialectic of the cross in Pauline theology, Moltmann turns back from the resurrection to the cross and discovers God's salvific presence not just in "exaltation" but also in "humiliation and lowliness."[63] In a central passage of *The Crucified God*, Moltmann explains God's act of personal representation in terms of his "giving up of the Son" as a divine enactment of "self-surrendering, self-emptying love":

> So what did God do in the crucifixion of Jesus? . . . God himself delivered him up. In the passion of the Son, the Father himself suffers the pains of abandonment. In the death of the Son, death comes upon God himself, and the Father suffers the death of his Son in his love for forsaken man. Consequently, what happened on the cross must be understood as an event between God and the Son of God. In the action of the Father in delivering up his Son to suffering and to godless death, *God is acting in himself. He is acting in himself in this manner of suffering and dying in order to open up in himself life and freedom for sinners.* Creation, new creation and resurrection are external works of God against chaos, nothingness and death. The suffering and dying of Jesus, understood as the suffering and dying of the Son of God, on the other hand, are works of God towards himself and therefore at the same time *passions of God.*[64]

According to Moltmann, this divine passion or suffering love acts for us in the cross-event, transforming the human situation by acting inwardly upon itself. In the act of the Father delivering up the Son, God suffers his own contradiction, godforsakenness, and embraces it within God's very being.

At this point we can pause to take note of how sharply Moltmann has revised his cross-resurrection dialectic since *Theology of Hope*. Whereas in his earlier book the cross-resurrection dialectic signified the harsh antithesis between the world and divine eschatological reality, in *The Crucified God* this antithesis is taken up into God's self. The cross is no longer a sign of divine absence in history but its very opposite—a sign of God's passionate presence in the midst of human history. Moreover, the suffering of the cross is not an external action of the Son of God who is sent into the world but is immanent to God—"God acting in himself." In sum, we see the author drive his theology of the cross to its radical conclusion: God's self-surrendering love on the cross is such that God encompasses this contradiction in God's self.

For the purposes of this study, what is crucial about Moltmann's resignification of the cross-event in *The Crucified God* is that this event now defines the nature of the biblical God who is love. Moltmann draws this clear ontological link between divine love and the cross-event in passages such as this one: "The cross of Jesus, understood as the cross of the Son of God, therefore reveals a change in God, a *statis* within the Godhead: 'God is other.' And this event in God is the event on the cross. It takes on Christian form in the simple formula which contradicts all possible metaphysical and historical ideas of God: 'God is love.' "[65] Here we begin to see how Moltmann's theology of the cross stipulates his early notion of divine love as a form of unconditional love for the other. The cross-event reveals God identifying God's self dialectically with his opposite and yet maintaining divine identity. To comprehend more fully what this dialectical concept of divine love entails, we need now to take up the question that we had earlier laid aside, that is, the ontological significance of the cross-event for the being of God.

The Cross-Event as Trinitarian Dialectic of Love

As we turn to investigate Moltmann's development of an explicitly trinitarian concept of God, let us first briefly recall why the author views the cross-event as uniquely disclosive of God's being. As I noted in my introduction to *The Crucified God*, Moltmann's theological epistemology is very much influenced at the time by Luther's theology of the cross. He takes up the Reformer's trenchant critique of natural theology as a "theology of glory," as well as his dialectical approach to divine revelation in the paradox of the cross from the *Heidelberg Disputation*. Moltmann had already voiced criticisms of the possibility of obtaining natural knowledge of God in the *Theology of Hope*. There he concluded that cosmological and anthropological proofs for God's existence were flawed, since they rested on false inferences drawn from the present state of the world (or the human subject) to the eschatological being of God.

In *The Crucified God*, Moltmann deepens this earlier critique of natural theology by adding to it Luther's critical perspective on the devastating noetic effects of sin. Moltmann adopts fully Luther's position that although natural knowledge of God had been "potentially open to men,"[66] it had been rendered impossible for humankind due to their perverse tendency toward self-divinization and idol worship. Given humankind's present fallen state, the only direct knowledge of the God of love is that which is made visible in the cross, because this is where God addresses the situation of fallen humanity. The cross reveals who God is "for us": the suffering God of love who liberates humankind from its compulsions toward self-delusion and self-deification.

In *The Crucified God*, Moltmann formalizes this dialectical revelation of God at the cross into the first principle of his theological epistemology. He defines this general "dialectical principle of knowledge" broadly as "like is known by unlike" and explains it with a controversial formulation borrowed from Schelling: "'Every being can be revealed only in its opposite. Love only in hatred, unity only in conflict.' Applied to Christian theology, this means that God is only revealed as 'God' in his opposite: godlessness and abandonment by God. In concrete terms, God is revealed in the cross of Christ who was abandoned by God."[67] Many interpreters have stumbled over Moltmann's formulation here (as well as his citation of Schelling), since at first glance Moltmann seems to be suggesting that God is the opposite of what God reveals himself to be.[68] On closer inspection, however, Moltmann's dialectical principle prescribes only that God reveals himself where he is contradicted by his very opposite. As Richard Bauckham points out, Moltmann's dialectical principle is "the epistemological corollary of the nature of God's love"; it corresponds to his notion of divine love as love to the other, a love that is revealed in God's act of solidarity with God's other—the godless sinner and godforsaken victim—at the cross.[69] Put differently, the cross-event bears a double significance for Moltmann: it is the locus of God's dialectical self-revelation, and it manifests the dialectical character of divine love itself as love for the other, the unlike.

In *The Crucified God*, Moltmann contrasts this dialectical principle of knowledge sharply with the "analogical principle of knowledge" ("like is known only by like"), which he views as the foundational principle of classical Greek epistemology.[70] Just as he drew an opposition between the Hellenistic God of Parmenides and that of Exodus in *Theology of Hope*, Moltmann now opposes this Hellenistic principle to the dialectical biblical one. True biblical knowledge of God "is achieved not by the guiding thread of analogies from earth to heaven, but on the contrary through contradiction, sorrow and suffering."[71] Adopting Luther's rhetoric, Moltmann argues that the analogical method, if it is pursued in isolation, leads to a theology of glory, while the dialectical leads to a theology of the cross.[72] In a parallel fashion, he contrasts the Hellenistic concept of love, *philia*, which he depicts as a conditioned analogical principle of love ("the love for what is similar and beautiful") to the biblical principle of love, *agape*, which he describes as an unconditional dialectical form of love ("creative love for what is different, alien and ugly").[73]

Despite his negative portrayal of a purely analogical approach to knowledge of God, Moltmann does not altogether exclude that knowledge of God can be gained by analogical means. He argues only that the dialectical revelation of God at the cross must be the soteriological condition for its possibility. This crucifying knowledge is what, in Moltmann's words, "brings [humankind] into correspondence with God, and, as 1 John 3.2 says, enables them even to have the hope of being like God."[74] The cross overcomes the absolute contradiction between God and humanity and, in so doing, restores through grace the very possibility of humanity's correspondence to God; only in this way does analogical knowledge of God once again become a real possibility for humankind.

In *The Crucified God*, Moltmann leaves many questions unanswered about the exact relationship that obtains between analogical and dialectical forms of knowledge of God. These ambiguities quickly brought criticisms against the book, ones that eventuated in Moltmann's clarification of his position in his later works. Significant for this study is the fact that even in the most dialectical phase of his thinking, Moltmann opens the door to the possibility of analogical knowledge of God. That is to say, he sees the possibility of transformation in the human situation through the sanctifying work of grace, and this, in turn, opens up the possibility for true analogies to exist between the divine and created orders. As I will argue in the chapters ahead, such analogies or correspondences between the divine and human realms became a more pronounced reality in Moltmann's mature trinitarian theology. Once he develops a full-blown doctrine of creation and accords the sanctifying work of the Spirit a more central role in the economy of salvation, Moltmann has the theology of grace in place that can support such analogies between the divine and created orders.

With this dialectical theological epistemology fully in view, we are now in the position to consider how Moltmann's soteriology leads to his initial trinitarian concept of God. As I demonstrated earlier, the crux of Moltmann's soteriology is that the cross-event represents a divine act of suffering love, in which God undergoes death in solidarity with and in personal representation of humanity. The cross becomes an event in God, in which divine love embraces and overcomes its opposite within itself. To grasp the full meaning of this event in and for God, Moltmann contends that we cannot speak generically of God acting in Christ or in *theopaschite* terms of the suffering or death of God.[75] The cross-event necessitates a trinitarian differentiation in the concept of God. In Moltmann's words, "The more one understands the whole event of the cross as an event of God, the more any simple concept of God falls apart. In epistemological terms it takes so to speak trinitarian form."[76]

By advancing the cross-event as the starting point for his trinitarian concept of God, Moltmann undertakes a radical reformation in how trinitarian doctrine had been formulated since the time of the early church. To clear the way for his reconstruction of the doctrine, Moltmann argues that the doctrine's development had gone seriously awry in the West. The doctrine of the Trinity had become slowly divorced from its roots in the *oikonomia* (how God acts for us in Christ) and instead treated as part of *theologia*—or speech about "the divine majesty."[77] Once this distinction had become an accepted part of the Western theological tradition, the Trinity was slowly transformed into a speculative mystery of the faith without soteriological and practical relevance.

In mounting this critique, Moltmann largely took over Karl Rahner's highly influential analysis of the demise of the doctrine that had been published a few years prior.[78] Moltmann agrees fully with Rahner's contention that the doctrine of the Trinity had becoming increasingly isolated from salvation history, especially since the Middle Ages, at which time the scholastic distinction between the articles *De Deo uno* and *De Deo trino* in the Christian doctrine of God was formalized.[79] This fateful division between the truths of natural theology and those of special revelation only reinforced the ancillary status of trinitarian claims to the doctrine of God as a whole. To Rahner's analysis of the doctrine's demise, Moltmann adds his own parallel Protestant version of the story. This scholastic division was incorporated into Protestant orthodoxy and eventually led to the "surrender of the doctrine of the Trinity" in the Protestant Enlightenment when the doctrine was dubbed a "theological speculation with no relevance for life."[80]

In developing a trinitarian theology of the cross, Moltmann set out essentially to rehabilitate the organic connection between the doctrine of the Trinity and soteriology. To this end, he applies Rahner's famous rule to his own trinitarian theology of the cross: "The economic Trinity *is* the immanent Trinity, and the immanent Trinity is the economic Trinity."[81] Moltmann radicalizes Rahner's rule by insisting that this is more than an epistemological restriction; it is an ontological rule. Put differently, Moltmann defends the ontological identification of the cross-event with the trinitarian being of God: "The cross stands at the heart of the trinitarian being of God; it divides and conjoins the persons in their relationships to each other and portrays them in a specific way."[82] In other words, the cross-event not only reveals the trinitarian God who is "for us" but actually constitutes the Trinity. And therefore, Moltmann (at least at this early stage of his theological development) argues against the need for this classical distinction between the immanent and the economic trinities altogether.[83]

Although Moltmann takes this decisive step toward reformulating the classical trinitarian doctrine, his initial trinitarian proposal is in fact quite rudimentary. Essentially Moltmann's proposal is for a "trinitarian understanding of kenosis," in which the kenotic act of self-surrender or "delivering up" differentiates the various relationships within the trinitarian God.[84] The bare outlines of this trinitarian model of divine kenosis were already present in our earlier discussion of the cross as a scene of abandonment between the Son and the Father. In a later passage of *The Crucified God*, Moltmann elucidates more clearly how the trinitarian distinctions take place in this self-surrendering act at the cross:

> In the surrender of the Son the Father also surrenders himself, though not in the same way. For Jesus suffers dying in forsakenness, but not death itself. . . . But the Father who abandons him and

delivers him up suffers the death of the Son in the infinite grief of love. . . . To understand what happened between Jesus and his God and Father on the cross, it is necessary to talk in trinitarian terms. The Son suffers dying, the Father suffers the death of the Son. The grief of the Father here is just as important as the death of the Son.[85]

Here Moltmann picks up on two of Paul's formulations of Jesus' death as a "delivering up" (Rom. 8:31–32; Gal. 2:20) and differentiates between the various acts of "delivering up" (*Hingabe*) that occur at the cross-event. Not only does the Father deliver up the Son, but also the Father himself is delivered up in the loss of the Son. Quite significantly, the Son is not a passive object in this kenotic act but actively delivers himself up, too. In this way both the Father and the Son appear as active agents and as the affected "persons" of the cross-event; only together do they assume the estrangement of the world as a "death *in* God."[86]

As I noted earlier, Moltmann interprets the cross-event as a deep rupture or estrangement in the personal relations between the Father and the Son. In a controversial formulation, Moltmann describes this division in highly agonistic terms as "God against God": "The cross stands between the Father and the Son in all the harshness of its forsakenness. If one describes the life of God within the Trinity as the 'history of God' (Hegel), this history of God contains within itself the whole abyss of godforsakenness, absolute death, and the non-God. '*Nemo contra Deum nisi Deus ipse.*' "[87] Moltmann's intent in this passage is clear: to include all of history's suffering, evil, and death within God's loving being. And yet, as Moltmann's critics were quick to point out, by speaking in dramatic terms of this "death in God," Moltmann risked introducing a paradox into the very being of God that would disrupt the unity of the Godhead.[88]

Here the Holy Spirit plays two decisive roles for Moltmann in overcoming this threatened disunity in the Godhead. First, the Spirit overcomes this contradiction (at least eschatologically) in the being of God by serving as the bond of love that joins the Father and the Son. Despite the deep division between the Father and the Son at the cross, the Holy Spirit (itself acting in self-surrendering love) joins the two in a "conformity" or "community of wills"; by mutually enacting this event, the two remain "most inwardly one in their surrender."[89] Second, this same Spirit of love acts as a unifying power between humankind and God, overcoming the breach caused by sin and thereby enabling the world's participation in this divine life of love. The common Spirit of the Father and Son processes forth from the cross-event in what I term an expression of "creative love" that breathes new life into humankind:

> Whatever proceeds from the event between the Father and the Son
> must be understood as the spirit of the surrender of the Father and

the Son, as the spirit which creates love for forsaken men, as the spirit which brings the dead alive. *It is the unconditioned and therefore boundless love* which proceeds from the grief of the Father and the dying of the Son and reaches forsaken men in order to create in them the possibility and the force of new life.[90]

It is crucial to note here that the Holy Spirit incarnates the same essence of divine *agape* as the Father and Son. As the power of love that "creates new life" and "creates similar patterns of love in man in revolt," the Spirit manifests the same unconditioned "love of the other" that the Father and Son also reveal at the cross event.[91]

As part of the backdrop to Moltmann's mature social trinitarian theology, it is significant to note that the author's early trinitarian dialectic of the cross-event actually resembles closely the dominant Western Augustinian model of the Trinity. Just as in Augustine's model, here too the Holy Spirit assumes the role of the *vinculum caritatis*—the bond of self-surrendering or kenotic love—that unites Father and Son, and processes forth from both to unite humankind to God. Moltmann also inherits the weak points of Augustine's model, namely, whether this understanding of the Spirit as the bond of love can assure the Spirit's full personhood and equal status to that of the Father and the Son. Moltmann's trinitarian theology of the cross especially seems liable to this criticism, since the Spirit clearly does not assume the same active role of delivering up or *kenosis* that distinguishes the personhood of both the Father and the Son at the cross.[92]

Where the Spirit does play an essential role in Moltmann's early trinitarian schema is in opening the trinitarian cross-event to include the world and, most particularly, to include human history. Through the activity of the Spirit, the trinitarian God-event becomes, in Moltmann's words, "an eschatological process open for men on earth":

> For eschatological faith, the trinitarian God-event on the cross becomes the history of God which is open to the future and which opens up the future. . . . it seems clear that the divine Trinity should not be conceived of as a closed circle of perfect being in heaven. This was in fact the way in which the immanent Trinity was conceived of in the early church. Barth also uses this figure of the "closed circle" for God. In contrast to this, though, one should think of *the Trinity as a dialectical event, indeed as the event of the cross and then as eschatologically open history.* The Spirit, love, is open to the future for the whole of forsaken humanity; in positive terms, for the new creation.[93]

Just as we saw previously with the God of hope, the trinitarian God of the cross is not a transhistorical reality or what Moltmann characterizes negatively here as a closed circle. This Trinity is rather itself an event in history that both impacts upon the present and is open to the future.

Moltmann appropriates a key concept from Hegel's philosophy of religion, namely, that of the Trinity as the history of God, to give conceptual expression to this historical-eschatological nature of the trinitarian God. By utilizing Hegel's schema, Moltmann introduces the same historical dynamic into his trinitarian theology of the cross that we saw in his model of divine revelation in *Theology of Hope*. Once reformulated as the history of God, the trinitarian relationships, which were first revealed at the cross-event, are set into a wider historical framework of God's salvific engagement with the world. This history of God begins now with the sending of the Son in the incarnation and extends to the Son's eschatological handing over of the kingdom to the Father.[94] Most significantly, the cross-event is no longer the conclusion of the "history of God," for this history remains open until the eschatological consummation of the kingdom, at which time "the 'Trinity may be all in all.' "[95]

By portraying the Trinity in the conceptual form of the "history of God," Moltmann abandons a crucial mode of speaking about God as *adventus*, the mode of God's activity that we saw in *Theology of Hope*. Instead of speaking about God breaking into history from its end, Moltmann now characterizes the world as being taken up into the "history of God" (the Trinity) and "integrated into the future of the 'history of God.' "[96] While Moltmann describes this "history of God" as inclusive of the world, at the same time he cautions against a pantheistic identification of God and world on the grounds that this would ignore the negativities of the world and negate divine transcendence over them. Moltmann advances instead an explicitly "panentheistic"[97] model of the world in the "history of God" as the most adequate way of expressing how the entire history of the world (including all its negativities) will be eschatologically reconciled within God's loving being.

At this point let us pause to note some of the controversial aspects of Moltmann's early trinitarian model and the criticisms that he received of it. First and foremost, Moltmann's dialectic of the cross-event as the history of God resembled closely the dialectical movement of Hegel's concept of absolute being: a dialectical historical process, in which God becomes divided in God's self at the cross, only to be eschatologically reunited through the Spirit. This parallel was not lost on Moltmann's critics, who found his trinitarian concept of God liable to many of the same theological problems from which Hegel's suffered. Chief among the suspicions raised about Moltmann's trinitarian "history of God" was that it jeopardizes divine sovereignty over God's creation. For example, Hermannus Miskotte argued that Moltmann's God appeared first to become Trinity in the process of world history—a position that rendered the course of world history necessary to God's being. Recalling Barth's critique against Hegel's schema, Miskotte pointed to the dangerous implications of

Moltmann's early trinitarian proposal: "In the end, however, God appears to have become the prisoner of this history."[98]

Other prominent critics such as Walter Kasper charged that Moltmann's presentation of the Trinity as the history of God appeared not only to open God's being to human history but also to dissolve God in it. Kasper traced the root of this problem to his Protestant colleague's dialectical "Denkform," which—with its uncritical dependency on German Idealism—ended up treating evil and salvation as necessary moments in the historical dialectic of divine being.[99] In Kasper's view, Moltmann's dialectic threatened to collapse into a dangerous identity: "Are we not faced here with the danger that the miracle of the love of God, the cross, is dissolved in a dialectic, which turns over into identity?"[100]

We will return to these specific criticisms of Moltmann's early work in our next chapter, where we will see how Moltmann engages them in *The Church and the Power of the Spirit* (1975) and in other key essays written during the same period. Similar questions about God's freedom in relationship to history and God's goodness in relationship to created evils will also occupy our attention in *The Trinity and the Kingdom*, where Moltmann develops most fully his views on the relationship of God and the world. At this point, however, we can venture one firm conclusion about Moltmann's early trinitarian theology development, namely, that his dialectical vision of the trinitarian life is driven more by soteriological than conceptual necessity. As I have argued previously, Moltmann's trinitarian turn in his concept of God was precipitated by a combination of his interpretation of the passion narrative and his theological epistemology that committed him to the position that direct knowledge of the divine came from God's self-revelation in the cross-event. These theological commitments rather than Moltmann's philosophical appropriation of dialectical idealism best explain his early formulation of the doctrine. Despite the strong family resemblances between Moltmann's dialectics and German Idealism, Moltmann certainly does not fall prey to the charge of a speculative dissolution of trinitarian doctrine—what Michael Welker incisively describes as making "the doctrine of the Trinity a vestigium of the 'absolute method.'"[101] Although Moltmann appropriates aspects of Hegel's speculative framework into his theology, his concept of the trinitarian God remains firmly rooted in the economy of salvation, and most particularly in the cross-event. The passion narrative not only determines Moltmann's early concept of the Trinity but also helps to distinguish the biblical God of love from rival philosophical concepts or moral ideals of love.

The Biblical God of Suffering Love

In the preceding section I traced how Moltmann's concept of divine love emerges from his interpretation of the passion narrative as a trinitarian event

of self-surrendering love. This event of love constitutes a form of divine suffering, which not only is an activity of God in the world but is internal to the
trinitarian life itself; it is an inward passion of God, that is, an act that God
undertakes toward God's self. I also elucidated how Moltmann differentiates
between the Father's and the Son's forms of suffering at the cross. We saw the
Son's suffering described in existential terms as the pain of dereliction or
godforsakenness, and as a death in solidarity with and personal representation
of humankind. And we saw how the Father is equally pained by an infinite
grief at the loss of his Son.

From these descriptions of the trinitarian dialectic at the cross-event, a
rather clear picture emerges of Moltmann's understanding of divine love. Most
broadly stated, it is an unconditional form of divine compassion—a "suffering
with" the other that occurs in and among the personal relations. As Richard
Bauckham explains well, for Moltmann, "God's love is his 'passion' in the
double sense of passionate concern (*Leidenschaft*) and suffering (*Leiden*). Love
is not just activity on others but involvement with others in which one is moved
and affected."[102] In other words, divine love expresses not only God's boundless
beneficence toward the world but also how God's very being is affected by
God's personal relationship to God's creation. At the cross human beings discover that this divine passion is utterly boundless. Paraphrasing Bonhoeffer,
Moltmann writes: "God allows himself to be forced out. God suffers, God
allows himself to be crucified, and is crucified and in this consummates his
unconditional love that is so full of hope."[103]

Even as Moltmann insists that the cross-event is the ultimate measure of
divine love in the New Testament, he identifies key antecedents for this same
love in the Old Testament. Just as he defends a fundamental continuity between
the resurrection and the promissory nature of God's revelation to Israel in
Theology of Hope, Moltmann now emphasizes the continuity between the "suffering love" of the crucified God and the ancient Hebrew understanding of
divine pathos (and the modern Jewish one). To build this case, Moltmann draws
especially upon Abraham Heschel's study of divine pathos in the prophetic
literature and on the rabbinic theology of the *Shekinah*, or the "self-humiliation
of God." Following Heschel, he describes divine pathos as the passionate concern and indeed suffering that arises from God's relationship to his covenant
people of Israel: "He is affected by them because he is interested in his creation,
his people and his right. The *pathos* of God is intentional and transitive, not
related to itself but to the history of the covenant people."[104] Stated differently,
the suffering love of the God of Israel is an active and freely chosen form of
passion; it is an act of divine freedom that arises out of God's relationship to
his creation.

For Moltmann, the rabbinic theology of the *Shekinah* or self-humiliation
of God profoundly deepened the Hebrew understanding of divine pathos. According to this tradition, God's covenantal relationship to Israel led to God's

actual indwelling in the midst of its situations of hardship, including situations of both guilt and innocent suffering. The *Shekinah* incarnates the same dialectical pattern that we have already traversed with the cross-event: a divine act of self-humiliation or of "self-surrender" in solidarity with the guilt and suffering of the human situation, through which human liberation is accomplished. Just as the divine suffering of the cross-event was internal to God's being, so, too, the history of Israel's suffering is embraced within God's loving being.[105]

This convergence between Hebrew and christological understandings of divine *pathos* proves extremely significant to Moltmann's later development of his trinitarian theology. By establishing the divine *pathos* of God already in God's history with Israel, the author insists that suffering is intrinsic to the biblical God's covenantal relationship with his creation. In Moltmann's later works, this claim becomes central to his defense that the doctrine of the Trinity (and with it the notion of a suffering God) has Jewish roots and therefore is not, as liberal Protestantism had previously argued, an intrusion of Hellenistic metaphysics into biblical faith.[106]

The link between Jewish and Christian notions of divine pathos is also central to Moltmann's project of developing a credible Christian theology after Auschwitz. As I noted in my introduction to *The Crucified God*, the horrors of Auschwitz presented Moltmann with the deepest challenge to his belief in a righteous God. For a Christian theologian to take this challenge seriously, Moltmann concludes, he or she must speak of a "God in Auschwitz," that is, affirm that the one God of Jews and Christians was present in the midst of the present sufferings of the people of Israel. As one can see in the following passage, Moltmann draws his own trinitarian theology of the cross to the dramatic and controversial conclusion of including the horrors of Auschwitz into its midst:

> Like the cross of Christ, even Auschwitz is in God himself. Even
> Auschwitz is taken up into the grief of the Father, the surrender of
> the Son and the power of the Spirit. That never means that Ausch-
> witz and other grisly places can be justified. . . . only with the annihi-
> lation of death will the Son hand over the kingdom to the Father.
> Then God will turn his sorrow into eternal joy. . . . God in Auschwitz
> and Auschwitz in the crucified God—that is the basis for a real
> hope which both embraces and overcomes the world, and the
> ground for a love which is stronger than death and can sustain
> death.[107]

In passages such as this one, Moltmann does not seek to explain the radical evil of Auschwitz but rather to embrace its horrors in the midst of the loving being of God. In so doing, he aims to offer meaningful hope both for its victims and for the future of the world.

By depicting the biblical God as a God of "suffering love," Moltmann challenges directly two alternative responses to the theodicy question, that of theism and that of protest atheism. Although Moltmann refers to several versions of theism in *The Crucified God*—metaphysical, philosophical, or classical—they all represent for him variations on the theism of classical antiquity, in which God is defined as "pure causality" or the "unconditioned mover."[108] Here, as he does repeatedly in his later works, Moltmann casts this Hellenistic God of theism in an extremely harsh light. He spotlights those classical attributes that are *negations* of finitude (for example, indivisibility, immutability, and, most important, impassibility) to emphasize how the God of classical theism is a remote and impersonal being.[109]

Moltmann's critique of theism follows the lead (although not uncritically) of two of his Protestant colleagues at the time, Eberhard Jüngel and Hans-Georg Geyer.[110] For Moltmann as well as the others, the cross-event challenges basic Hellenistic metaphysical presuppositions that exclude suffering and death from God. The early church advanced furthest toward realizing this metaphysical revolution by positing a doctrine of the Trinity that spoke of God in terms of the incarnation and cross-event. This theological revolution had been halted, however, by the "intellectual barrier" of the "Platonic axiom of the essential *apatheia* of God."[111] Once suffering was limited to the human nature of Jesus at the Council of Chalcedon and *theopaschitism* was subsequently rejected at the Council of Constantinople, the God of theism triumphed again. Although Moltmann does not state this explicitly in *The Crucified God*, he appears to conclude that the Hellenized God of theism has (with few exceptions) eclipsed the truly trinitarian concept of the suffering God in Western theology ever thereafter.

Regardless if one agrees with this historical judgment or not, the heart of Moltmann's critique of theism is not philosophical but soteriological; in his view, theism fails to address meaningfully the problem of evil. On this issue Moltmann sides with the "protest atheism" of Camus and Dostoyevsky, who rejected the existence of an omnipotent and gracious God who remains impassive in the face of the deep injustice and human suffering in the world. Moltmann agrees with them that an apathetic God is deficient in being, rather than its supreme perfection. A God who remains unmoved by his creation's suffering jeopardizes the very goodness of God. In the author's words, "A God who cannot suffer is poorer than any man. . . . But the one who cannot suffer cannot love either. So he is also a loveless being."[112]

Even as Moltmann assumes the protest atheist's critique of theism, he subjects it to equal criticism. He charges it with naive anthropocentrism and nihilism: protest atheism either divinizes humanity or succumbs to meaninglessness.[113] At its root, protest atheism suffers from the same false assumption as theism; it assumes that the reality of God and suffering are contradictions to one another.

For Moltmann, the trinitarian theology of the cross overcomes these two alternatives by overturning the *apatheia* axiom. As he asserts, "God's being is in suffering and the suffering is in God's being itself, because God is love."[114] The key to grasping Moltmann's argument here lies in how he defines divine love not as a freedom *from* suffering but as a freedom *for* suffering. To appreciate the significance of this shift, it is important to recall that for the classical Christian tradition, divine love was viewed as an act of benevolence or goodwill in which God affects us, but in which God remains unaffected in God's self.[115] For classical theologians such as Augustine and Aquinas, all forms of vulnerability were excluded from the concept of divine love because they would indicate that God had changed or been determined by an alien force. Such an idea was simply inconceivable for a God defined in terms of perfect being and pure causality. Likewise, all forms of emotion were excluded from the divine being, since they were perceived as a form of passivity and hence as an imperfection in the divine being.

On the basis of the divine passion revealed in the cross-event, Moltmann argues otherwise. Although he agrees that God cannot be subject to involuntary suffering, he proposes an alternative notion of divine love: "active suffering," in which God chooses or allows himself to be affected by others of his own free will.[116] If divine love is understood as "active suffering," God can be affected by his personal relationship to the world without this becoming a deficiency in his being. In a crucial passage Moltmann presents his argument succinctly:

If love is the acceptance of the other without regard to one's own well-being, then it contains within itself the possibility of sharing in suffering and *freedom to suffer as a result of the otherness of the other.* . . . *The one who is capable of love is also capable of suffering, for he also opens himself to the suffering which is involved in love, and yet remains superior to it by virtue of his love.* The justifiable denial that God is capable of suffering because of a deficiency in his being may not lead to a denial that he is incapable of suffering out of the fullness of his being, i.e. his love.[117]

Central to Moltmann's argument here is that as freely chosen or "active suffering," divine love maintains its transcendence over human suffering. In other words, there is an asymmetry between God's will and the evils of the world. Given this asymmetry, divine passibility does not have the negative consequences that the classical theist suggests, namely, that God becomes a victim of human finitude.

This concept of divine love as "freedom *for* suffering" responds equally to the protest atheist's accusation against a God indifferent to the concrete suffering of humankind. By embracing the contradictions of death in love itself, God's suffering love offers solidarity with human suffering and real hope for a different future. Although the active suffering of the cross does not offer any sort of answer (or, even worse, a justification) to the question of evil's existence, it does offer a soteriological response. Moreover, this notion of active suffering nullifies the protest atheist's claim that a theology of the cross inculcates passive submissiveness to suffering because it implies that the human protest against evil and suffering remains alive in God. Divine suffering does not silence the rightful protest against human suffering; on the contrary, it intensifies it by making it God's own.

One final observation is in order about Moltmann's depiction of the biblical God of suffering love in *The Crucified God*. If we cast our minds back to the *Theology of Hope*, we can see how Moltmann's dichotomy between the suffering God of the cross and the apathetic God of classical theism in *The Crucified God* corresponds to his juxtaposition of the biblical and Hellenistic concepts of God in his earlier work. There the author juxtaposed the biblical God of Exodus and of the resurrection-event to the God of Parmenides, and also the eschatological paradigm of biblical revelation as a promissory event in history to the transcendental Hellenistic paradigm of an "epiphany of the eternal present." Moltmann makes this same historical-eschatological distinction between the biblical and Hellenistic views of the divine in *The Crucified God*, but now he adds another dimension to his argument—divine passibility. Here we encounter the divine pathos of the God of Israel and of the "Crucified God," directly challenging antiquity's ideal of *apatheia* as the metaphysical and ethical perfection of God.

Moltmann's opposition between the biblical concept of God and the Hellenistic concept develops one step further in *The Crucified God*. He no longer contrasts these as two rival theistic concepts as he previously had in *Theology of Hope* but instead advances an explicitly trinitarian concept of the biblical God over and against that of philosophical theism. If we are to grasp the history of this biblical God of hope as the crucified God, Moltmann insists that we must make an ontological differentiation within a strictly monotheistic understanding of God. This initial differentiation in the being of God sets the stage for what we will see emerge in his later work, namely, the author's juxtaposition of his social trinitarian proposal to any undifferentiated and monarchical form of monotheism.

The Dialectic of Crucified and Creative Love

In this chapter I have explored Moltmann's earliest major works in order to discover the specifically biblical origins of his trinitarian theology and to identify his early concept of divine *agape* as a foil for the notion of trinitarian love that emerges in his later work. Moltmann's "dialectical christology" has been at the center of this chapter's investigation, as I looked first at the author's eschatological interpretation of the "resurrection of the crucified Christ" in

Theology of Hope and then at his complementary interpretation of the "cruci-fixion of the risen One" in *The Crucified God*.

In *Theology of Hope*, I uncovered what I termed a prolegomena to Molt-mann's doctrine of God, that is, his distinctive model of biblical revelation as a dialectical, historical, and eschatological promissory-event. Here I empha-sized in particular Moltmann's interpretation of the resurrection as an uncon-ditional yet eschatological promise of victory over death and of new creation. As a restless promise (*promissio inquieta*), the resurrection-event produces an ongoing dialectic that draws history—curiously enough, from its anticipated end—toward its consummation in the eschatological kingdom of God. We could only gather a few clues to the nature of this biblical God from Molt-mann's early descriptions of God's activities in history: God appears as the power of the future, the dialectical principle of creative transformation, and the source of creative possibility and freedom. From these descriptions, I con-cluded that Moltmann saw the biblical God in this earliest work chiefly as the eschatological source of hope and new life.

I pursued Moltmann's dialectical christology further in *The Crucified God*, where the cross-event became the new focal point of Moltmann's theological investigation. Here I showed how the author replaced his earlier interpretation of the cross-event as sheer negativity and divine absence with a quite different one: God's dialectical identification with that which contradicts God's very be-ing—godforsakenness and the evils of the world. Moltmann took this radical theology of the cross a step further in response to the challenge raised by the theodicy question. The cross-event becomes an event in God through which divine love embraces and eschatologically overcomes its very opposite within itself. This soteriological interpretation of the cross-event as a death in God provided the impetus for Moltmann's shift toward a trinitarian concept of God in this period.

Despite Moltmann's stated aim to radically reform the classical doctrine of the Trinity, we saw that his initial trinitarian theology was in fact quite rudimentary. He offers a trinitarian understanding of kenosis at the cross-event, in which the Father and the Son mutually enact this self-surrendering act of love. Although cast in a highly subordinate role, the Spirit appears also at the cross-event as divine *agape*—as the bond of love joining the Father and the Son, and as the gift of creative love that reconciles the world to God. When viewed together, these differentiated acts of love provide the underlying dialect-ical structure of Moltmann's early trinitarian history of God, a history that traces an ontological division in God's being that is reconciled through the eschatological work of the Spirit. In keeping with the promissory nature of divine revelation that he introduced in *Theology of Hope*, Moltmann describes this trinitarian history of God as an open dialectic. The trinitarian cross-event is open to humankind and to all of human history, and it remains so until the eschatological consummation of the kingdom of God, when all things will be taken up into the midst of the trinitarian life.

At this point in his career, Moltmann has yet to develop his mature social doctrine of the Trinity. Already prominent, however, in this early period is the inextricable link between the author's trinitarianism and his soteriological vision of divine love. The doctrine of the Trinity is nothing other than the story of God's unconditional and salvific love acting on behalf of humankind. In Moltmann's words, "The doctrine of the Trinity can be understood as an interpretation of the ground, the event and the experience of that love in which the one who has been condemned to love finds new possibility for life because he has found in it the grace of the impossibility of the death of rejection."[118] It is the story of the victory of divine love over the depths of human suffering.

Through careful investigation of this trinitarian dialectic at the cross-event, we have been able to disclose the shape of Moltmann's early view of divine love. On my reading of his works, divine *agape* manifests itself in two forms—as crucified and creative love. By crucified love, I am referring specifically to the divine compassion or suffering with the other that we saw enacted by the Father and the Son at Christ's death at the cross. Moltmann presents this crucified love as an unconditional form of divine pathos, in which God in God's self suffers the grief of abandonment on behalf of (personal representation) and in solidarity with his creation. The other side of this dialectic, creative love is clearly more of a minor theme than that of suffering love in the author's early work. The notion of divine love as creative love is already present, however, in the author's discussion of God as the source of creative possibility in *Theology of Hope*. In *The Crucified God*, creative love manifests itself more explicitly in and through the liberating activity of the Holy Spirit, who creates new life in humankind and, in so doing, returns humankind to the embrace of divine love.

From this dialectic of trinitarian love as crucified and creative love, we can draw one significant conclusion about Moltmann's early understanding of divine love. He holds to a personal and relational notion of divine *agape*, by which I mean that divine love includes being affected by one's personal relation to the other. In this respect the author's concept of divine *agape* as divine pathos or freedom for suffering departs significantly from the classical tradition's notion of divine love as active beneficence, a notion that excludes God from being affected by the other.

In conclusion, allow me to raise two unresolved questions with regard to this early trinitarian concept of divine *agape*. First, do the two sides of Moltmann's dialectic of divine love—crucified love and creative love—cohere with one another to provide a unified vision of God's being as love? We might state this question polemically in terms of Moltmann's dialectic: wherein lies the identity in this dialectical contradiction? One solution to this question lies in

Moltmann's proposed notion of *agape* as an unconditional love for the other; both crucified and creative love could be subsumed under this general principle. And yet this begs the further question: Can one capture the history of God under such a dialectical principle without obscuring both the biblical and the soteriological root of Moltmann's notion of divine love?

A second important question remains with regard to the exact relationship that obtains between divine and human loves. Should we understand God's love on analogy to our own human expressions of love, or is God's love of such a qualitatively different order that we come to know it uniquely and exclusively through revelation? Moltmann seems to presume some degree of analogy between divine and human loves, because in several places he freely characterizes divine love in highly anthropomorphic terms.[119] Most obviously, Moltmann explicates God's suffering love at the cross in terms of the all-too-human feelings of grief and abandonment. And yet, Moltmann also seems in *The Crucified God* to follow Luther's theological epistemology, in which the knowledge of God obtained at the cross-event destroys the illusion of any true knowledge of God obtained through analogies to the human situation.

Sorting out whether there are analogies between the divine and human forms of love, and if so, to what degree, is more than an epistemological question for this study. As we will see in chapters 4 and 5, this question returns to us in considering the trinitarian patterns of the Christian life: To what degree and through what powers (our own or through grace) can human beings pattern themselves after the love of God? Can we realize any kind of *imitatio Trinitatis*, imitation of the trinitarian life, in the fragile and finite realities of human relations and communities?

3

The Relational Ontology of Love in the *Messianic Theology*

This chapter investigates Moltmann's social reconstruction of the doctrine of the Trinity in the first volume of his *Messianic Theology*, *The Trinity and the Kingdom*, and how it alters his concept of divine love. Both methodological and doctrinal issues will claim our attention in this chapter. On the methodological side, I will point to new scriptural resources to which Moltmann appeals in support of his social trinitarian proposal. Identifying these scriptural patterns and how they function in his doctrine will help to evaluate one of the central criticisms raised against Moltmann's social trinitarianism that I noted at the outset, namely, whether his doctrine is governed more by the author's social and political agenda than by the biblical witness.

In addition to Moltmann's use of scripture, I will also be identifying several new theological conversation partners from which he draws inspiration for his doctrine. During this period Moltmann became increasingly engaged in ecumenical dialogues and as a result became more critical of weaknesses in his own Reformed tradition. At the same time, he developed a new appreciation for Eastern Orthodox theology, especially for its doctrines of the Holy Spirit and of salvation, and sought creative ways to appropriate these tradition's insights into his theological proposals.

On the doctrinal side, our primary task will be to uncover the conceptual framework of Moltmann's social reconstruction, in particular, his concepts of the divine persons, their relations, and their unity with one another. These concepts not only structure Moltmann's trinitarian doctrine but also provide the building blocks for his theological anthropology and his views on redemption and sanctification, to which we will turn in chapters 4 and 5. Related to this doctrinal development we will also pursue several questions concerning God's eternal nature as love: How does the author's concept of divine love materially change from what he presented in his early dialectic of crucified and creative love? What are the implications of his messianic perspective of God's nature on his claims about God's being as love? Finally, how does Moltmann relate claims about God's being as love to those about God's freedom, especially in relationship to the creation and redemption of the world? In answering these questions, we will be returning to another one of the most contested aspects of Moltmann's theology, namely, whether his construal of the God-world relationship compromises divine sovereignty to the vicissitudes of human history.

Toward an Eschatological Doctrine of the Trinity

The Turn to Trinitarian Pneumatology

The years between the publication of *The Crucified God* (1972) and the start of his work on *The Trinity and the Kingdom* in 1978–79 represent a transitional phase in Moltmann's thinking. He presented no major trinitarian proposals on the order of what he had set forth in *The Crucified God*. He did, however, make significant emendations and expansions on his earlier dialectical trinitarianism in certain programmatic essays and in his major work during this period, *The Church in the Power of the Spirit* (1975). The most significant among these shifts is Moltmann's development of a robust pneumatology, which, in turn, revitalized the eschatological dimension of his theological program.

Just as with the theology of the cross in the late sixties, a mixture of church-political and theological issues prompted Moltmann's renewed interest in pneumatology during the early and midseventies. In terms of church politics, Moltmann continued to be troubled by the ongoing crisis of relevance that the German Protestant church was experiencing.[1] Like most established or state churches in Europe, the Protestant church in Germany found itself in a rapidly secularizing society that looked to the church neither to address its spiritual needs nor to answer its pressing social and political questions of the day. Moltmann saw the church's crisis as an opportunity for a radical reformation of the church's self-understanding and its organizational structure. As he explained years later, the German Protestant church found itself at a crossroads: either it would continue down this same institutional path and become the "organized religion of the state," or it would reform itself into "a community church of the people of God."[2] With the hope of contributing to such a radical reformation of the post–World War II *Volkskirche* into a free church structure, Moltmann devoted the third volume of his trilogy, *The Church in the Power of the Spirit* (1975), to the theme of ecclesiology.

From the very first, Moltmann's ecclesiology did not enjoy the critical success of his two prior works; nor did it achieve his hoped-for reformation of the *Volkskirche* into a free church structure. It proved fruitful, however, in focusing Moltmann's attention once again on the role of the Holy Spirit, especially in the processes of justification and sanctification—what he calls bringing about the promised new creation.[3] For Moltmann, the church quickly became a subordinate doctrinal theme to the wider messianic activity of the Holy Spirit in realizing the kingdom of God in the world.

Specific criticisms of *The Crucified God* also provoked Moltmann's return to pneumatology in this period.[4] In the previous chapter we already saw some of these criticisms of Moltmann's trinitarian theology of the cross emerge: the ambiguities in his dialectical epistemology and the Hegelian tendencies that others had identified in his trinitarian theology. Underlying both of these criticisms is a concern about Moltmann's assertion that the cross is the constitutive event for the Christian doctrine of God. Many of Moltmann's critics interpreted this statement to be suggesting that God first became Trinity in the cross-event. For example, Hermannus Miskotte challenged Moltmann's staurocentric approach to trinitarian doctrine on the grounds that it eclipsed the distinctive work and persons of the Father and the Spirit in the economy of salvation. Miskotte asks whether, if "the cross is the beginning of the trinitarian history of God," then "the Son appears to have become the *'fons deitatis.'*" He drew particular attention to the indefiniteness of the person and work of the Holy Spirit in *The Crucified God* as indicative of Moltmann's flawed trinitarian theology of the cross; the Spirit, he criticized, appeared more like a "divine power" than actually a personal "mode of being of the Trinity."[5]

In his 1979 response to critics of *The Crucified God*, Moltmann reaffirmed his position that the cross-event is the soteriological starting point for trinitarian doctrine, because this is where the human being first experiences his or her liberation from God's judgment and abandonment.[6] Moltmann did think that his critics had discovered a neuralgic point in his trinitarian theology of the cross. His one-sided focus on the cross-event's implications for the Godhead had eclipsed the distinctive activity of the Holy Spirit within the economy of salvation. As Moltmann wrote many years later about his trinitarian proposal in *The Crucified God*, "I did not get further than seeing a binity of God the Father and Jesus the Son of God. Where was the Holy Spirit, who according to the Nicene Creed is to be worshipped and glorified together with the Father and the Son?"[7]

In conjunction with these shortcomings in his trinitarian theology of the cross, Moltmann began to question whether a certain subordination of the Spirit was endemic to the Western trinitarian tradition. He noted, for example, how his binitarian interpretation of the cross-event followed closely the Western Augustinian love analogy for the Trinity, in which the Father and Son appear as the lover and the beloved, and the Spirit as the bond of love (*vinculum amoris*) that joins the two. Just as in his own trinitarian theology of the cross, here, too, in Augustine's triad of love, the Spirit is more a "hypostatization of a relation" than its "own personality," and thus never emerges as a divine person equal to the Father and Son.[8] In the end Moltmann concluded that his trinitarian interpretation of the cross-event had simply recapitulated this Augustinian pattern of the Spirit as the bond of love that unites the Father and the Son at their point of deepest separation and mutual forsakenness.[9]

Moltmann links this subordination of the Spirit in Augustine's and his own trinitarian schemas to a further problem that he pinpoints in the Western formulation of the Trinity: its singular emphasis on the sending of the Son and the Spirit into the world and on the corresponding internal processions in the Godhead. Troubling to Moltmann about this way of formulating trinitarian doctrine—what the author describes as moving from the "Trinity in the sending" to the "Trinity in the origin"—is that it overlooks the eschatological aspects of the trinitarian history of God with the world.[10] In other words, it does not take into account the still outstanding history of God that reaches beyond the initial sending of the Son and the Spirit into the world. This traditional "protological" approach to the doctrine assumes further that all intradivine activities stem from the Father and the Son, and never from the Holy Spirit. While the Spirit may be active in terms of her mission toward the world, she appears merely passive as the one who is being sent by the Father and Son.[11]

Moltmann discovers this traditional structure of the "Trinity in the sending" and the "Trinity in the origin" repristinated in his trinitarian theology of the cross. He, too, had extrapolated from the Father's and Son's actions in the cross-event a description of their inner relations. As a result, the Spirit had been guaranteed neither its own distinct activity in the economy of salvation nor an active relationship toward the Father and the Son. Despite these subordinationist tendencies, Moltmann did not altogether abandon his trinitarian theology of the cross. Instead, he sought to resolve this imbalance by developing a history of the Spirit that complemented his earlier history of the Son. Through this history of the Spirit, Moltmann sought to do justice to the full divine personhood of the Spirit while at the same time recovering the crucial eschatological dimensions of the Trinity's engagement with the world.

The Eschatological Spirit of New Creation and the Trinity in the Glorification

Moltmann develops the basic outlines of his history of the Spirit in his programmatic essay "The Trinitarian History of God" (1973) and fills it in subsequently with much greater detail in *The Church in the Power of the Spirit*. He essentially begins where he left off in *The Crucified God*—with the history of Christ—but now approaches this history as it were from the other side of his christological dialectic. He focuses on the divine activity in the resurrection-event and looks toward its eschatological goal.[12]

Moltmann draws together a mosaic of Pauline texts in order to interpret the resurrection-event as a revelation of the Father's glory—as "the divine unfolding of splendour and beauty"[13] through the activities of the Son and the Spirit. Integral to the Father's glorification is the eschatological transfiguration and participation of all of creation within the glory of the Godhead. "The mission of Christ," Moltmann contends, "achieves its purpose when men and creation are united with God. In this union God is glorified through men and in it they partake of the glory of God himself."[14] Although the glory of the Father has already been anticipated in the Son's resurrection, it will first be brought to its ultimate conclusion with God's eternal indwelling in his creation.

The heart of the Holy Spirit's mission is to accomplish this eschatological goal of divine glorification and unification. The Spirit does not simply apply the justification of the sinner that is already fully accomplished in Christ, but in fact consummates or completes salvation by glorifying creatures and drawing them into joyful fellowship with God. The Spirit creates fellowship between God and human beings, and in so doing sparks freedom and joyfulness in God's creatures. As Moltmann formulates this, "The Spirit glorifies the Father and the Son by freeing men for fellowship with them, filling men in their freedom with joy and thanksgiving. The glorifying of the Son and the Father through the Spirit sets men on the road towards the glory for which they themselves are destined."[15] Here the Holy Spirit acts not only as that bond of love that unites humanity to the atoning love of Father and Son at the cross but also as the creative power of God's eschatological future. Through the glorifying activity of the Spirit, humankind experiences not simply freedom from its sinful past but also freedom for the creative transformation of this life.[16]

Moltmann's description of the work of the Holy Spirit builds on much we have already seen in *Theology of Hope* and *The Crucified God*. There the Spirit already appeared as the "power of the future" and as the "creative love" of God that brings new possibilities and life into the world. Genuinely new, however, is the author's attention to the transfigurative work of the Spirit, which creates the possibility for humankind's intimate fellowship with God. This new emphasis on the transformative energies of the Spirit can be traced to a crucial influence on Moltmann's thinking during this period—that of Eastern Orthodox theology. Throughout the seventies, Moltmann grew increasingly fascinated by Eastern Orthodox theology through his involvement in ecumenical dialogues with the Faith and Order Commission of the World Council of Churches, as well as through his personal friendship with Romanian Orthodox theologian Dimitru Staniloae.[17]

What especially captured Moltmann's interest was the Orthodox model of salvation as deification, and particularly its emphasis on the Holy Spirit's role in transfiguring the life of the believer. In *The Church in the Power of the Spirit*, Moltmann integrates this new model of salvation alongside of his Reformed tradition's classical emphases on the forgiveness of sinners through the work of Christ and the justification by faith of the believer. Although Moltmann never abandons either of these central Reformed tenets as the starting point of the Christian life, he now views them as incomplete without an equal emphasis on sanctification and the liberated life of the believer.[18] Moreover, he derives from the Orthodox understanding of faith as doxology another important element that he found largely absent from Protestant notions of the Christian life—an attitude of joyful thanksgiving and delight in the goodness of God.[19]

Based on the deepened understanding of the Spirit's mission in the economy of salvation, Moltmann develops a second schema of trinitarian relations in history, "the Trinity in the glorification," that completes his earlier narrative of the Son's and the Spirit's missions into the world. If the "Trinity in the sending" traces the divine persons' missions into the world, the "Trinity in the glorification" corresponds to the reverse of that pattern; it represents the divine persons' gathering and uniting of the world into the heart of God's loving being.[20] Where in the former schema all divine activity originates in the Father and moves toward the sending of the Spirit, in the latter one all activity proceeds from the Spirit toward the glorification of the Father.

Although Moltmann does not himself make specific reference to the Neoplatonic emanation-return (*exitus-reditus*) paradigm in explaining his expanded version of the trinitarian history of God, one can hardly mistake its resemblance to this ancient pattern. The "Trinity in the sending" traces the "love of God issuing from itself," while the "Trinity in the glorification" follows the return of divine love with all of creation into God.[21] Instead of the incarnation, here the cross- and resurrection-events become the turning point in Moltmann's revision of this emanation and return schema, for these events represent the historical juncture at which the seeking love of God is transformed into the gathering love of God.

Most significant about Moltmann's formulation of the Trinity in the glorification is that it crystallizes for the first time the eschatological goal of his trinitarian history of God: the indwelling of all of creation within the trinitarian life. Moltmann roots this vision of God "becoming all in all" in the scriptures by combining aspects of Pauline eschatology with the apocalyptic vision of the Book of Revelation.[22] According to these biblical traditions, God will no longer stand over and against creation in the eschatological kingdom but will indwell in its very midst. At the same time, all of creation will be so transfigured so as to participate fully in the life and glory of God.

There were already glimpses of Moltmann's "eschatological panentheism" in *The Crucified God*, where the cross-event appeared as an open event awaiting its consummation through the inclusion of the world in the embrace of divine love.[23] In *The Church in the Power of the Spirit*, Moltmann takes one step further, however, and integrates this panentheistic vision into the midst of the trinitarian life itself. Just as the cross-event is an event in the divine life, now the eschatological consummation of creation becomes equally for him a "happening within the Trinity."[24] In taking this theological step, Moltmann ties the glorification of the Trinity directly to the eschatological destiny of creation. Divine glorification arrives only through the liberation of and fellowship with creation.

The Doctrine of the Trinity and the Nature of Divine Love Revisited

Moltmann's newly proposed "eschatological history of the Spirit" has significant implications for his reconstruction of Western trinitarian doctrine and his understanding of divine love in his later work. In examining these implications, it is essential to bear in mind the fundamental methodological principle that structures Moltmann's reconstruction of trinitarian doctrine, namely, that God is who God is *pro nobis*. As we saw earlier in *The Crucified God*, this soteriological principle means that Moltmann claims quite radically that God's salvific activity on behalf of humankind in the cross-event does not just manifest the true being of God but actually constitutes it. This is why Moltmann abandons (at least provisionally in *The Crucified God*) the traditional distinction between the immanent or eternal Trinity and the economic or revealed one. In its place he proposes his one unified concept of the trinitarian history of God, in which trinitarian being is to be found in the unfolding dialectic of God's history with the world.

The addition of new pneumatological dimensions to this trinitarian history of God renders Moltmann's soteriological reconstruction of trinitarian doctrine at once much more complex. There is no longer the single event of the cross, but now an entire narrative of divine activities that constitutes this history. This narrative stretches back in time from the cross to the sending forth of the Son and Spirit from the Father; similarly, this narrative continues on from the cross to the consummation and glorification of creation into the trinitarian being in the eschaton. As a result, the Trinity now appears as open to the world not simply at the rupture of the cross-event but, in Moltmann's words, from its "very origin,"[25] that is, from the sendings of the Son and Spirit into the world from the Father. Moreover, the Trinity remains open until the gathering, uniting, and glorifying of the world in the glory of God.

Given this fundamental openness of trinitarian being to history, Moltmann abandons altogether the classical Western structure of the doctrine in terms of eternal processions and temporal missions. He does so on the grounds that no single set of relations among the Father, the Son, and the Spirit can be specified that will correspond to the eternal trinitarian being as such. In place of such a fixed conceptual reformulation of the doctrine, Moltmann turns instead to various narrative depictions of this dynamic trinitarian movement in history. These narratives recount the changing relationships among the Father, the Son, and the Spirit that reflect both the various operations of the Trinity in history and "the divine experience of history."[26] In other words, these narratives recount how the three divine persons affect the history of the world and how that history conversely affects the trinitarian being.

At this point in Moltmann's emerging trinitarian theology, he construes just two narratives of trinitarian relations—the Trinity in the sending and the Trinity in the glorification—to describe this entire trinitarian history of God. In *The Crucified God*, he had already explored at length the Trinity in the sending and drew forth a vision of God's being as passionate self-giving and suffering love. To this Moltmann now adds the Trinity in the glorification, which reveals the divine delight over the liberation of creation and its freedom for new life. In the author's words: "If we think in the direction of the glorification, then . . . we must talk about God's joy (as already in Isa. 62.4–5; Zeph. 3.17), God's happiness and felicity (I Tim. 1.11; 6.15; Luke 15.7; Matt. 25.21; John 15.11; 16.20; Rom. 14.17; 15.13)."[27]

We saw glimpses of these liberative and joyful dimensions of trinitarian love in Moltmann's few references to the Holy Spirit's activities in *The Crucified God*. These were, however, very much eclipsed by his cross-centered focus on divine *agape* as freedom for suffering. This picture shifts dramatically in *The Church in the Power of the Spirit*. With this eschatological interpretation of the resurrection-event, the creative and joyful side of trinitarian love not only occupies center stage but gains preeminence as the telos of the entire history. Now Moltmann describes God's suffering in the passion of the Son and the Spirit in service to the "history of God's joy in the Spirit and his completed felicity at the end."[28]

One final implication of Moltmann's trinitarian pneumatology deserves our careful attention, namely, how it lends an eschatological openness to the trinitarian history of God. Although Moltmann does not quite go so far as to state explicitly that the Trinity is presently incomplete in its being, he does describe it metaphorically as open for the gathering of restored creation into its midst. To the degree that the trinitarian history of God awaits eschatological completion through the glorifying and unifying of creation through the Spirit, so, too, we can say that the trinitarian Godhead itself awaits eschatological unification.

In light of this eschatological horizon of trinitarian being, Moltmann revises his whole notion of divine unity. He pointedly rejects the two different ways that the Eastern and the Western church fathers have traditionally construed divine unity, that is, either in terms of the Father as the source of the Godhead or in terms of a common essence that can be logically abstracted from the three divine persons. Neither schema, in his view, corresponds adequately to this trinitarian history of God.[29] Moltmann proposes instead that divine unity be construed as an "eschatological goal" rather than an "eternal premise" of divine being.[30] In other words, divine unity emerges in and through the consummation of the economy of salvation, that is, through the glorification and unification of the Father, the Son, and the Spirit with each other and the world.

In *The Church in the Power of the Spirit*, Moltmann offers only a preliminary sketch of how to reconceive divine unity in such eschatological terms. He depicts it as the "union of God"—a union that includes all of creation. He looks specifically to the Spirit to accomplish this consummating work in the world: "Just as [God's] glory is presented to him from creation through the Spirit, so his unity through the union of creation is also brought to him through the Spirit."[31] As his precedent for this notion of divine unity as unification with creation, Moltmann turns to the rabbinic notion of divine *Shekinah*, the indwelling presence of God, especially as it has been reinterpreted by the modern Jewish thinkers Franz Rosenzweig and Abraham Heschel. Just as the unity of the Hebrew God is, in Rosenzweig's words, a "Becoming Unity"[32] that includes the return of God's people to him, so, too, Moltmann argues, the "unity of the triune God is the goal of the uniting of man and creation with the Father and Son in the Spirit."[33]

Moltmann's initial proposal for an eschatological concept of divine unity as the union of God raises a series of pressing new questions for his emerging doctrine of the Trinity. For example, what is the nature of divine unity in the eschaton—an ontological unity among the Father, the Son, and the Spirit, or merely a volitional unity that is constituted by their shared activity of glorification? Moreover, if God's unity is to be understood as a "becoming unity," can one speak meaningfully at all about a divine unity in the Trinity in the origin? And if so, how does one relate this protological unity of God to the eschatological one? Should one speak here of a quantitative or a qualitative difference between the two? Finally, if the world's unification is part and parcel of the eschatological union of the Father, the Son, and the Holy Spirit, does this mean that creation becomes an eternal necessity of trinitarian being?

Answers to this range of questions will have to await Moltmann's formal reconstruction of the doctrine in *The Trinity and the Kingdom*. Nevertheless, Moltmann's description of the eschatological unity of trinitarian being as the "becoming unity" of the indwelling *Shekinah* illumines our path forward. It reminds us that the hermeneutical key to Moltmann's vision of trinitarian love lies in God's passion for the world, its salvation, and its new creation. It belongs to the essence of that divine passion to undertake a pilgrimage in history in order to return God's beloved creation to God's self. Like the *Shekinah*, the trinitarian God puts the unity of divine being at risk by linking its eschatological destiny to that of creation.

The Trinity and the Kingdom: A New Starting Point
for Trinitarian Doctrine

A New Method of Procedure

With the completion of his early trilogy of works in 1975, most of the building
blocks for Moltmann's reconstruction of the doctrine of the Trinity were in
place. He not only had integrated both sides of his dialectical christology into
his trinitarian framework but also had remedied his earlier subordination of
the Spirit within his trinitarian theology of the cross; in so doing, he had filled
in the pneumatological and eschatological dimensions of his trinitarian economy of salvation. In sum, Moltmann had fleshed out the bare skeleton of his
dialectical trinitarian history of God so that it now encompassed the changing
relationships among the trinitarian persons from the sending of the Son and
the Spirit into the world to their eschatological consummation.

What was still missing, however, was an adequate doctrinal framework—
one that represents adequately the nature of the trinitarian God who both
affects this messianic narrative and is affected by it. As Moltmann envisioned
it, such a doctrine would be able, in his words, to "integrate all of the historical
experiences and therefore speak of the persons, their relations and the changes
in their relationships, i.e., of their history. This would be a doctrine of the
Trinity with—abstractly formulated—changing vectors."[34] By 1979 Moltmann
had determined the course for this doctrine's future development. Without
abandoning any of his trinitarian proposals from his earlier trilogy, he set out
to represent their contents in a different systematic form—within what he
originally called a "*messianic Dogmatics*" that would have as its goal the freedom
of humankind in the kingdom of God: "From the guiding perspective of the
Trinity and the kingdom of God," Moltmann wrote, "the way will be marked
out from history into freedom."[35]

Moltmann launched his full-scale reconstruction of the doctrine with the
1980 publication of *The Trinity and the Kingdom*, the first volume of his *Messianic Theology*. There he develops for the first time his "social doctrine of the
Trinity" as a fundamental critique of the dominant trajectory of the doctrine
in the West.[36] Since the patristic period, Moltmann contends, Western formulations of the doctrine have placed an undue emphasis on the unity of divine
essence at the expense of the differentiated relationships among the persons
in the Godhead. As a result, Western trinitarianism has devolved into what the
author terms a form of "monarchical monotheism," which does justice neither
to the full personhood of Father, Son, and Spirit nor to the biblical understanding of divine sovereignty in the kingdom. Furthermore, Moltmann charges
that this monarchical doctrine of the Trinity has provided a divine legitimiza-
tion for political orders and ecclesial structures that have undermined Christian
notions of freedom and of fellowship in community.[37]

Moltmann seeks to overturn the monarchical trajectory of Western trinitarianism by developing his social doctrine with a different conceptual framework: "The Western tradition," he explains, "began with God's unity and then went on to ask about the trinity. We are beginning with the trinity of the Persons and shall then go on to ask about the unity."[38] In other words, Moltmann's overall program is to begin with the activities and the changing patterns of relationships among the Father, the Son, and the Spirit—both with each other and in relation to the world. From these various trinitarian activities in the world (opera ad extra), Moltmann derives what he calls various "trinitarian forms."[39] These trinitarian forms serve, on the one hand, to distinguish the three persons from one another and, on the other, to describe the nature of divine triunity as the dynamic sociality of the Godhead—what he terms the "Trinity's relations of fellowship."[40]

In The Trinity and the Kingdom, Moltmann continues in many respects exactly where his earlier trinitarian theology left off. Not only do many of the key motifs from these earlier works recur in this new work, but also the same methodological criteria are applied to the doctrine's reconstruction. Most important, Moltmann's fundamental methodological principle of revising the doctrine in light of the biblical witness remains unchanged.[41] He pursues a trinitarian hermeneutics of the scriptures that follows the same basic lines as the one that we introduced earlier in The Crucified God; he defends the doctrine of the Trinity as a legitimate interpretation of the various narratives that are contained in the scriptures.

In terms of the actual content of this trinitarian narrative, The Trinity and the Kingdom does represent a significant advance upon the earlier versions of the trinitarian history of God. Here for the first time Moltmann integrates (at least in a compressed form) all the Trinity's activities in the world from the act of creation to eschatological consummation into his trinitarian history of God. As we will see ahead, the author's new trinitarian interpretations of both creation and the event of the incarnation are of particular significance, since these interpretations deepen Moltmann's account of the "Trinity in the sending" and in so doing contribute to his reinterpretation of the nature of the trinitarian love.

Coupled with Moltmann's expansion of the trinitarian history of God is a more comprehensive and variegated use of the biblical texts. From The Trinity and the Kingdom onward, Moltmann weaves together an ever more complex tapestry of biblical texts to which he appeals in order to illuminate the different roles of the Father, the Son, and the Spirit in the trinitarian history. To take a central case in point: in The Crucified God Moltmann relied chiefly on the Gospel of Mark and on Pauline letters as the scriptural resources for his history of the Son. Many of these same interpretations of key biblical texts reappear intact in the new version of the "history of the Son" presented in The Trinity and the Kingdom. They are now enhanced, however, by biblical interpretations drawn from the other synoptic gospels (particularly from Matthew) and even more from the Gospel of John. In a similar fashion, Moltmann appeals to a broader range of biblical resources to give more definition to the activities and personhood of the Spirit and, most noticeably, to that of the Father. These further differentiations among the trinitarian persons and their particular activities within the trinitarian history of God prove crucial to Moltmann's social reconstruction of the doctrine, since he concludes from these the distinct personhood of each of the three, as well as the nature of their common love.

In addition to appealing to a greater variety of biblical texts, Moltmann also engages in an intensified dialogue with the history of trinitarian traditions. In *The Trinity and the Kingdom* and in the ensuing volumes of his *Messianic Theology*, Moltmann addresses a range of unsettled theological issues from the past, while also sifting through the history of doctrine for new insights to contemporary questions. As I suggested in my earlier discussion of his methodology, Moltmann has always insisted that it is the particular nature of theological truths to emerge only in a free and ongoing dialogue. We saw ample evidence of the dialogical character of his theology in his earlier works, in which he engaged in a lively conversation with his contemporary culture and church situation and with his Reformed theological tradition.

What distinguishes Moltmann's dialogical approach in his mature theology is that his conversation partners greatly expand to include an *"ecumenical fellowship"* of theologians from the past.[42] Of course, certain key theologians who already appeared in *The Crucified God* remain center stage in *The Trinity and the Kingdom*. Schleiermacher's modalism and Barth's and Rahner's monarchianism still represent the key antipodes in modernity to Moltmann's social trinitarianism. They are now joined, however, by a chorus of other pivotal figures from the patristic and medieval periods of Eastern and Western trinitarian theology, most notably Origen, the Cappadocian Fathers, Augustine, Boethius, Joachim of Fiore, and Richard of St. Victor. This eclectic group provides Moltmann with an array of conceptual resources for reconstructing his doctrine.

Keeping in mind these introductory remarks on Moltmann's methodology and his aims in formulating a social doctrine of the Trinity, let us turn to the unusual structure of *The Trinity and the Kingdom* and our method of proceeding through its argument. Even for those who are already familiar with Moltmann's earlier trinitarian theology, the structure of *The Trinity and the Kingdom* appears at first glance utterly opaque. Moltmann neither begins in the traditional way with a prolegomena that introduces his theological method and outlines his resources nor provides a formal introduction to the order and structure of the topics about to unfold. In a brief opening chapter Moltmann does situate his trinitarian project in the contemporary debate by raising the major modern objections to any human knowledge of the trinitarian God—namely, that such knowledge is speculative and of no moral value.[43] He also presents a cursory overview of the two Western models of the unity of God, "God as Supreme Substance" and "God as Absolute Subject," that appear within the proofs for the existence of God.[44] Both of these discussions serve as a foil for the author's own soteriological starting point of the doctrine, but they do little either to explain Moltmann's methodology or to illuminate the unfolding logic behind this work.

In my view, the key to unlocking the overall program in *The Trinity and the Kingdom* lies in Moltmann's construal of the relationship between the immanent and the economic Trinity—a construal that we saw emerging in *The Church in the Power of the Spirit*. There we saw how Moltmann reinstated a version of the immanent and economic distinction after his radical identification of the two in *The Crucified God*. Specifically, Moltmann argued that one could make certain inferences about the eternal nature of the Godhead from the missions of the Son and Spirit into the world. This so-called Trinity in the origin serves as the ontological condition of the possibility of the Trinity in the sending. He argued similarly that other inferences about the eschatological nature of the immanent Trinity could be made on the basis of the glorifying and consummating activities of the divine persons in history. In this way, Moltmann's trinitarian history of God points to an eternal trinitarian reality both at its origin and at its end.

On my reading, the structure of *The Trinity and the Kingdom* recapitulates this very order of trinitarian being. The book begins with a preliminary investigation of the nature of divine passion, in which Moltmann anticipates various aspects of the entire trinitarian history of God to come and then weaves these aspects together into an initial concept of divine passion. This initial concept of trinitarian love represents the ontological condition for the possibility of the trinitarian history of God to follow. In other words, his initial model of love crystallizes the nature of the Trinity in the origin that can be inferred from the history of the sendings. Moltmann then traces in a nearly sequential order (except for discussing christology before creation) the sending forth and the returning back of this divine passion in the trinitarian economy of salvation. Only after narrating the entirety of this trinitarian history of God does the book conclude with Moltmann's proposed social reconstruction of the doctrine of the Trinity.

Given Moltmann's unusual approach to developing his doctrine, I pursue this same order of presentation in interpreting the work. Such a procedure recommends itself because it allows us to consider the different facets of trinitarian love that emerge as one passes through the various changing relationships among the divine persons and the world that constitute the trinitarian history of God. Since much of Moltmann's discussion of divine *pathos* and the trinitarian history of God in *The Trinity and the Kingdom* retraces ground that he covered in his earlier trilogy, I will be highlighting only those aspects of the book's narrative that advance or significantly revise the author's earlier position. In particular, we will be exploring the new formal aspects of his social doctrine of the Trinity—his concepts of divine personhood, relations, and unity, all of which appear for the first time in *The Trinity and the Kingdom*.

Trinitarian Love in the Origin: Divine Passion
as the Self-Communication of the Good

Moltmann begins his reconstruction of trinitarian doctrine with an analysis of the nature of divine passion—what he terms "a doctrine of *theopathy*."[45] In choosing divine passion as his starting point, the author invokes his same premise that he elaborated at length in *The Crucified God*, namely, that the Christian theologian asks the question of God first and foremost as a soteriological rather than a philosophical question. At the heart of the experience of faith is knowledge of God's suffering representation of humankind in Christ. In Moltmann's words, "The person who believes owes his freedom to Christ's representation. He believes in God for Christ's sake. God himself is involved in the history of Christ's passion."[46]

Moltmann creates an unusual mosaic of theological and philosophical traditions in order to elucidate the nature of divine passion. The rabbinic and kabbalistic doctrine of the *Shekinah*, the Anglican theology of Richard Rolt, the Spanish mysticism of Miguel Unamuno, and finally the thought of Nikolai Berdyaev, the Russian Orthodox philosopher of religion, all contribute to Moltmann's explanation of divine passion. A primary clue, however, comes from Origen's interpretation of the giving up of the Son in Romans 8:32 in terms of the "passion of love (*Caritas est passio*)."[47] In many respects Origen's exegesis coincides exactly with Moltmann's earlier interpretation in *The Crucified God* of divine passion as the active suffering of love between the Father and the Son. As Moltmann explains, "When Origen talks about God's suffering, he means the suffering of love, the compassion which is at the heart of mercy and pity. . . . at the same time [he] points to a divine passion between the Father and the Son in the Trinity."[48] Yet Origen also takes a further step beyond Moltmann's earlier argument by describing this divine *pathos* as having its ultimate source in the "superabundance and overflowing of his being."[49]

Moltmann's initial exploration of Origen's notion of divine *pathos* returns us to the familiar territory of *The Crucified God*, in which the nature of trinitarian *agape* first emerged as kenotic or crucified love. There Moltmann developed a key analogy between the active suffering of love at the cross-event and the rabbinic and kabbalistic *Shekinah* tradition, in which divine *pathos* appears as a form of self-differentiation and self-humiliation in history. Moltmann returns to the *Shekinah* tradition again in *The Trinity and the Kingdom* as his prototype for the divine passion of Christ. Here, however, his portrayal of the *Shekinah* dramatically shifts as he focuses on the eternal purpose behind this divine self-humiliation. He concludes that divine passion points ultimately to God's desire for a beloved counterpart who will freely return his love. As Moltmann explains, it is God's desire for the freedom of humankind that ultimately lies behind his suffering love in history: "Love humiliates itself for the sake of the freedom of its counterpart. The freedom towards God of the human being whom God desires and loves is as unbounded as God's capacity for passion and for patience. Love of freedom is the most profound reason for 'God's self-differentiation.' "[50] Moltmann's new emphasis on the love of freedom as the telos of divine passion corresponds well to the eschatological development that we traced earlier in his trinitarian history of God. Just as we saw there how creative love gains a certain eschatological preeminence over the suffering love in the trinitarian history, so here, too, the dominant aspect of divine passion shifts to the creative and liberating love of God who desires the freedom of his beloved counterpart.

Alongside appeals to these ancient Jewish and Christian traditions, Moltmann draws support for this new view of divine passion from his other modern theological and philosophical resources. Miguel Unamuno, for example, describes the infinite sorrow of the Father as something that arises from God's own self-limitation in order to enable the freedom of creation.[51] Similarly, in Nikolai Berdyaev's philosophy of history Moltmann discovers the idea that the essence of history is God's desire or inner longing for the freedom of creation. Berdyaev's depiction of divine desire proves especially congenial to Moltmann's project, since the Russian philosopher, too, describes desire as arising not from a deficiency or need but out of the overflowing creative goodness of God; in Moltmann's words, it "is a movement in God himself, which leads him out of himself and brings him to his counterpart, his 'Other'—man."[52] Like Moltmann, Berdyaev also saw this divine ecstatic movement as theologically rooted in an affirmation of God's triune nature.

On the basis of these theological and philosophical traditions, Moltmann formulates his initial trinitarian interpretation of divine passion in a series of concluding theses. In his first thesis he sets into conceptual form this new understanding of divine passion that we saw emerging previously. Moltmann redefines love as *"the self-communication of the good.* It is the power of good to go out of itself, to enter into other being, to participate in other being, and to give itself for other being. . . . Love wants to live and to give life. It wants to open up the freedom to live."[53] Here divine passion still takes the form of a self-gift, but the essence of this gift is transformed from *kenosis* into *ecstasis*— the overflow or creative superabundance of being.

From this ecstatic concept of divine love as the self-communication of the good, Moltmann deduces both the trinitarian nature of God and the creation of the world as God's beloved Other or counterpart. I use the term "deduction" here only loosely to describe Moltmann's argumentation, since the brief arguments that he sets forth for God's trinitarian nature and for the creation of the world are hardly on the order of formal proofs for these claims. Nor does

Moltmann appear to intend them as such. On my reading, he infers the trinitarian self-communication of love to humankind from proclamations that are rooted in revelation, that is, either in the biblical witness or in the experience of faith. This soteriological foundation of Moltmann's trinitarian theology of divine passion is not, admittedly, readily apparent to the casual reader, especially given the fact that these deductions from the concept of divine passion actually precede his account of the trinitarian economy of salvation in the book's order of presentation.

With this cautionary note in mind, let us look more closely at Moltmann's deduction of the Trinity from his ecstatic concept of love. He analyzes this self-communication of the good in dialectical terms as the eternal process of self-differentiation and self-identification. Since such a process cannot be accomplished by a single subject, Moltmann concludes that divine love must be understood in trinitarian terms: "If God is love he is at once the lover, the beloved and the love itself. Love is the goodness that communicates itself from all eternity."[54] The logic of Moltmann's analysis of the concept of love here is quite straightforward. The self-communication of the good requires the differentiation of a subject and object of self-communication—a lover and a beloved. Joining these two in the act of self-communication is a third, their self-identification or the love that they share with one another.

What comes as quite a surprise here is Moltmann's renewed appeal to this dialectical concept of love and the Augustinian love analogy as the backbone of his argument for the trinitarian nature of divine love. We already saw how the author had criticized his implicit reliance on this Augustinian love analogy in *The Crucified God*, since it could not guarantee the full personhood of the Holy Spirit. Yet the same binitarian tendencies reappear in Moltmann's appropriation of the analogy here. His dialectical analysis of the self-communication of the good focuses chiefly on the relationship between the lover and the beloved, with little mention of how the Holy Spirit fits into the schema.

This time, however, this love analogy serves quite a different purpose in Moltmann's overall argument; it grounds God's passionate love for creation within the trinitarian relations of love. Here the inner-trinitarian love between the Father and the Son provides the springboard for this second deduction. Moltmann defines the engendering and responsive love of Father and Son as "the *love of like for like*, not the love for one who is essentially different. It is necessary love, not free love."[55] If divine love is the ecstatic self-communication of the good, Moltmann contends, then it must pass beyond this necessary love between the Father and the Son. The eternal passion of love must presuppose an Other—creation upon which it can bestow the freedom to love. In the author's formulation, "If his free and creative love is responded to by those whom it calls to life, then it finds its echo, its answer, its image and so its bliss in freedom and in the Other. God is love. That means he is engendering and creative love. . . .*Creation exists because the eternal love communicates himself creatively to his Other.*"⁵⁶

Here we can see the most radical implication of Moltmann's redefinition of divine passion as the self-communication of the good, namely, that the creation of the world belongs to the essence of divine love. As we investigate in detail the different aspects of the trinitarian economy, we will look much more precisely at how Moltmann anchors creation within the eternal intra-trinitarian relations of love. Already apparent at this point is how Moltmann's description of God's relationship to creation as love to the Other departs from his earlier definition of divine *agape* as love to the Other in *The Crucified God*. While retaining the same formal definition of divine *agape*, Moltmann has shifted its locus in revelation from cross to creation, and in so doing has significantly altered its meaning from suffering love to creative love—the gift of life and freedom.

This is not to suggest that divine passion now redefined as the self-communication of the good lacks the aspect of suffering love. Rather, from *The Trinity and the Kingdom* onward, Moltmann subsumes this notion of suffering love within the larger compass of God's ecstatic goodness. The suffering of God with, from, and for the world appears now as the highest form of creative love acting on behalf of its beloved's life and freedom. In Moltmann's words, "Creative love is ultimately suffering love because it is only through suffering that it acts creatively and redemptively for the freedom of the beloved. Freedom can only be made possible by suffering love."⁵⁷ Just as creative love attained a certain preeminence over suffering love in the eschatological trinitarian history of God, so here, too, suffering love is included within the trajectory of creative love that aims at the freedom of his beloved counterpart. This trajectory of creative love reaches its fulfillment when a liberated and transfigured creation returns to its dwelling place with God—"when it finds its beloved, liberates them, and has them eternally at his side."⁵⁸

In sum, Moltmann's new concept of divine passion as the self-communication of the good and the deductions that he draws from it contain *in nuce* the entire trajectory of the trinitarian history of God from creation to eschatological consummation. As I proposed in my introduction to the book's structure, this first discussion of divine passion represents trinitarian love in the origin. It explains the original openness of divine being to the world, history, and time in such a way that it includes the entire economy of creation and redemption. In this regard Moltmann's new definition of divine passion as self-communication of the good represents a conceptual advance beyond his earlier dialectic of crucified and creative love. It synthesizes the two sides of the pilgrimage of love into the world into a teleological concept of love that points to its messianic goal—the freedom of humankind in the kingdom of God.

God as the "One Who Is Free in Love"
and the "One Who Frees in Love"

Before we turn to Moltmann's expanded presentation of the trinitarian economy of creation and redemption, one aspect of Moltmann's ecstatic notion of
trinitarian love bears our attention, namely, its relationship to the author's
concept of divine freedom. As we already saw in chapter 2, the issue of divine
freedom had become a driving concern in Moltmann's work ever since the
publication of *The Crucified God,* when several of his critics challenged the
ontological implications of his radical identification of divine being with
the cross-event. If the immanent Trinity was strictly identified with the economy of salvation, as Moltmann implied, then it seemed to many of his readers
that divine being had been equated with a world process.[59] In *The Trinity and
the Kingdom,* Moltmann responds fully to his critics on this issue by setting
forth his understanding of divine freedom in critical discussion with that of
Barth.[60] This discussion proves significant to our study because it discloses not
only further differences between Barth's and Moltmann's root models for the
Trinity but also how the two Reformed theologians differently relate the divine
attributes of love and freedom to one another.

Moltmann critically investigates Barth's concept of divine freedom as it
appears within his doctrine of election. There Moltmann describes his predecessor's notion of divine freedom as self-determination or an "absolute freedom of choice."[61] In support of this reading, Moltmann points to how Barth
depicts God's primordial decision to elect humankind to be his covenant partner as an utterly groundless divine decree. Although God elected in love not
to remain self-sufficient, he could have used his absolute freedom to elect
otherwise.

Moltmann challenges Barth's notion of divine freedom here with two intertwined arguments. First, he criticizes the "nominalist fringe"[62] to Barth's
insistence on God's primordial decision. This notion of God's absolute freedom—either to love or not to love—introduces the possibility of a difference
or, even worse, a contradiction between God's eternal nature and his self-
revelation.[63] Stated differently, Moltmann charges that Barth suggests that God
has "two natures": one prior to the election of humankind, in which freedom
is understood as pure "self-determination," and another after this election, in
which divine freedom is defined in terms of being for humankind.[64] With this
temporal before-afterward (or hidden-revealed) structure, Barth disrupts the
perfect correspondence between divine revelation and divine being.

Beneath this first line of argumentation lies Moltmann's central objection
to his predecessor's model of divine freedom: it contradicts God's self-
revelation as love. On Moltmann's reading, Barth's concept of divine freedom
follows "the concept of *absolute power of disposal,*" a concept that is derived from
Roman property law rather than the scriptural notion of love. This notion of

freedom lies beneath Barth's repeated insistence on God's lordship: "Then 'God's liberty' means his sovereignty, and his power of disposal over his property—creation—and his servants—men and women."[65]

On closer inspection, one sees that the heart of Moltmann's disagreement with Barth lies where it did earlier in *The Crucified God*, namely, with how Barth defines the biblical root of the Trinity in terms of divine lordship in his doctrine of revelation. In that doctrine Barth portrays divine freedom in terms of God's absolute power of self-determination—to reveal or not to reveal God's self. In Moltmann's view, this early concept of divine freedom as absolute sovereignty is at odds with Barth's later claims of God's revelation as love in his gracious election of humankind. Although Barth attempts to mediate between divine love and freedom by defining God later in his *Church Dogmatics* as "the One who loves in freedom," Barth still privileges divine freedom over love, insofar as he retains the notion that God's highest freedom lies in the choice either to love or not to love.[66]

Moltmann distinguishes his position from Barth's by developing a concept of God's being in which love and freedom coincide with one another. He appeals to Augustine to support his claim that the highest freedom is not free choice but a teleological concept of freedom as freedom for the good.[67] As he explains in this passage, divine freedom rests not in absolute power but in the self-communication of the good: "So total power is by no means identical with absolute freedom. Freedom arrives at its divine truth through love. Love is a self-evident, unquestionable 'overflowing of goodness,' which is therefore never open to choice at any time. We have to understand true freedom as being the self-communication of the good."[68] Given this notion of love as overflowing goodness, Moltmann argues further, one cannot speak of there being any necessity in God's love for the world. "Self-communication of the good" occurs from neither "compulsion" nor "arbitrary resolve," but rather out of "inner pleasure of his eternal love."[69] If true freedom lies in the self-communication of goodness, then God is most free in the bestowal on his creatures of the gifts of life and freedom. Although Moltmann himself does not offer a summary formula for his doctrine of God, one might characterize his understanding of God as the one who *is free* in his love, and the one who *frees* in love.

Moltmann uses his disagreement with Barth as a springboard from which to offer his own positive formulation of freedom in accordance with his notion of love. The freedom that God offers as a gift to his beloved creation is the opposite of lordship ("Herrschaft"); it is "friendship" ("Freundschaft") or "fellowship" ("Gemeinschaft").[70] For Moltmann, such freedom corresponds fully to God's very being—it is truly God's self-gift: "The triune God reveals himself as love in the fellowship of the Father, the Son and the Holy Spirit. His freedom therefore lies in the *friendship* which he offers men and women, and through which he makes them his friends."[71] This initial formulation of God's gift of freedom to his beloved creation in terms of the friendship or fellowship of the

Father, the Son, and the Spirit is highly revealing for our path forward. This formulation not only points to the nature of the intra-trinitarian relations of love as relations of fellowship but also indicates the consummation of the freedom of the Christian in divine friendship. In this regard, Moltmann's initial discussion of trinitarian love as the self-communication of the good not only represents trinitarian love in the origin but also anticipates its messianic consummation—the freedom of creation in the fellowship of God.

The Pilgrimage of Trinitarian Love in the World

If we read Moltmann's initial discussion of divine passion as a description of the nature of the Trinity in the origin, we can view the rest of the book as an unfolding of this divine pilgrimage of love into the world. Moltmann first explores in detail the various trinitarian activities in the world and then deduces from these divine operations the nature of the Father, the Son, and the Spirit. By developing his doctrine in this way, Moltmann abandons a central tenet of the classical Western tradition, namely, Augustine's doctrine of appropriations. The doctrine of appropriations prescribes that the whole Trinity acts as a unity toward the world and that its individual works in history are merely ascribed to one of the three divine persons. In contrast, Moltmann contends that all three persons have distinct and nonexchangeable roles in the trinitarian history of God. Each of these roles reveals, indeed constitutes, the being of the Trinity.

In what follows I do not rehearse the entire plotline of these trinitarian operations in the world, since much of it repeats what we have seen in Moltmann's previous works. Instead, I emphasize only those new aspects of his trinitarian history that are critical to Moltmann's social reconstruction of trinitarian doctrine and to its three central themes: the nature of divine passion, the trinitarian kingdom, and its eschatological telos in the return of humankind into the divine fellowship.

A New Christological Root for the Doctrine of the Trinity and for Divine Rule

As noted earlier in the discussion of methodology, Moltmann roots his interpretation of the pluriform activities and relations among the trinitarian persons in a trinitarian hermeneutics of the biblical witness. He sifts through the key events in biblical history and isolates various patterns of trinitarian relations—what he calls the "trinitarian forms"[72]—that are displayed in the scriptures. Although this trinitarian narrative now includes many different actors and events, christology still provides the anchor for his doctrinal interpretation.

In defending this christological root of the doctrine, Moltmann sides with his Reformed predecessor Karl Barth over and against the liberal Protestant historian of doctrine Adolf von Harnack, who interpreted the doctrine of the Trinity as a Hellenization of Jesus' proclamation of the kingdom. At the same time that Moltmann agrees with Barth that the doctrine's root lies in Jesus' life and ministry, he challenges the substance of Barth's christological interpretation. Already in *The Crucified God* Moltmann had taken issue with how Barth rooted the doctrine in Christ's exaltation—an exaltation in which God reveals God's self as Lord. At the time, Moltmann's counterproposal was to anchor trinitarian doctrine in the cross-event, where God reveals himself not as Lord but as the suffering love of the Father and the Son.

In *The Trinity and the Kingdom*, Moltmann pursues a different line of argumentation against Barth's biblical root for the doctrine. The author no longer rejects the notion of christological rooting in the notion of divine rule per se but rather disagrees with Barth's interpretation of divine rule in terms of the self-revelation of God as Lord. Moltmann contests this interpretation on the grounds that it reduces the entire biblical history to the work of one absolute divine subject. It ends up flattening out the distinctive agency of the three divine persons in the christological narrative, thereby reducing all three to repetitions of the same single subject—God's self-relation. The heart of Moltmann's objection is that Barth imports a notion of divine lordship that does not spring from the biblical text but rather comes from a preliminary hermeneutical decision about the nature of divine sovereignty. Rather than allowing the notion of divine rule to emerge from the co-working of the three persons as depicted in the biblical witness, Barth, according to Moltmann, imports an extrabiblical notion of divine rulership that dictates an undifferentiated monotheistic shape to trinitarian doctrine.[73]

If one is to develop a truly trinitarian concept of divine rulership, Moltmann argues, one must investigate the various stages in the history of the Son and see the distinctive patterns of trinitarian relationships revealed therein. We already saw Moltmann pursue this course in his early trilogy, where he focused exclusively on the cross- and resurrection-events in the history of the Son. Now Moltmann widens his christological lens to include the full range of events in Jesus' life, from his initial sending in his baptism to his eschatological handing over of the kingdom to the Father.

The first true glimpse of the nature of trinitarian rule appears in Jesus' baptism and call. Moltmann highlights Jesus' eschatological proclamation of the kingdom and its link to Jesus' unique relationship with the God he calls Abba. Here we discover that the kingdom of God is a place of merciful compassion and liberation: "In this kingdom God is not the Lord; he is the merciful Father. In this kingdom there are no servants; there are only God's free children. In this kingdom what is required is not obedience and submission; it is love and free participation."[74] For Moltmann, Jesus' relationship to the Father signals the utter transformation of God's relationship to his creation in the kingdom; these are no longer relationships of lordship and obedience but of mercy and freedom. Jesus not only proclaims this "joyful message" of the divine compassion and freedom of God the Father but also manifests the Father's kingdom in his own life "by gathering the oppressed into the liberty of his fellowship."[75]

Moltmann appeals to the Gospel of Matthew and the Johannine corpus for this depiction of the intimate fellowship of the Father and Son. In particular, he draws on the Johannine-like text in Matthew 11:27 and combines it with a number of other texts from the Johannine corpus (e.g., John 10:30; 17:21;1 John 2:22–24) in order to describe the intimate relationship between the Father and the Son as "an exclusive and mutual knowing, loving and participating."[76] Pauline theology then fills in the pneumatological dimensions of this trinitarian fellowship. Drawing on Romans 8:15, Moltmann ascribes to the Spirit the role of opening this intimate fellowship of the Son and Father to humankind. The Spirit communicates " 'the spirit of sonship' "[77] to human beings so that they, too, experience the merciful compassion and liberation of the Father.

Moltmann's interpretation of the other key stages in the history of Son—the author's kenotic interpretation of the Son's surrender in the cross-event and eschatological interpretation of the Son's exaltation in the resurrection—resembles closely those in *The Crucified God* and *The Church in the Power of the Spirit*. There are, however, two new aspects of Moltmann's presentation of the history of the Son that contribute significantly toward the author's reformulation of the doctrine of the Trinity. First, Moltmann draws from each stage of the history of the Son a particular sequence of trinitarian relations that have been revealed therein. These patterns describe who among the Father, the Son, and the Spirit are the agents and who are the recipients of the divine activity. For example, in the sending, surrender, and resurrection of the Son, the Father appears as the origin of all activity, the Son is the receiver, and the Spirit is the means by which this activity occurs. In contrast, in the exaltation of the Son and the sending of the Spirit, the Father and the Son act as the two agents, while the Spirit is the sole recipient. Finally, in the eschatological consummation, the Spirit and the Son appear as the two agents, while the Father becomes the recipient of the kingdom and the glory.[78]

Given all these varying patterns of divine activity in the world, Moltmann concludes that no single pattern or order of trinitarian relations can be chosen as the one that corresponds to the intra-trinitarian life. In contrast to Western trinitarian doctrine that has been predicated upon one single pattern of divine processions, Father–Son–Spirit, Moltmann depicts all three persons coworking in changing patterns of divine activity and receptivity. Eventually Moltmann will return to these trinitarian patterns of activity as the basis for his differentiations among the three divine persons. But in this context, these various trinitarian forms serve a more limited function; they show how the coworking of all three divine persons is vital to the realization of the trinitarian rule in the kingdom. In other words, the kaleidoscope of changing relations among the divine persons reveals how the dynamic fellowship among the three is constitutive of the divine life.

The second utterly new aspect in Moltmann's presentation of the history of the Son is his trinitarian interpretation of the kingdom's eschatological consummation. As we saw earlier, Moltmann had already placed his eschatological panentheism in a trinitarian frame in *The Church in the Power of the Spirit*. There the author emphasized the Spirit's role in unifying and glorifying creation with God. In *The Trinity and the Kingdom*, Moltmann for the first time assigns to the Father and the Son distinctive roles in the eschatological consummation of the divine rule. Here the Pauline text 1 Corinthians 15:22–28 provides the chief biblical clue to the eschatological future as trinitarian event.[79] Moltmann argues that the eschatological mission of the Son concludes in an inner-trinitarian process—in which the Son actually delivers the kingdom over to God the Father:

> The divine rule was given by the Father to the Son through Christ's resurrection. In the final consummation it will be transferred from the Son to the Father. . . . According to Paul, the whole Christian eschatology ends in this inner-trinitarian process, through which the kingdom passes from the Son to the Father. Eschatology accordingly is not simply what takes place in the Last Days in heaven and on earth; it is what takes place in God's essential nature.[80]

Moltmann draws two significant conclusions about the nature of divine rulership from this eschatological inner-trinitarian process. First, the kingdom of God is consummated and exercised through the co-working of the Father, the Son, and the Holy Spirit. Second, the nature of the divine rule actually changes in its eschatological transferral from one divine subject to another. The Son destroys all the powers of death to make room for the kingdom of life and love of the Father. Divine rule is thus not an eternal and fixed reality imposed on the world but a historical reality that emerges in and through the eschatological consummation of the world.

If we gather together the diverse strands of Moltmann's new trinitarian interpretation of the history of the Son, a vision of divine rule emerges that diverges from Barth's model of lordship in two dramatic ways. First and foremost, Moltmann insists that divine rule is a communal property or attribute of the Trinity, whose nature is determined in and through the dynamic movement—the changing relations among the three persons. In Moltmann's words, divine rule "cannot be a monadic unity," "the identity of a single subject"; it is, rather, the *"fellowship"* or *"union* of the Father, the Son and the Spirit."[81] This rule of fellowship is an interpersonal union, a form of mutual indwelling and participation that not only preserves but also creates personal distinctions.

Second, divine rule is a historical-eschatological reality. The trinitarian kingdom cannot be understood as the inbreaking of the eternal divine lordship in the midst of the world. Rather, the kingdom is consummated in and through the world, with the kingdom ultimately becoming an intra-trinitarian reality that includes the world in its midst. In Moltmann's words, "[The kingdom] does not merely run its course on earth—which is to say outside of God himself—as dogmatic tradition ever since Augustine has maintained. On the contrary, it takes place in its earthly mode within the Trinity itself, as the history of the kingdom of the Father, the Son and the Spirit."[82]

This vision of divine rule as the union of God with creation hearkens back to the eschatological notion of divine unity that Moltmann suggested earlier in *The Church in the Power of the Spirit*. It also coincides with the telos of divine passion as the fellowship or friendship of creation with God, a telos that emerged in our prior discussion of the God who frees in love. Now for the first time Moltmann roots this fellowship in his christology: the personal relationship between the Father and Jesus the Son manifests this rule of fellowship that is promised in the kingdom.

The World of the Trinity

With his christological anchor for his doctrine of the Trinity in place, Moltmann expands his focus from the history of the Son to take in all the key events of the trinitarian economy: the creation of the world through the Father of Jesus Christ, the incarnation of the Son, and the transfiguration of the world through the Holy Spirit. Moltmann does not exhaustively treat any of these different doctrines in *The Trinity and the Kingdom*; he reserves this task to his investigation of the individual loci in his subsequent volumes of the *Messianic Theology*. His aims here are more limited. On the one hand, he seeks to frame creation, incarnation, and transfiguration as trinitarian events, that is, to see how these events can be understood as the unfolding of the divine passion and fellowship that he discovered in the history of the Son. On the other hand, Moltmann seeks to identify the implications of this entire economy of creation and salvation for the nature of the immanent trinitarian relations—in the author's words, "What does the creation of the world and its history mean for God himself?"[83]

In pursuing Moltmann's answers to these questions, we need to recall that for the author the so-called economic and immanent trinities never correspond to one another in any straightforward fashion. Ever since *The Crucified God*, Moltmann has boldly argued that the Trinity not only affects the world but also is affected by its activities in the world. In *The Trinity and the Kingdom*, he grounds this interdependence in terms of the logic of God's self-communication of fellowship and freedom to the world. Moltmann argues that the world "is not a matter of indifference for God himself, but ... represents an object, a counterpart of his love for freedom."[84] Since the world is the beloved recipient of God's self-communication of loving freedom, God also opens God's self to the world's loving response. Although Moltmann immediately qualifies that the world does not affect God in the same way that God affects the world, he nonetheless insists that the triune God enters into a real relation with the world, a relation in which God too suffers.

Given this real relationship between God and the world, the nature of the divine persons *ad intra* cannot be simply inferred from any particular work *ad extra*. Moltmann declares that deducing the actor from the act, the master from his work, is an ill-suited method of analyzing the living relationship between God and the world.[85] He pursues instead a twofold tactic: first, he analyzes the various operations in the world on the basis of the nature of trinitarian love; second, he analyzes the impress of these various activities *ad extra* on the relations of love among the Father, the Son, and the Spirit *ad intra*. In Moltmann's preferred terminology, he traces the "inward acts" or "sufferings" (*passio Dei*) within the Trinity, which correspond to the outward acts.[86]

Bearing Moltmann's methodological approach in mind, let us turn to the author's analyses of the key events of creation, the incarnation, and the transfiguration or renewal of creation. Moltmann begins his trinitarian interpretation of creation by first anchoring it in the biblical witness. He observes that in the scriptures, the act of creation is always mediated within the compass of the experience of salvation and the messianic hope of salvation's completion. For example, Israel thematizes creation retroactively from its central experience of salvation, the "exodus experience," and proleptically in terms of "*the messianic hope* for the new" or as "the scene of his coming glory."[87] In the New Testament, faith in Christ provides the basis for a soteriological understanding of creation. If Christ is creation's goal, he must be at its foundation and its mediator for all of eternity.[88] The New Testament also witnesses to a messianic relationship between God and creation that is mediated by the Holy Spirit. The Spirit's presence in creation is distinct from that of either the Creator or the incarnate One, insofar as it is a form of divine indwelling in humanity itself.[89] This divine indwelling instills the messianic hope for a future in which all of creation will be transfigured into the dwelling place of God.

On the basis of these soteriological and messianic relations of the Son and the Holy Spirit to creation, Moltmann concludes that to understand the divine act of creation we need to view it in terms of all three persons' actions. The author explains the actual trinitarian terms of creation in terms of the eternal love of Father and Son. The creation of the world results from the overflowing love of the Father for the Son: "His self-communicating love for the one like himself opens itself to the Other and becomes creative, which means anticipating every possible response."[90] Since creation results from the Father's overflowing love for the Son, Moltmann reasons that creation cannot be viewed as an act of God's arbitrary will, but rather of God's will to goodness. The Father creates the world out of his good pleasure, and with the ultimate aim that creation will respond to his love with gratitude and praise. Furthermore, argues Moltmann, the world is created not only *for* the Son but also *through* the Son. The Son represents the "divinely immanent archetype of the idea of the world,"[91] insofar as his responsive love of the Father becomes the archetype for humankind's own love.

By describing creation as an intra-trinitarian act between the Father and the Son, Moltmann seeks an alternative to either a theistic or a pantheistic approach to creation. Against theism, he contends that creation is not an external act of God's arbitrary free will but belongs to the eternal essence of God as the self-communication of the good. Against pantheism, he argues that the world's creation does not itself coincide with an aspect of the intra-trinitarian process, for example, the begetting of the Son out of the Father's divine love.[92] In place of either of these two options, Moltmann advances a trinitarian panentheism, in which creation belongs to the eternal love of the Father and Son yet remains distinct from it. The Holy Spirit provides the linchpin for this panentheistic proposal. Through the "pouring out" of its creative energies, the Spirit bridges the distance between the eternal love of the Father for the Son and that for the world: "This Spirit is the divine breath of life which fills everything with *its own life*."[93] Here the Spirit's breath of life enables creation to participate in a mediated way in the intra-trinitarian life by binding creation within the eternal love relation of the Father and the Son.[94]

This trinitarian analysis of the outward act of creation provides the basis for determining the inward impress of creation on the trinitarian God. Moltmann postulates that in order for God to go forth "creatively 'out of himself,' " there must have been an inward act of "*self-limitation*."[95] Here the zimsum theory of the kabbalist Isaac Luria provides Moltmann with a way of conceiving of this inward divine act. In a variation on the idea of the indwelling presence of the *Shekinah* in the temple, Luria claimed that a concentrated inversion or self-withdrawal, a zimsum, had taken place in God for the purpose of making room for creation. Appropriating this idea into his trinitarian framework, Moltmann postulates that a divine self-limitation occurs in the love between the Father and the Son through a "contraction" or "inversion of the Spirit."[96] This alteration in the intra-trinitarian relations creates the space, the time, and the freedom for the creation of the world: "Eternity breathes itself in, so as to breathe out the Spirit of life."[97]

Moltmann's theological move to postulate such an eternal self-limitation is certainly a highly speculative move that lacks any direct support in the biblical witness. This notion of eternal self-limitation does explain, however, some of the most puzzling features of Moltmann's portrayal of the pilgrimage of trinitarian love in history. It helps account for the author's claim that the trajectory of divine passion, once reconceptualized as the self-communication of the good, still begins with an act of suffering love or divine *kenosis*. The notion of an inward divine self-limitation that makes room for creation and for human freedom shows how suffering love could be the initial moment in the overall trajectory of a God who frees in love. Moreover, Moltmann's notion of a trinitarian contraction in the moment of creation leaves space for talk of the Trinity's sending into the world from its eternal origin. That is to say, the zimsum theory provides a conceptual framework for inscribing the entire trajectory of the history of the world in God without simultaneously falling prey to pantheism.

Moltmann's depiction of the other two key events in the trinitarian economy—the incarnation of the Son and the transfiguration of creation by the Spirit—builds squarely on the foundation of his trinitarian analysis of the act of creation. He presents the incarnation as the fulfillment of God's outward act of creation rather than treating it as a remedy for sin. The ultimate end of the incarnation is to return the beloved creation into eternal fellowship with God. In Moltmann's words: "Love does not merely want to vanquish the death of the beloved; it wants to overcome the beloved's mortality too, so that he may be eternally beside the beloved and so that the beloved may be eternally beside himself."[98] This trinitarian interpretation of the incarnation renders explicit the evolution in Moltmann's model of salvation that we detected earlier in *The Church in the Power of the Spirit*. Without minimizing the soteriological significance of the Son's act of reconciliation in the cross-event, Moltmann now places an ever-greater emphasis on the process of sanctification that works toward the perfection or renewal of creation.

Moltmann relates the initial act of creation to its consummation in the incarnation through the notion of the *imago Dei*. As the Logos through whom the world was created, the Son represents the "true 'ikon'" or the *"primordial image"* of God.[99] In the incarnation the eternal Son becomes human, thus fulfilling the destiny of creation as the *imago Dei*. As the representative of true humanity, Christ communicates to creation his own perfect responsive love of the Father: "He gathers them into his relationship of sonship to the Father and communicates to them his own liberty, which is above the world."[100] This mediation of divine love occurs not only through the passion of the cross-event but also through the Son becoming *"the prototype"*[101] of true sonship in his entire way of life. In Moltmann's preferred Pauline formulation, the Son becomes "the first-born among many brethren" (Rom. 8:29), who invites all humankind into fellowship with the Father and into participation in his own mission of liberating creation.

Just as the outward act of creation makes an inward impress on the trinitarian being in the form of self-limitation, Moltmann postulates that the incarnation likewise entails an *"inward self-humiliation."*[102] This inward self-limitation surpasses that of creation, since God now fully accepts humanity and its situation into his eternity: "Not only does he enter into this state of being man; he accepts and adopts it himself, *making it part of his own, eternal life. He becomes the human God."*[103] This inward kenosis reaches its highest point in the cross-event, in which God takes the darkest depths of the human situation, sin and death, into his very being. The inward impress of this outward act of kenotic love is a concession of divine freedom. "For the sake of freedom, and the love responded to in freedom," Moltmann explains, "God limits and empties himself."[104]

Moltmann draws his account of the trinitarian history of God to a close with a brief investigation of the transfigurative work of the Spirit. Unlike his elaborate new trinitarian interpretations of the acts of creation and incarnation, his description of the Spirit's activity is more like an abbreviated form of his pneumatology that he already presented in the midseventies. Moltmann describes the work of the Spirit with the same rubrics that we saw in *The Church in the Power of the Spirit*: the glorification of the Father through the Son's resurrection, and the renewal of creation and its eschatological unification with the trinitarian fellowship.

In terms of his evolving trinitarian theology, two aspects of Moltmann's pneumatology are significant. First, Moltmann represents the Spirit's work as the consummation of its work in creation rather than as a remedy for sin, that is, as the forgiveness of sins and as justification by faith. Just as we saw the Spirit as the life-giving presence of God indwelling in the world in creation, so, too, we discover the Spirit now renewing its life-giving presence among creation. Here the Spirit manifests the same divine passion that we saw in the workings of the Son and the Father in the world: the Spirit expresses the overflowing love of God that offers fellowship and freedom to its beloved creation. Through the transfiguration of the world, the Spirit acts ultimately to glorify the Son and the Father; the Spirit gives delight and joy to the other persons of the Trinity by drawing creation into their life of fellowship.

Second, Moltmann insists that the human being's experience of the Spirit is a this-worldly and indeed physical experience. He rails against any spiritualized interpretation of the Holy Spirit that might suggest that the Spirit draws human beings out of their history and into an eternal timeless realm. Rather, the Spirit indwells in the fabric of human beings' lives, renewing them and drawing them into deeper fellowship with one another and with God. In so doing, the Spirit acts to consummate the original intent of creation, that is, to make all things "the home of the triune God."[105]

Moltmann describes the inward impress of the Spirit's work as a reverse movement of the divine operations in the world. The movement of the Spirit outward into the world is actually a gathering of the world inward—into the inner-trinitarian life: "In the glorification of the Spirit, world and times, people and things are gathered to the Father in order to become *his world*."[106] Here one ceases altogether to speak meaningfully of God *ad extra* and *ad intra*, since the world returns to its true dwelling place within the trinitarian relations of love. Moltmann describes the inward impress of the Spirit's glorifying and unifying of all creation as the very opposite of divine self-limitation or humiliation. The God of passionate love attains fulfillment in the eternal delight and blissful love of creation: "This is the eternal feast of heaven and earth. This is the dance of the redeemed. This is 'the laughter of the universe.' "[107]

In conclusion, if we glance back over the key events in the trinitarian economy—creation, incarnation, and transfiguration—we detect here the same twofold pattern of movement of the Trinity in the sending and the Trinity in the glorification that we discovered in Moltmann's earlier trilogy. Here, too, we discover the overall pattern of emanation and return. Where this account of the trinitarian economy advances beyond the author's earlier ones is in painting a much richer picture of the Trinity in the sending, which now includes the pivotal events of creation and the incarnation along with the cross-event. As I have suggested previously, these new aspects of the trinitarian missions in the world alter the meaning of trinitarian love. The earlier dialectic of crucified love and creative love becomes now a divine passionate longing for the Other, creation, that expresses itself in the gift of life and freedom to that Other.

This trinitarian economy offers a transformed picture not only of God's love *pro nobis* but also of its inward impress on the intra-trinitarian relations of love. Although divine suffering and self-limitation or *kenosis* still mark the effects *ad intra* of God's relationship with the world, Moltmann now qualifies this inward suffering by emphasizing its messianic telos in the love and freedom of creation. We discover that the ultimate impress of this trinitarian history of God with the world is an increase of eternal joy and bliss in the eschatological homecoming of God's beloved creation.

A Social Reconstruction of the Doctrine of the Trinity

A Critique of the Western Doctrine and Christian Monotheism

The changing patterns of the trinitarian relations in the economy of creation and redemption provide all the materials for Moltmann's reconstruction of trinitarian doctrine. Equally important to his dogmatic reformulation, however, is the author's critique of the dominant Western structure of the doctrine— what he refers to usually either as "monotheistic monarchianism" or, borrowing Barth's formulation, as "Christian monotheism."[108] Moltmann's terminology can easily be misleading here because he is not objecting to monotheism per se. As he clarifies in an explanatory footnote, the target of his critique is a strict or undifferentiated form of monotheism, that is, a form of "theism," which construes divine unity in monadic or nonrelational terms.[109] With respect to trinitarian proposals, Moltmann directs this charge of monarchianism toward any form of the doctrine in which divine unity is conceptually independent and logically prior to the trinitarian nature of God.

In *The Trinity and the Kingdom*, Moltmann offers a highly schematized

account of this monarchical and monistic trajectory as he sees it develop in
Western trinitarian thought.[110] According to this account, ever since Tertullian
laid the foundation for the Western doctrine in terms of his formula of one
substance and three persons, there has been a tendency in Western doctrine
for the concept of the one undivided unity of the Godhead to prevail over the
three persons. Moltmann traces this monistic tendency originally to Christianity's appropriation of the Greek philosophical concept of supreme substance
as a way of depicting the divine essence. The early conflicts that arose over
Arianism and Sabellianism provide ample evidence for the difficulties involved
in differentiating the three persons on the basis of this notion of divine essence.
Even Tertullian, who tried to overcome both subordinationism and modalism
through making careful terminological distinctions, reinforced a certain mo-
nism in the doctrine through his insistence on the monarchy of the Father.[111]

   According to Moltmann, both Augustine and Aquinas, the chief architects
of Western trinitarian thought in the patristic and medieval periods, respectively, deepened this monistic and monarchical trajectory by assigning a certain
logical and epistemological primacy to the one divine essence. Because the
divine essence could be argued for through natural reason, it was attributed a
logical precedence over the trinitarian persons, who could only be known in
light of special revelation. This precedence of the divine unity over the three
persons was officially codified in the manual theologies of Catholicism and in
Protestant orthodoxy; in both branches of Christian tradition, the doctrine of
God was formally split into the treatises *De Deo uno* and *De Deo trino*. This
twofold division of the doctrine established a notion of divine unity that was
independent from and actually competed with the unity constituted by the
three persons. Eventually, natural knowledge of the one God eroded the doctrine of the Trinity in the Enlightenment period into a form of undifferentiated
and abstract monotheism.[112]

   Despite the renewed interest in trinitarian theology in the early twentieth
century, Moltmann argues that these proposals, too, suffer from the same
monarchical tendencies. In the wake of German idealism, the notion of God
as absolute subjectivity has replaced that of absolute substance. Here the concept of the person applies to the one divine subject, and the Father, the Son,
and the Spirit are differentiated according to the process of self-differentiation
and self-identification, by which a modern subject comes to self-conscious-
ness.[113] Moltmann charges that this modern version of the Western doctrine
dispenses with the particularities of Christian revelation and replaces them
with a general philosophical concept of transcendentality. This Idealistic model
of the Trinity represents "a late triumph for the Sabellian modalism,"[114] in
which the divine subject disappears as a hidden reality behind the cloak of the
three modes of being.

   Moltmann identifies the highly influential proposals of Karl Barth and Karl

Rahner as falling prey to different versions of this Idealist modalism.¹¹⁵ In Barth's case, Moltmann points to how his predecessor deduces his earliest version of the doctrine from an Idealist concept of self-revelation, a concept that he appeals to in order to secure the absolute sovereignty of God over the human act of knowing.¹¹⁶ His threefold structure of revelation as Revealer, Revelation, and Revealedness cannot, in Moltmann's eyes, ensure the true differentiation among the three persons that Barth seeks. First of all, the Spirit appears only in the role of the bond of love that joins the Father and the Son; such a role is redundant, however, because the Father and Son are utterly one in their relationship to one another.¹¹⁷ Ultimately, Moltmann questions whether even a duality of divine persons can be sustained on Barth's model. Barth's trinitarian formula, " 'God reveals himself as the Lord,' "¹¹⁸ implies actually one absolute personality, a personality that must be ascribed either to the Father or, in Sabellian fashion, to a fourth subject behind the three manifestations. In either case, this monistic and monarchical concept of divine essence as absolute subject eclipses the trinitarian nature of divine being.

Moltmann discovers different symptoms of German Idealism at work in Rahner's proposed trinitarian model of "a single divine subject in three 'distinct modes of subsistence.' "¹¹⁹ He challenges in particular Rahner's contention that we need to abandon personhood language on the grounds that the modern concept of personhood leads inevitably to a tritheistic understanding of the Godhead. Here Rahner reveals his indebtedness to a notion of personhood as "an independent, free self-disposing center of action," a notion that corresponds to the Idealist notion of a self-reflexive subject.¹²⁰ Moltmann charges that instead of challenging this notion of personeity altogether, Rahner capitulates to this Enlightenment model by applying it to the Father as the source of the Godhead. In support of this claim, Moltmann points to Rahner's telling trinitarian formula, "the Father gives us himself in absolute self-communication through the Son in the Holy Spirit," in which the Father appears as the "single God-subject," while "the Son is the historical instrument, and the Holy Spirit 'in us' is the place of God's self-communication."¹²¹

Moltmann identifies a host of further problems that flow from Rahner's model of the Trinity as the absolute self-communication of God the Father. For one, Rahner's redefinition of divine personhood as "mode of subsistence" does not permit personal differentiation within the Godhead itself; the Son and Spirit are reduced to actualizations of the one self-communication of the Father.¹²² Moreover, Moltmann charges that Rahner's model of divine self-communication endangers a real distinction between God and creation. Moltmann points to Rahner's description of the Holy Spirit as "the salvation that deifies us . . . in the innermost centre of the existence of an individual person"¹²³ as evidence that human beings become themselves a moment in the divine process of self-communication. In sum, Moltmann charges that Rahner

offers a "mystical variant of the Idealistic doctrine": "Here the absolute subjectivity of God becomes the archetypal image of the mystic subjectivity of the
person who withdraws into himself and transcends himself."[124]

Before we move on to Moltmann's reconstruction of the doctrine, we
should pause to note that Moltmann's criticisms of Rahner and Barth raise as
many questions for his own trinitarian proposals as they do for his rivals. For
example, there are strong parallels between Moltmann's concept of divine passion as the self-communication of the good and the deductions that he draws
from this concept about the sendings of the Son and the Spirit, and his predecessors' models of divine revelation. Both the dialectic of self-differentiation
and self-identification and the Augustinian analogy of the lover, the beloved,
and their bond of love inform Moltmann's trinitarian deduction from his concept of love. Like Barth and Rahner, he also has difficulty assigning equal
personal status to the Holy Spirit, or else not reducing the divine persons to
modes of the same being.[125]

Despite these Idealist traces in his own work, Moltmann takes a very different route than that of his predecessors when it comes to the formal structure
of the doctrine. Rather than beginning with a general postulate of divine unity
and then differentiating the trinitarian persons, he follows the reverse procedure. He begins with the concrete revelation of the three persons and their
relations in the biblical history and looks to establish the nature of their unity
with one another at the conclusion of his doctrine. In so doing, he sides explicitly with those in the trinitarian tradition that have preferred a social or
interpersonal analogy for the Trinity to a psychological one. He does so on the
grounds that only a social analogy can adequately depict the differentiated
relations among the three divine persons and eliminate the subordinationist
or modalist traces that he sees plaguing his predecessors' trinitarian doctrines.[126]

Moltmann also opts for a social analogy for the Trinity as the best way to
represent the distinctive nature of divine unity that is realized in the trinitarian
history of God with the world. The notion of a becoming unity that includes
not only the sending forth and gathering back of the Son and the Spirit but
also the transfiguration and inclusion of creation in the trinitarian fellowship
requires a different conceptuality of unity than either of the notions of one
substance or the self-identical subject. Unlike these dominant Western concepts of unity, Moltmann argues, a social concept of triunity as "unitedness"
can better include difference in its midst without collapsing into identity.[127]

If Moltmann's critique of traditional and modern formulations of trinitarian doctrine aims to expose their recurring monarchical and modalist tendencies, his own social reformulation of trinitarian doctrine must withstand criticisms from the opposite problem that often troubles social approaches to the
doctrine, namely, the danger of tritheism. That is to say, does Moltmann's
social reconstruction so emphasize the distinctions among the divine persons

that it becomes difficult for him to secure the divine unity? As we examine his conceptual reconstruction of the doctrine, in particular how Moltmann develops the notions of divine personhood and divine unity, we will need to judge how successfully Moltmann eliminates this threat of tritheism from his doctrine.

The Doxological Trinity: The Three Persons and Their Unity

THE IMMANENT TRINITY IN A DOXOLOGICAL PERSPECTIVE. In turning to Moltmann's formal reconstruction of the doctrine, we need to return to a epistemological issue that has accompanied our analysis of his doctrine from the outset, namely, how the author draws inferences from the economic trinitarian relations to God's immanent relations. We have already seen that Moltmann contests the classical distinction between the immanent and the economic Trinity on the grounds that such a distinction cannot do justice to the real relationship that exists between the trinitarian God of love and the world. The notion of an immanent Trinity whose personal relations to one another are utterly self-sufficient contradicts the revealed essence of the Trinity as the self-communication of the good. At the same time, Moltmann does not utterly relinquish this distinction by simply equating the Trinity with its history of relations to the world, as he appeared to do in *The Crucified God*. Rather, he seeks a legitimate way of making claims about the essence of God that both respects the dynamic ongoing real relation of the Trinity to the world and upholds its distinction from the world.

In *The Trinity and the Kingdom*, Moltmann proposes for the first time a conceptual distinction that will meet both of his aims. He suggests that we can make claims about God's eternal nature if we do so within the context of doxology. In doxology human beings offer praise and adoration of God that spring from God's beneficence toward humankind. At the same time, believers also move beyond praise for God's good works to offer praise for God's very goodness in and of itself—for God's own sake. As Moltmann explains, "In doxology the thanks of the receiver return from the goodly gift of the giver. But the giver is not thanked merely for the sake of his good gift; he is also extolled because he himself is good."[128] We can rely on the truthfulness of doxological claims about God in God's self so long as they remain anchored in that economy of salvation; we cannot presume, however, a second doxological Trinity that in any respect contradicts God's revelation in history. Moltmann formulates this epistemological rule most clearly in a doxological revision of Rahner's axiom: "Statements about the immanent Trinity must not contradict statements about the economic Trinity. Statements about the economic Trinity must correspond to doxological statements about the immanent Trinity."[129]

Even with this basic epistemological rule in place, the reciprocal relationship that Moltmann describes between the Trinity and the world obviously complicates any one-to-one pattern of correspondence between the trinitarian history of God and the doxological Trinity. Since the trinitarian history of God affects the immanent Trinity, the full nature of the doxological Trinity—who God is in the fullness of his goodness—is only realized at the conclusion of history. In other words, there will first be a perfect correspondence, even more, a unity between the two in the eschaton, when the entire trinitarian history of God draws to a close. As Moltmann puts it: "When everything is 'in God' and 'God is all in all,' then the economic Trinity is raised into and transcended in the immanent Trinity."[130] Given this eschatological perspective on the immanent being of God, the doxological Trinity may well correspond to our present experience of salvation, but it also always surpasses it. For this reason Moltmann places an eschatological proviso on all theological statements about the doxological Trinity. Only in a "fragmentary way" do our concepts and ideas actually point to the eternal nature of the Trinity; they must, in Moltmann's words, "suffer *a transformation of meaning* if they are to be applied to the mystery of the Trinity."[131]

THE ETERNAL RELATIONS OF FATHER, SON, AND SPIRIT. Bearing this eschatological proviso in mind, let us turn now to consider Moltmann's model of the eternal relations and the processions among the three persons. In keeping with his epistemological rule (to keep his doxological claims anchored in the narrative of biblical revelation), Moltmann first describes each of the three divine persons and their eternal relations as inferences that he draws from his economy of creation and redemption; only thereafter does he develop his general concepts of divine personhood, relationality, and unity for his social doctrine.

In developing his concept of the eternal Father, the author takes his cue from the Father's revelation in and through his relationship to the Son. Moltmann spotlights again the distinctive Abba relationship that the Father shared with the Son, for example, as it is witnessed to in the Lord's Prayer. Moltmann draws the contrast sharply between his theological notion of fatherhood and the cosmological God the Father who is the creator or origin of the universe. Whereas the latter represents the God of patriarchy—an almighty ruler who is to be feared as well as worshiped, the former reveals a God whose gifts are mercy and compassion, freedom and fellowship.[132]

On the basis of their intimate relationship of fellowship, Moltmann considers the Father's primordial relation to the Son as his eternal source or begetter. Here, too, Moltmann's primary interest is in showing the profound difference between his trinitarian notion of God the Father and that of other monotheistic and patriarchal religions. He highlights in particular how the sexist image of God the Father is utterly transformed in the Christian narrative through the imagery of birth or begetting. Quoting with approval the Orthodox tradition's description of the Son being born out of the Father's womb, Moltmann concludes that the Christian concept of God the Father is really that of a "motherly Father" or a "fatherly Mother."[133] This utterly transformed Father language delegitimates the whole notion of patriarchal rule in society and proclaims in its place a rule of egalitarian fellowship. Paraphrasing Galatians 3: 28, Moltmann writes, "It leads to fellowship of men and women without privilege, and subjection, for in fellowship with the first-born brother there is no longer male or female, but all are one in Christ, and joint heirs according to the promise."[134]

While many aspects of this interpretation of the Father return to themes we have seen previously, two aspects are especially significant for the overall shape of Moltmann's social doctrine. First, he conceives of the personeity of the Father primarily in relational terms; we simply cannot know the Father except insofar as he is in relationship to the Son. Although Moltmann does not draw any further conclusions for his doctrine at this point, this provides us with an early sign of the fact that personeity and relationality are mutually constitutive concepts within his doctrine. Furthermore, Moltmann's primary concern in describing the relationship of eternal begetting is identifying the nature of the relationship that the Father shares with the Son—one of freedom and fellowship. To invoke the terms that I introduced earlier, the eternal procession of the Son reveals the Father as the one who frees in love and who offers this kingdom of freedom to humankind through our adoption into the Son's fellowship with the Father.

Second, Moltmann introduces a caveat to his definition of the Father in terms of his eternal relationship to the Son. The author acknowledges that a second definition of fatherhood as the unoriginate origin, the *"principium sine principio,"* is also needed.[135] He invokes this definition of Father as eternal origin to avoid the danger of Sabellianism, that is, the idea that there might be a fourth entity independent of the three divine persons who is their true origin and source of their being. Moltmann applies this cosmological term to the Father reluctantly, however, because it reintroduces the notion of monarchy that he was anxious to circumvent at all costs in his doctrine. He restricts this monarchy of the Father as applicable only to the divine relations of origin, the "inner-trinitarian constitution of God," and having no bearing on the Father's relationship to the world.[136] In terms of the Trinity's relationship to the world, all three persons are equally primordial.

In contrast to his description of the Father, Moltmann's depiction of the second person of the Trinity follows very traditional lines. He readily adopts the language of eternal generation and its traditional meaning as affirming that the Son is the one and the same essence of the Father. Through this eternal begetting the Father "communicates everything to the eternal Son—everything except his fatherhood. The Father communicates to the Son his divinity, his power and his glory."[137] Moreover, Moltmann affirms that the Father's eternal communication of being to the Son is not a matter of free choice but belongs to the essence of the divine nature; in other words, there is no essence of God apart from the personal differentiation between Father and Son.

Moltmann's depiction of the eternal relations of Father and Son goes beyond traditional affirmations by suggesting that these personal relations of love contain from eternity both the Father's acts of creation and the Son's sacrifice of love, activities that return creation into the midst of the Father's and Son's love for one another. Moltmann accounts for these activities by positing an eternal differential between the creative love of the Father and the responsive love of the Son. In the author's words, "They do not stand in an equal reciprocal relationship to one another. The Father loves the Son with engendering, fatherly love. The Son loves the Father with responsive, self-giving love."[138] Out of the positive surplus or overflow of the Father's love for the Son, the Father creates a world that is destined to return this love and give God delight. Similarly, Moltmann argues that the Son's responsive love of the Father, what the author calls the Son's "eternal obedience," always already includes the "sacrifice of boundless love of Golgotha" that justifies and saves creation.[139]

Given the binitarian tendencies that we have noted all along the way in Moltmann's trinitarian theology, it comes as no surprise that the author has the most difficulty explicating the personhood of the Spirit, especially within the framework of the personal relationship of the Father and the Son. Moltmann contends that this problem is not his alone; the scriptures themselves obscure the distinctive personhood of the Holy Spirit, since the Spirit usually appears in them either as a divine energy or as a sanctifying force. Moreover, he argues that the trinitarian traditions in both the East and the West also offer unsatisfactory definitions of the Spirit's personhood. On the one hand, the East's strategy of defining the persons in terms of their relations of origin leads only to a negative definition of the Spirit's personhood—as being "not without origin, like the Father," and "not generated, like the Son."[140] On the other hand, the Western definition of the Spirit as the bond of love between the Father and the Son is also fraught with difficulties, since the Spirit is defined solely in terms of its relation to the other two persons and does not have its own distinctive pattern of love relations.

Moltmann resolves the issue of the Spirit's personhood, its procession and eternal relations to the Father and Son, through a series of complex arguments involving both the scriptures and theological tradition. He turns first to the Johannine schema of the Word and the Spirit in order to demonstrate the Spirit's full divinity. There he notes that since the breathing out of the Holy Spirit is always bound to the utterance of the eternal Word, we can infer from the eternal procession of the Word that the Spirit also eternally proceeds from the Father, and is thus of equal divinity.[141] Second, Moltmann clarifies the Holy Spirit's eternal relations to the Father and the Son by offering a creative compromise solution to the *Filioque* debate between the Eastern and Western churches. To recall, the *Filioque* debate concerns whether the Spirit proceeds from the Father alone as the Eastern church maintains, or from both the Father and the Son as the Western church insists. With the East Moltmann affirms that the Spirit processes only from the Father as the sole Origin of the Godhead. The Spirit receives its full divinity from the Father, or, in Moltmann's preferred terminology, has its "divine existence (hypostasis)" from the Father.[142] At the same time, Moltmann gestures toward the Western position by recalling that God the Father is "in all eternity solely the Father of the Son,"[143] so that one can genuinely speak of the Spirit's proceeding "from *the Father of the Son*."[144] Since the eternal procession of the Son is the "logical presupposition" of the Spirit's procession, one can speak of the Son's participation in the Spirit's procession as "from the Father in the eternal presence of the Son."[145]

To specify the inner-trinitarian relationship of the Spirit to the Son and the Father, Moltmann introduces a distinction between the Spirit's *hypostasis*, an ontological category, and her relational form, *eidos* or *prosopon*, an aesthetic category.[146] The relational form depicts the Spirit's role in the inner divine life as glorifier of the Father and the Son: the Holy Spirit's face "is manifested in his turning to the Father and to the Son, and in the turning of the Father and the Son to him. It is the Holy Spirit in her inner-trinitarian manifestation of glory."[147] While the Spirit receives its hypostasis or divine being from the Father, she receives its glorifying form from the Son and the Father. Thus, Moltmann concludes that the Holy Spirit is the one "who proceeds from the Father of the Son, and who receives his form from the Father and the Son."[148]

A SOCIAL RECONSTRUCTION OF THE CONCEPT OF DIVINE PERSONS: THEIR RELATIONS AND THEIR UNITY. Although Moltmann's concept of divine personhood has been implicit throughout his presentation of the trinitarian history of God and of the doxological Trinity, he first clarifies his formal concept of personhood after engaging in critical discussion of various proposals from the history of the doctrine. Four theologians—Augustine, Boethius, Richard of St. Victor, and Hegel—provide the chief dialogue partners and also the building blocks for Moltmann's own constructive proposal.

Moltmann's starting point is Boethius's definition of personhood as *"persona est rationalis naturae individua substantia"*; as Moltmann states, "As individual substance, the person is characterized by substantiality, intellectuality and incommunicability."[149] The author begins with Boethius's substantial concept of personhood because it provides an important corrective to the modalist concept of personhood as a "mode of being" that has prevailed in modern trinitarian proposals: "The trinitarian Persons are not 'modes of being'; they are individual, unique, non-interchangeable subjects of the one, common divine substance, with consciousness and will. Each of the Persons possesses the divine nature in a non-interchangeable way; each presents it in his own way."[150] Moltmann emphasizes not so much the rational aspect of Boethius's concept as the weight that it assigns to the noninterchangeable agency of each person. This coheres well with the author's own picture of the trinitarian history of God in which each divine person enacts a distinct set of activities in the world that establishes its particular identity.

Although there are indubitable strengths to a substantial notion of personhood, Moltmann points equally to its significant limitations: it neither provides a way to identify the uniqueness of the divine persons nor clarifies their interdependence with one another. To remedy these deficiencies, Moltmann turns to Augustine's relational concept of personhood. Here the particular identity of each of the three divine persons is constituted by its unique and nonexchangeable set of relationships to the others. Moltmann points out that by defining the persons in terms of their relationships to one another as *paternitas, filatio, spiratio,* Augustine differentiates among the three in such a way that also binds them inextricably to one another; in Moltmann's words, "The three Persons are independent in that they are divine, but as Persons they are deeply bound to one another and dependent on one another."[151] Despite these advantages in a relational understanding of personhood, Moltmann concludes that a relational definition of personhood alone does not suffice as well. If we define persons strictly in terms of their relationships to one another, nothing can prevent the threat of modalism, that is, that the three become subordinate to a monolithic divine subject.[152]

Given the shortcomings of either a purely substantial or a purely relational definition of personhood, Moltmann offers a definition of divine personhood that combines both aspects: "The trinitarian Persons *subsist* in the common divine nature; they *exist* in their relations to one another."[153] With this definition, he affirms on the one hand that the divine persons are constitutive of the divine essence: one does not exist without the other. On the other hand, the divine persons are only given in their relationships to one another. In Moltmann's words, "The two [personality and relationships] arise simultaneously and together."[154]

Moltmann develops his concept of divine personhood one step further by specifying the nature of these divine relations. He does so by adopting a concept of personhood that was first introduced by Richard of St. Victor and subsequently developed by Hegel. From Richard of St. Victor the author gleans the notion that the persons exist in ecstatic relations of love in which they give themselves fully to one another: "By virtue of the love they have for one another they ex-ist totally in the other. . . . Each Person finds his existence and his joy in the other Person. Each Person receives the fullness of eternal life from the other."[155] Hegel furthers Richard of St. Victor's notion of ecstatic love relations with the idea that the divine persons do not simply exist in being for the other but actually consummate or realize their personhood through these reciprocal acts of self-giving and receiving; in this way, Hegel introduces the essential dimension of historicity to the essence of divine personhood. One cannot have the divine persons apart from the history of the self-surrendering love that is given and received from the other persons.

Although Moltmann does not draw out the correspondences himself, it is not difficult to see that this concept of divine persons as ecstatic historical relations of love corresponds to the relations among the divine persons that were manifest in the trinitarian history of God. As we have seen earlier, Moltmann interprets all the major events within the trinitarian economy—creation, incarnation, cross-resurrection, and transfiguration—as permutations of the self-giving love that is exchanged among the Father, the Son, and the Holy Spirit. Although these relationships are ever changing in the sense that different persons of the Trinity take on the role of giver and receiver of the divine action of love, the common denominator in each is this ecstatic exchange of one's self in love.

The final and arguably most distinctive aspect of Moltmann's social reconstruction of the doctrine is his concept of divine unity. Divine unity is the dynamic communion shared among the divine persons through their reciprocal relationships of indwelling. Moltmann appeals to an ancient concept from John the Damascene, the notion of *perichoresis* (περιχωρησις), to depict this unique concept of unity as communion or fellowship in the Trinity.

Three aspects of this concept are essential elements for Moltmann's notion of triunity. First, *perichoresis* is a dynamic concept. As Moltmann explains in the following passage, this concept signifies a unity or at-oneness that is constantly created anew through the acts of self-giving and receiving among the three persons: "An eternal life process takes place in the triune God through the exchange of energies. The Father exists in the Son, the Son in the Father, and both of them in the Spirit, just as the Spirit exists in both the Father and the Son. By virtue of their eternal love they live in one another to such an extent, and dwell in one another to such an extent, that they are one."[156] Although the term *perichoresis* has often been translated in the West as "coinherence," a term that connotes a static form of indwelling, Moltmann's use of it is more akin to "interanimation," that is, a dynamic being and acting among the divine persons.

Second, *perichoresis* involves an ongoing dialectic of self-differentiation and self-giving that establishes both particularity or otherness in the Trinity and the unity of the three persons with one another. In Moltmann's words, "In the *perichoresis*, the very thing that divides them becomes that which binds them together."[157] This means that the unity or oneness of God does not compete with the threeness of God for ontological precedence. They emerge together because these relationships of mutual indwelling at once distinguish the persons and form their unity with one another. As such, this notion of divine unity does not subsume the three persons under a generic concept of divine being; divine unity understood as *perichoresis* is truly a communal attribute that can only be predicated of all three persons together.

Third, this notion of perichoretic unity lacks any hint of subordination among the divine persons. This dynamic movement rests entirely on perfect reciprocity and equality among the three persons. Neither hierarchy nor patterns of domination and subjugation exist in this eternal giving and receiving of trinitarian fellowship. As such, the notion of *perichoresis* corresponds perfectly to Moltmann's vision of divine rule in the eschatological kingdom of God—a form of mutual and personal indwelling that is based on relationships of perfect equality.

While Moltmann heralds the concept of *perichoresis* as the solution to how the three persons can truly be one, critical questions remain about his notion of divine unity. First, as several critics have pointed out, there remains the evident danger of tritheism in Moltmann's social reconstruction.[158] Moltmann's social doctrine invites this criticism, especially because of his emphasis on the noninterchangeable identity of the divine persons in the trinitarian history of God. As we have seen, the persons each carry out different roles in the trinitarian economy, roles that are not simply appropriated to them but that actually constitute their personal identities. Given this notion of divine personhood, it becomes easy to liken the three to independent subjects, whose unanimity is merely volitional. Moltmann's descriptions of divine unity as a union (*Einigkeit*) among the three divine persons—a union that is open to humankind's inclusion in its midst—also furthers such a suspicion. The notion of union suggests that these are distinct entities that join together in acts of common will.

Moltmann seems to recognize this threat of tritheism, since he seeks to ward it off from the very first in *The Trinity and the Kingdom*. He defends his view of triunity against this picture of the three divine persons as fully separable agents, "who only subsequently enter into relationship with one another."[159] He insists that their triunity is an ontological unity that rests in their constitution as persons. To follow Moltmann's argumentation here, it is important to call to mind the second concept of divine unity that he invokes in his social doctrine, namely, the unity in the origin or in the monarchy of the Father. Although Moltmann does not render this explicit, it appears that it is this notion of the Father as the source of the Godhead that actually guarantees the common divine essence of the three persons, rather than his notion of fellowship through the three persons' mutual indwelling.

This leads directly to a second critical question concerning Moltmann's doctrine: What is the relationship between this protological concept of divine unity in the Father and the eschatological notion of divine unity in the *perichoresis* of the doxological Trinity? We can formulate this question more broadly in terms of divine love: Is there an ontological difference between the Trinity in the origin as the self-communication of the good and its telos in the intratrinitarian fellowship and freedom of the eschatological kingdom?

Moltmann's writings do not give an unambiguous answer to these questions. As I have pointed out throughout this chapter, there are clearly deep correspondences between the various aspects of his doctrine—his notion of trinitarian love in the origin, his presentation of its pilgrimage in the history of the world, and its anticipated eschatological end in the kingdom. All point to a triune God whose essence is that of an ecstatic, intimate, and mutual fellowship. And yet, Moltmann's statements about the unfinished nature of the divine life until the world is gathered into its midst also leave such issues finally unresolved in history. All we can affirm is that the doxological Trinity corresponds to what we have come to know of the Trinity in the origin through the trinitarian history of God, but that this messianic reality will also infinitely surpass it.

4

A Social Trinitarian Theology of the Human Person

Chapters 2 and 3 of this study have traced the historical development of Moltmann's trinitarian theology and the corresponding evolution within his concept of divine love. In this chapter and the next,
we will step beyond the strict domain of Moltmann's doctrine of the
Trinity and his construal of divine love to enter the broader terrain
of the author's trinitarian anthropology and his theology of grace.
Here our task will be to explore how Moltmann appeals to his social
trinitarian theology to reconfigure the notions of human personhood
and the relations among God, the individual, and the human community. We will be asking toward what kind of attitudes and forms
of actions the believer is inclined when he or she comprehends his
or her life *coram Deo*—in the presence of this trinitarian God of
love.

By posing this set of questions to Moltmann's theology, we will
be testing the second theological wager that the author makes on behalf of his social trinitarian concept of love, namely, that it reflects
not only who God is but also who human beings as *imago Trinitatis*
are called to become. We will be evaluating both the promise and
the limitations of Moltmann's social trinitarian concepts of relationality, persons, and communion as a normative model—what I
termed in the opening chapter as a "social trinitarian analogy of fellowship"—for the right relationships among individuals and society
and their God. In so doing, we not only will be contributing a distinctive hermeneutic for reading Moltmann's *Messianic Theology* but
also will be critically assessing the practical significance of Moltmann's social trinitarian theology.

This chapter takes the first step toward addressing this agenda. Here I focus primarily on Moltmann's social trinitarian anthropology, which lays the cornerstone for his vision of the Christian life that we will consider in chapter 5. In what follows, I turn first to the author's criticisms of Western theological anthropology and demonstrate how these correspond to his earlier critiques of the Western doctrine of the Trinity. In particular, I show the parallels between Moltmann's concerns over the atomism and hierarchicalism of Western views of the human person, and the monarchianism that has dogged Western trinitarianism.

In the second section of this chapter, I introduce the author's distinctive pneumatological and messianic approach to the doctrine of creation, which supplies the doctrinal framework for his theological anthropology. Here we will see how Moltmann appeals to the dynamic fellowship of the Spirit as the Trinity's immanent presence in creation. The Spirit engenders the possibility for a range of correspondences—what I term "analogies of fellowship"—between the trinitarian life and that of humankind. Second, we will consider how Moltmann revises traditional Western schemas of creation and redemption by replacing the classical twofold structure of nature and grace with a tripartite eschatological dialectic of nature, grace, and glory. This theological move lends a messianic trajectory to human life, so that it remains open—prepared but not yet perfected—for its messianic destiny of becoming the glory of God.

In the third and concluding section of this chapter, I consider Moltmann's messianic interpretation of the *imago Dei* in humankind: its created designation as *imago Trinitatis*, its messianic calling as *imago Christi*, and its eschatological telos as *gloria Dei*. Here I examine in detail the distinctive aspects of our created destiny as *imago Trinitatis*. Moltmann interprets the image of God in humankind as an *"analogia relationis,"* that is, a theological analogy between the inner-trinitarian relations of fellowship and human interpersonal relations. With this relational model, the author treats our created destiny as *imago Trinitatis* as a social and embodied likeness that the individual can realize through the various constellations of relationships that constitute her existence. Humankind's potential for creating such social trinitarian analogies provides the stepping-stone for Moltmann's sweeping social trinitarian vision of the Christian life that I will take up in the next chapter.

Atomism and Hierarchicalism in Theological Anthropology

In many ways Moltmann's critique of Western theological anthropology resembles closely his critique of the Western doctrine of the Trinity explored in the previous chapter. He exposes the same monistic and monarchical tendencies in the "possessive individualism" and "hierarchicalism" of Western theological anthropology and its political theology that have plagued its doctrine of God.[1]

Just as the unity of God takes precedence over the differentiated relationships among the divine persons in the Western doctrine of the Trinity, Moltmann contends that so, too, the sovereignty of the individual prevails over the various constellations of interpersonal and sociopolitical relations in the human community.

In *The Trinity and the Kingdom*, Moltmann develops this monarchical critique of Western theological tradition first in the realm of political theology. He investigates how certain patterns of absolute power and rulership in Christian monotheism are transposed into what he terms "political monotheism," that is, forms of governance in which a single ruler exercises absolute sovereignty over his subjects.[2] While Moltmann does not see the relationship between religious and political ideas as simply unilateral, he nonetheless argues that models of divine sovereignty very often supply the sacred legitimation for earthly monarchical orders. "The notion of a divine monarchy in heaven and on earth," contends Moltmann, "for its part, generally provides the justification for earthly domination—religious, moral, patriarchal or political domination— and makes it a hierarchy, a 'holy rule.'"[3] The theological root behind such political monotheism is the notion of absolute rulership that Moltmann has previously identified in Western monarchical models of the Trinity, most notably in those of Barth and Augustine. In Moltmann's words, the "Lord of the world," who "is defined simply through his power of disposal over his property, not through personality and personal relationships," provides the divine prototype for political monarchianism.[4] As we saw earlier, the author objects to such definitions of divine lordship in terms of absolute power and self-determination because, in his view, they do not correspond to the biblical views of lordship. Rather, these are secular and legal notions of power that have been transposed into the theological realm.

Moltmann offers a number of classical examples from Western political history as evidence to support his case. He points first to the ancient Constantinian empire as a prime example of how the notion of divine sovereignty legitimated the absolute rule of the Christian emperors in the early church. There Moltmann recalls how the emperor was "to a pre-eminent degree *the visible image* of the invisible God. . . . His rule represents God's rule. Hence the one God is venerated in him. He is not merely the regent; he is the actual lord and possessor of the imperium."[5] Moltmann identifies a similar monarchical analogy between divine and earthly authorities in seventeenth-century French absolutism; the French Calvinists defended the absolutist power of the earthly sovereign as the "complete reflection or 'portrait' of the majesty of God."[6]

Moltmann shifts his monarchical critique from the realm of politics to that of personal anthropology in *God in Creation*, the second volume of his *Messianic Theology*. Here as elsewhere Barth serves as Moltmann's preferred target of critique. He identifies two symptoms of monarchianism in Barth's theological anthropology—what Moltmann terms "spiritualization" and "instrumentalization."[7] With these terms he describes how Barth identifies the human being's essence with its ruling soul and how the body serves as an instrument of this soul. For Moltmann, the structure of domination that is implicit in this soul-body relation mirrors Barth's understanding of rulership and the absolute freedom of the will in his doctrine of the Trinity. What links the two is the notion of the human being as *imago Dei*. Moltmann contends that Barth's model of the *imago Dei* rests on an analogy between the absolute lordship of God over the world to the lordship of the human spirit over the body. As we already saw in chapter 3, Moltmann charges that Barth's concept of divine freedom in terms of lordship is incommensurate to that of the scriptures. In his theological anthropology, the author advances an analogous critique of Barth's model of the inner sovereignty of the individual as *imago Dei*. The *imago Dei* amounts to a form of absolute self-possession: "The human being is the image of God his Lord in that he belongs to himself, controls himself and disposes over himself. . . . *The rule of the soul over its body is an expression of the rule of God, and the self-control of the human being is its parable.*"[8]

Nor do the ill effects of Barth's trinitarianism on his theological anthropology end there. Moltmann argues that Barth recapitulates the Son's pattern of perfect obedience to the Father's rule in the inner-trinitarian life in the ordered division of the human person as a "dominating soul" and the "subservient body."[9] This inner-trinitarian order of rule and obedience sacralizes a rigid order of superiority and subordination that has ripple effects throughout Barth's doctrine of creation. The relations of heaven and earth, male and female, humankind and nature all correspond to this hierarchical order of relations.[10]

While Barth may be Moltmann's preferred modern example of the monarchical and monistic tendencies in Western theological anthropology, Moltmann roots the problem in Augustine's trinitarian theology. We already saw how in *The Trinity and the Kingdom* Moltmann links the monarchical monotheism of Western trinitarian theology with Augustine's psychological analogy. In *God in Creation*, Moltmann offers a series of related objections to Augustine's psychological analogy for the Trinity. The author challenges Augustine's interpretation of the *imago Dei* in humankind and outlines its deleterious implications for his theological anthropology and view of the Christian life.

Moltmann takes issue with the fundamental premise of Augustine's *imago Dei* anthropology, namely, that each human person is created in the image of the whole Trinity, rather than in the image of one divine person or as part of an interpersonal or social image of the Trinity. Quoting Augustine's words, "Man is the image of the one true God. For this Trinity is itself the one true God," Moltmann contends that for the church father, "the human being corresponds to the single Being of the triune God, not to the threefold nature of

God's inner essence."[11] In other words, by locating the image of the Trinity in an individual's rational soul, Augustine construes the analogy between God and humankind primarily in terms of divine sovereignty.

Now Moltmann does acknowledge that Augustine's psychological analogy implies that there is a trinitarian differentiation among the individual soul's faculties, for example, in the triad of "spirit–knowledge–love."[12] This does not relieve Augustine's psychological analogy (or Aquinas's subsequent reception of it), however, of its monarchical tendencies. On the contrary, Moltmann argues that once Augustine locates the *imago Trinitatis* in the intellectual nature of human being, the human subject devolves into a thinly veiled model of the single lordship of God the Father: "[Augustine and Aquinas] seem to see the Trinity as a single subject with two 'processions,' and to interpret the human soul correspondingly, as also a subject of reason and will. This means that as the image of God the human being corresponds to God the Father."[13] Just as the monarchy of the Father prevails over the trinitarian community of persons in Augustine's doctrine of God, so, too, Moltmann argues, the monarchical unity of the individual rational soul dominates over its internal relationality in the church father's model of the *imago Dei*.

Moltmann rejects the rational soul as the seat of the *imago Dei* in humankind not only because it fails to do justice to the differentiated relationality of the Trinity but also because it supports what he calls an "analogy of domination" over the body akin to what he previously identified in Barth's doctrine.[14] With this term "analogy of domination," Moltmann refers to the implicit analogy that Augustine creates between God's absolute sovereignty over the world and an individual's spiritual sovereignty over the body; here, too, the relationship is one of domination and perfect obedience. Just as God exercises absolute power over his creation, so, too, the spirit preserves its omnipotence over the body's activities.

According to Moltmann, Augustine's hierarchical model of the *imago Dei* paves the way for a similar analogy of domination to be created between men and women.[15] On first glance this is quite a surprising claim, since one might well think that a spiritualized notion of the *imago Dei* would support the fundamental equality of men and women as creatures. Moltmann argues, however, the converse: the hierarchies, upon which the psychological analogy is constructed—the lordship of the one sovereign God over the world, the soul over the subordinate body—fit with an analogy of domination that exists between male and female relations. Without the positive affirmation that the whole human being, both soul and gendered body—male and female alike—is created in God's image, the equal dignity of women and men as *imago Dei* remains at risk.

Moltmann's most far-reaching critique of Augustine's psychological analogy for the Trinity is that it treats an individual's social relations as less significant than one's self-relation. By locating humankind's likeness to God in the self-reflexivity of the intellect, Augustine privileges the individual soul and its interior relations over that of the individual's relationships to other persons.[16] Although Moltmann grants that this psychological approach to the *imago Trinitatis* supports the dignity of each and every individual, it also helped generate the Western individualism that pits the individual and his or her interests over and against those of his or her community.[17]

In *The Spirit of Life*, the fourth volume of his *Messianic Theology*, Moltmann presents this same criticism of Augustine's theological anthropology in more pointed terms. Here he charges that the overall introspective character of Western spirituality—what Moltmann polemically describes as its "gnostic spirituality"—stems from Augustine's interiorization of the *imago Dei* in humankind; Augustine's turn inward led "to a devaluation of the body and nature, to a preference for inward, direct self-experience as a way to God, and to a neglect of sensuous experiences of sociality and nature."[18] In other words, Augustine's attempts to discern knowledge of the Trinity out of the inner depths of the soul not only enhance a soul-body dualism in the individual but also encourage the soul's retreat from its network of interpersonal relations and social responsibilities in the world. Moltmann charges that Augustine (and the mystics in the Augustinian tradition) set the individual on an interior spiritual journey to know and love her God and herself, a journey that withdraws the individual from love of the senses and love of one's neighbors. It generated a contemplative spirituality that was easily divorced from active discipleship—a spirituality that Moltmann portrays harshly as "non-sensuous, unworldly and non-political."[19]

Before we turn to Moltmann's social trinitarian reconstruction of theological anthropology, let me offer two critical observations about his presentation of Western anthropology. First, we need to question at several points the adequacy of Moltmann's interpretations of both Barth's and Augustine's theological anthropologies. In both of these cases Moltmann casts sweeping judgments that often rely on isolated passages from their complex works. For example, in Barth's case Moltmann draws attention to certain patterns of lordship and obedience in his predecessor's writings, while he skips over the countervailing themes of God's partnership with humankind and that of human beings with one another, themes that are woven throughout Barth's theological anthropology. Although one might rightly object to Barth's reliance on this rhetoric of lordship and service, one can equally argue that Barth seeks to redefine the significance of such terms by placing them in a kenotic christological framework.[20]

In Augustine's case, Moltmann's analyses are equally selective and often rely for their interpretation on modern commentaries that are highly critical of Augustine's position. As David Cunningham points out, Moltmann seems to fall prey here to "historical scapegoating."[21] That is, he saddles Augustine with views of human personhood, for example, as atomized and nonrelational, that are more appropriate to post-Cartesian views of the human subject than they are to Augustine's rational psychology.

The second observation is a related one. In my view, the more appropriate target of Moltmann's critique is the monarchical picture of the Christian God and the anthropocentric worldview that have dogged Christian theologies of creation since the early modern period. Moltmann suggests this critique of modernity in the opening chapter of *God in Creation*, as he points out how the emerging modern concept of God in the Renaissance (particularly under the influence of nominalism) dramatically shifted the paradigm both of God's relationship to the world and of human beings' relationship to nature. Through the rise of scientific methodology and industrialization, humankind came to view its relationship to the rest of creation in terms of exploitative domination—in terms of possession and absolute power over its resources. Just as absolute power became the "pre-eminent attribute of [God's] divinity," so, too, the modern human being is urged "to strive for power and domination so that he might acquire *his* divinity."[22]

In essence, Moltmann's polemic against Western theological anthropology parallels that which he launched earlier against modern theism: he objects to its ideal of freedom as self-sufficiency and absolute power over others. Modern theological anthropology adopts this false understanding of divine freedom and, as a result, fosters a range of destructive relationships of domination in and among human communities and toward the rest of creation. Above all, Moltmann's doctrine of creation and theological anthropology seek to dismantle this modern analogy of domination by reconfiguring both the divine and human relationship and the pattern of human relationships in terms of the communal and life-giving patterns of trinitarian fellowship. As we turn to his constructive proposal ahead, we will evaluate how successful Moltmann is in providing an alternative paradigm for Christian existence built on the dynamics of trinitarian fellowship, a paradigm which will foster human flourishing and healthy interpersonal relations of interdependence.

A Pneumatological and Messianic Theology of Creation

Before we turn to Moltmann's *imago Dei* anthropology, let us look first at two overarching principles operative in his doctrine of creation: first, how the Spirit bestows the Trinity's life-giving immanent fellowship in the world; and second, Moltmann's messianic revision of the classical creation-redemption (nature-grace) model of God's relationship to the world.[23] As I argue later, these two aspects of his doctrine have important methodological implications for how Moltmann presents the relationship between the Trinity and creation, and particularly for the human being's capacity to model the trinitarian life in and through her various relationships in the world.

The Spirit's Creative Fellowship with the World

As we recall from our discussion of *The Trinity and the Kingdom,* Moltmann anchors the original act of creation in the inner-trinitarian love of the Father for the Son. The overflow of the Father's engendering love for the Son calls creation forth into life through the power of the Holy Spirit. Moltmann retains essentially the same trinitarian theology of creation in *God in Creation,* but he now expands significantly on its pneumatological dimensions. He does so by appealing to various biblical traditions, particularly the Wisdom literature, the Psalms, and the Book of Acts, as well as two main sources from the theological tradition—the trinitarian pneumatology of the Cappadocian Fathers and Calvin's pneumatological doctrine of creation.[24]

In keeping with his trinitarian theology of love as developed in *The Trinity and the Kingdom,* Moltmann describes the Spirit as the overflowing love of God from which creation originally issues forth. The Creator Spirit represents the wellspring or, to quote Calvin, "the fountain of life (*fons vitae*)."[25] The Creator Spirit provides not only this initial energy of creation but also the continuous presence of the trinitarian God within creation. This indwelling Spirit of God, the *Shekinah,* permeates the entire cosmos with life-giving energy, preserving it in life and all the while transforming it into a new life. "Through the powers and potentialities of the Spirit," Moltmann writes, "the Creator indwells the creatures he has made, animates them, holds them in life, and leads them into the future of his kingdom."[26] In essence, the Spirit fulfills the three classical Reformed notions of God's providential agency—preservation, accompaniment, and governance of all creation.

Moltmann not only describes the agency of the Spirit in classical terms but also integrates insights from evolutionary and ecological theory into his pneumatology. The Spirit acts as "the principle of creativity" that creates "new designs and 'blueprints' for material and living organisms."[27] The Spirit is at once the "principle of individuation," differentiating the one into the many, and the "holistic principle," knitting creation into a community with each other and with their God.[28] Finally, the Spirit serves as a teleological principle, what Moltmann terms "the principle of intentionality,"[29] that orients the whole of creation toward its common future in the kingdom of God.

For our purposes, what is most significant about Moltmann's pneumatological approach to creation is how it redresses the hierarchicalism that structures modern theologies of creation. Through the Spirit's dynamic and continuous presence in the world, Moltmann replaces the hierarchical relationship between God and creation (and, derivatively, between the human community and its natural environment) with a pattern of relationality that corresponds to that of the trinitarian life itself. This trinitarian nature of the God-world relationship becomes explicit once Moltmann invokes the notion of *perichoresis* to describe the "dialectical movement"[30] of the Spirit in creation. Through its dialectical movement, the Spirit forms a pattern of relationships with creation that is analogous to the intra-trinitarian relations of mutual indwelling. In an essay written subsequently to *God in Creation*, Moltmann describes in greater detail how he envisions this perichoretic relationship between God and the world: "The coexistence of Creator and creature is also their mutual life, their cohabitation and influence on each other. The Creator finds space in the fellowship of creatures. The creatures find space in God. So creation also means that we are in God and God is in us."[31] Through these relationships of mutual indwelling, Moltmann replaces the power structure of absolute sovereignty implicit in a God who is wholly transcendent over creation with one based on mutual interdependence between God and creation.

Moltmann's description of the relationship between God and creation as perichoretic is one of the most controversial aspects of his doctrine. By using the term *perichoresis* without any qualifications to describe the relationship between Creator and creation, Moltmann blurs the clear ontological distinction between the two. His terminology suggests that the Holy Spirit and the world exist on an equal plane—on analogy to the mutuality and equality of relations that exist among the trinitarian persons. As I pointed out at the outset of this study, Moltmann's unqualified use of such trinitarian terminology has drawn fire from his critics, who argue that he thereby risks either divinizing creation or dissolving God's being into the world.[32] Although Moltmann does not spell out for his readers how the *perichoresis* between God and the world differs from that among the divine persons, he suggests in fact that it does so. He argues that the Holy Spirit remains transcendent over creation through its eternal unity with the Father and the Son in the inner-trinitarian life.[33] In this way, Moltmann intimates that there is an asymmetry in the Holy Spirit's relationship to humankind that distinguishes it from the mutual indwelling among the divine persons. The Spirit is intimately involved in creation but also exists infinitely beyond the world as its eschatological telos.

At this point we can helpfully return to one of the other critical debates about Moltmann's trinitarian theology that I raised at the outset of this study. There I made the point that contemporary theologians criticize Moltmann's depiction of the relationship between God and creation for virtually opposite reasons. Some such as Sallie McFague criticize Moltmann's doctrine of the immanent Trinity as a way of preserving God from any hint of dependency on creation. In McFague's view, Moltmann's trinitarian theology undercuts any real relationality between God and the world in favor of a distant and self-absorbed picture of the divine nature. Others, for example, Alan Torrance, contend that Moltmann's trinitarian history of God ties the Trinity too closely to the passage of world history and, in so doing, compromises the transcendence and sovereignty of the triune God over creation. For this reason it becomes difficult to protect the gracious nature of God's redemptive agency on behalf of humankind.

Since Torrance's criticisms focus more directly on questions of grace and the nature of doxology in the life of faith, I will wait until the next chapter to engage his particular criticisms. We can, however, address McFague's criticisms now that we have seen in greater detail how Moltmann relates his trinitarian theology to his doctrine of creation via his pneumatology. Here a couple of points can be made in favor of Moltmann's trinitarian theology of creation.

First, McFague's criticism seems shortsighted, insofar as she does not take into account how Moltmann's reconstruction of the doctrine of the Trinity creates a more differentiated picture of the relationship between God and the world than that of either radical transcendence or immanence. Through the dynamic self-giving (*kenosis*) of the Holy Spirit, there is a mediated presence of the Trinity in creation that guarantees a real and ongoing presence of God in the world without equating the two. Moltmann uses his trinitarian notion of the perichoretic relationship of God and the world to overcome both the alternatives of deism, a remote God who is uninvolved in the world, and of pantheism, dissolution of the distinction between God and the world. In his words, "The trinitarian concept of creation binds together the transcendence and the immanence of God. . . . In the panentheistic view, God, having created the world, also dwells in it, and conversely the world which he has created exists in him."[34]

Second, Moltmann's description of the God-world relationship via the fellowship of the Spirit, namely, that God is both transcendent to creation and radically present and engaged in all of creation, coheres well with the views of classical theologians such as Augustine, Aquinas, or Calvin. As has been recently argued by Kathryn Tanner and William Placher, only in modernity do doctrines of creation assume what McFague does, namely, a "contrastive definition" of divine transcendence in which transcendence and immanence become inverse terms in a "zero-sum game"; the more the one increases, the other decreases.[35] For Aquinas, Luther, or Calvin, it was not a logical contradiction to claim that God is both radically transcendent to creation and immediately present and at work in it, because God's freedom and agency are of a different order than those of finite creatures.[36] What was unacceptable was the notion that God exists in the world in the sense that the world becomes a necessary part of God's being. Although Moltmann's unqualified use of the term *perichoresis* to describe God's indwelling presence in the world might initially suggest that he espouses such a pantheistic view, Moltmann's insistence on the unbroken fellowship of the immanent Trinity, as well as the dialectical nature of the Spirit's presence, counters such an interpretation.

A Messianic Doctrine of Creation

The second distinctive aspect of Moltmann's doctrine of creation is its messianic character. As we recall from previous chapters, the term "messianic" is the author's way of qualifying his theology in terms of his eschatological chris-tology, that is, in light of Jesus' proclamation of the kingdom of God and its anticipation in his history. In *God in Creation*, Moltmann takes one step further and anchors his messianic interpretation of creation in the biblical accounts of creation. He focuses particularly on the Sabbath day, "'the feast of crea-tion,'"[37] as the central clue to the messianic structure of creation. Western doctrines of creation have largely overlooked the fact that according to the first account in Genesis, creation does not conclude with the six active days of creation and the creation of humankind. Creation is first crowned with the Sabbath on the seventh day, when God rests and rejoices in his creation. In this Sabbath feast we discover the future of creation when "God will dwell entirely and wholly and for ever in his creation, and will allow all the beings he has created to participate in the fullness of his eternal life."[38] The Sabbath gives us a foretaste of the kingdom of glory, in which God's people will joyfully come home to their permanent dwelling in God's midst.

This Sabbath vision is at the heart of Moltmann's theological agenda of developing an ecological doctrine of creation. Here Moltmann is motivated by more than a genuine concern of responding to the ecological crisis. He is equally concerned to recover the biblical perspective on nature as the house-hold (*oikos*) or the permanent dwelling place of God.[39] In the author's view, modern theologies of creation have lost the sense of God's real presence in nature and have thus paved the way for modern science's attitudes of domi-nation and exploitation of nature's resources. They have treated the world as humankind's possession rather than as God's sacred gift.

This messianic perspective permeates the whole of Moltmann's doctrine of creation. Most simply, it means that creation is not an event that occurred once and for all at the beginning of time; rather, creation is a continuous and open process that reaches its completion first in the eschaton. Moltmann sim-ilarly reconfigures redemption and the renewal of creation. Redemption does not restore creation to its original paradisiacal perfection; rather, it builds on the ongoing process of creation.[40] Although the kingdom of glory has been anticipated proleptically in the resurrection-event, the messianic tension in the world does not abate with the coming of Christ. On the contrary, the pouring forth of the Holy Spirit into the world intensifies the messianic restlessness in all of creation, drawing it onward toward its eschatological liberation.

Moltmann appeals to one of his oft-cited Pauline texts, Romans 8:19–23, in support of his view of "new creation in the Spirit" as a dialectical experience of liberty and of longing, of both joy and the sighs of pain: "'We have' the first fruits of the Spirit and yet 'wait' for the redemption of the body. . . . The point where the liberty of the children of God has come so close that we revive in hope is the very point where we become painfully aware of the chains of bond-age."[41] As we can see from passages such as this one, Moltmann views re-demption as a holistic transformation of the created realm. He rejects a spiritualized view of redemption that promises liberation or exodus from this world. Rather, redemption represents both solidarity with the woes of the world and a commitment to their transformation.

To conclude, I would like to lift up two significant implications of Moltmann's messianic approach to the doctrine of creation for our path ahead. The first concerns how Moltmann's messianic perspective affects the traditional division of the divine economy with the world in terms of nature and grace, creation and redemption—or, to use Barth's christological categories, "creation and convenant [sic]."[42] Moltmann rejects such traditional twofold schemas on the grounds that they conflate the grace offered in Christ with the consummation of eternal glory and, in so doing, ignore the unfinished history of creation. Not only is such an equation of eschatological redemption with the present experience of divine grace inconsistent with the New Testament's messianic vision, but it also fosters a dangerous Christian triumphalism that assumes humankind's destiny has already been fulfilled in Christianity.[43]

Moltmann replaces this traditional creation-redemption schema with a threefold eschatological dialectic, in which the coming kingdom of glory qualifies the realms of both nature and grace. He formulates this messianic framework by first taking the medieval principle that grace does not destroy nature but presupposes and perfects it (*"gratia non destruit, sed praesupponit et perfecit naturam"*) and revising it in messianic terms: "Grace does not perfect, but prepares nature for eternal glory. Grace is not the perfection of nature, but prepares the messianic world for the kingdom of God."[44] With this principle Moltmann orients the whole history of creation and redemption toward its fulfillment in the messianic kingdom. This does not mean that God's history with the world represents a steady evolutionary progress toward the messianic goal of God's permanent indwelling. As we will see more clearly in the next chapter, creation itself does not possess the potential for the realization of the kingdom. Rather, the messianic kingdom that is anticipated in Christ and thereafter mediated through the Spirit involves a cosmic struggle and vanquishing of all the negativities of history—of both natural and human evils. As Richard Bauckham formulates it, the "eschatological" is, for Moltmann, "a counter-movement which does not develop out of this present, transient reality, but contradicts the evil, suffering and transience of the world as it is, transforming it by bringing it out of the nothingness to which it tends into the eternal life of indwelling."[45] On this point Moltmann's messianic narrative of creation-redemption remains utterly consistent with his earlier dialectical eschatology of *Theology of Hope*: the inbreaking power of the future mediated through the Spirit brings genuinely new life-giving possibilities into history.

The second issue is a related one, namely, how this messianic and pneumatological approach to the doctrine of creation creates the conditions for and at the same time qualifies any correspondences between the Trinity and the created order. Here a couple of points are in order. First, Moltmann's pneu-

matological doctrine of creation secures the theological nature of all correspondences between Trinity and creation, including those among human beings. By this I mean that any and all correspondences to the trinitarian life
that emerge in the finite realm are reflections of God's indwelling presence.
Since the Holy Spirit suffuses creation always and everywhere with its gift of
life, there are no purely natural analogies or correspondences to the trinitarian
life in the created realm that are independent of God's gracious presence.

If Moltmann's insistence on the indwelling of the Spirit in creation appears to elevate all of creation into a potential symbol of divine life, his messianic perspective also qualifies all such analogies as anticipations of the kingdom of the glory to come. In the author's words, the created world reveals "the
real promises of the kingdom of glory. The present world is a real symbol of
its future."[46] This means that all reflections of the divine—what I call "analogies
of fellowship"—in the created order have a dialectical nature. They are real but
also broken symbols of the kingdom to come. In this light, all such signs of
the kingdom possess a certain dynamic toward their own revision; they always
point beyond themselves to their yet unrealized future.

The Human Being as *Imago Christi* and *Imago Trinitatis*

With this messianic and pneumatological approach to the doctrine of creation
as our framework, let us turn to Moltmann's *imago Dei* anthropology. In *God
and Creation*, Moltmann situates his *imago Dei* anthropology at the conclusion
of a detailed discussion of the human being's community with the rest of
creation. He does so to counter the prevalent anthropocentrism of modern
theologies of creation. Modern philosophical and theological analyses of the
human being have so emphasized the difference between humankind and
nature that they have masked human beings' dependence on as well as their
unique responsibility for the rest of creation. In contrast, Moltmann develops
what we might describe as a doctrine of creation from below. He begins by
highlighting the many affinities between humankind and the rest of creation
in the Genesis accounts of creation. For the author, humankind's organic relationship to the natural world is symbolized most basically in human beings'
creation from the earth and their return there upon death.[47] Humankind also
shares several key features with the rest of animal creation. Like other animals,
human beings are designated as "living souls" (Gen. 1:30)—a term that in
Hebrew means an "animated body,"[48] in contrast to the later Greek notion of
a soul as a spirit imprisoned in the body. Like the rest of creation, human
beings also find themselves dependent on the earth for its living space and its
food. Finally, human beings share with the rest of the animals the gift of "bi-
sexuality and fertility,"[49] for they receive the same blessing to be fruitful and
multiply.

Despite their similarities, human beings occupy a unique place within this fellowship of creation as *"imago mundi"* or as "a microcosm in which all previous creatures are to be found again."[50] Human beings recapitulate the whole evolutionary history of creation in their complex life systems. As the capstone of all earthly creation, human beings serve the unique function of being creation's representative before God. In this capacity human beings perform both the "priestly" and "eucharistic" functions of offering petition and praise on behalf of creation to God.[51]

Against this backdrop of the human being's community with the rest of creation, Moltmann presents an innovative interpretation of the human being as *imago Dei*, in which he weaves his trinitarian theology into a messianic interpretation of the creation accounts in Genesis. Moltmann departs from the traditional notion of the *imago Dei* as an ideal primordial state or property of human beings that has been damaged or utterly lost in the Fall and then restored through grace. He reconfigures this mythic story of paradise lost and regained into a messianic narrative, one in which the *imago Dei* appears as humankind's eschatological destiny instead of as its lost origin. "In the messianic light of the gospel," Moltmann writes, "the human being's likeness to God appears as a historical process with an eschatological termination; it is not a static condition. *Being* human means *becoming* human in this process."[52] Within this messianic narrative, the human being as *imago Dei* appears in the same tensive state of "already and not yet" that dynamizes the trinitarian history of God; human beings' likeness to God is both an ever-present reality and an unrealized promise. In Moltmann's words, it is "both gift and charge, indicative and imperative. It is charge and hope, imperative and promise."[53]

Moltmann divides this messianic narrative of the human being as *imago Dei* into three stages that correspond to his eschatological dialectic of nature, grace, and glory. First, humankind's original created destiny is to become *imago Dei*. Second, our messianic calling in history is to become children of God, a term that Moltmann defines christologically as *imago Christi*. Finally, our eschatological end is to become *gloria Dei*.[54] In what follows, we will investigate the first stage of this messianic narrative—humankind's created destiny as *imago Dei*—and will return to the second and third stages when we consider Moltmann's model of salvation and the life of faith in the following chapter.

Moltmann's guiding principle in defining the human being as *imago Dei* is that this must be a theological category as opposed to a general anthropological category, capacity, or property that distinguishes humanity from non-human creation. By theological category, he means that the *imago Dei* in humankind should be defined in terms of God's being and eternal purpose in creating humankind. "The human being's likeness to God," he insists, ". . . first of all says something about the God who creates his image for himself, and who enters into a particular relationship with that image, before it says anything about the human being who is created in this form."[55] If we recall our earlier discussion of God's being as divine passion in *The Trinity and the Kingdom*, God's purpose in creating human beings is to have a "counter-part" in love—a relationship to another who can receive and respond freely to the divine gift of love. Accordingly, Moltmann defines the human being's unique designation as *imago Dei* in terms of its role as recipient and respondent to the divine gift of love: "Men and women are beings who correspond to God, beings who can give the seeking love of God the sought-for response, and who are intended to do just that. As God's image, men and women are his counterpart in the work of creation."[56] Although the whole of the created order springs forth gratuitously from God's infinite self-giving, human beings are unique in their capacity to reciprocate (albeit in a creaturely manner) this divine self-giving. They are singularly destined to become the beloved Other, the trinitarian God's sought-after covenant partner whose fulfillment is found in returning this gift of divine love in freedom.

Moltmann goes on to describe the *imago Dei* in even more precise terms as an *analogia relationis*. Following the lead of Bonhoeffer and Barth, the author contrasts this "analogy of relations" to an "analogy of substance," the latter of which focuses on a single attribute inherent in human beings, such as the rational soul or the will.[57] Instead of fixing the likeness to God in the individual's possession of a certain capacity, Moltmann defines the image in terms of relationships that correspond to the trinitarian life. As *imago Dei*, human beings not only respond in love to God's gift of fellowship but are blessed with the possibility of expressing ecstatic and passionate fellowship toward one another. In Moltmann's words, "As the image of God on earth, human beings correspond first of all to the relationship of God to themselves and to the whole of creation. But they also correspond to the inner relationships of God to himself—to the eternal, inner love of God that expresses and manifests itself in creation."[58] To return to the terms for God's essence that I introduced in the previous chapter, human beings consummate their messianic destiny as *imago Dei* when they are "free in love" and become those who themselves "free in love."

Let me draw our attention to three aspects of this *imago Dei* anthropology that are crucial for our path ahead. First, this divine-human analogy of relations depends strictly on the gift of grace. Whatever likeness or correspondences to the trinitarian relations appear in and among human beings come as a response to God's prior self-giving; all our acts of self-giving love, however much they are our own, are offered in response to God's first initiating a relationship with us. In this respect, the *imago Dei* can never be taken for being a property that human beings can either possess or lose. It remains always and everywhere a gift that God offers freely and human beings receive in gratitude ever anew.

Second, Moltmann's analogy of relations stipulates that the *imago Trinitatis* in humankind is a social or interpersonal likeness. On this point Moltmann

parts ways with the dominant Augustinian strand of Western theological anthropology that locates the *imago Trinitatis* in the self-relationality of the individual psyche. In *God and Creation*, Moltmann directly challenges Augustine's
exegesis of Genesis 1:26–27 and interprets its alternating singular and plural
terms in such a way as to support his social rather than Augustine's individual
interpretation of the *imago Dei*. The fact that the verse speaks of God as an
internal plural in the singular suggests that God creates human persons in the
plural ("as man and woman he created them") to realize a single image of the
Trinity. "The one God, who is differentiated in himself and is at one with
himself," concludes Moltmann, "then finds his correspondence in a community of human beings, female and male, who unite with one another and are
one."[59]

Although Moltmann defends his social interpretation of the *imago Dei* as
a valid interpretation of the Genesis text, his social interpretation rests more
truly on his relational ontology of the trinitarian persons that he developed in
The Trinity and the Kingdom. There we saw that divine personhood only comes
into existence through ecstatic relationships of self-giving with one another.
Moltmann argues analogously here that true human personhood, that is, the
human being's likeness to God, comes into being only in and through relationships with other persons in community. As Moltmann states in the following passage, sociality and right relationships with others belong to the essence
of what it means to be human:

> From the very outset human beings are social beings. . . . They are
> gregarious beings and only develop their personalities in fellowship
> with other people. Consequently they can only relate to themselves
> if, and to the extent in which, other people relate to them. The iso-
> lated individual and the solitary subject are deficient modes of being
> human, because they fall short of likeness to God. Nor does the per-
> son take priority over the community. On the contrary, person and
> community are two sides of one and the same life process.[60]

Although social relationships are constitutive of true personhood in Moltmann's trinitarian anthropology, this does not mean that a form of collectivism
swallows up the individual or that an individual's identity is simply the sum
of her relations.[61] On closer examination, Moltmann's social trinitarian interpretation of the *imago Dei* in humankind prescribes the inseparability of personal identity and sociality, so that self-relation and social relations come into
existence together. Just as the unity of the Trinity does not take precedence
over the distinction among the three persons, so, too, the human community
and individual personhood are of equal status in the sphere of human relations.[62]

Moltmann does describe each individual as *imago Dei* insofar as each person's messianic calling is to become *imago Christi*. On this point Moltmann

cites Paul's notion of the risen Christ as God's true image and as the archetype of what it means for humankind to be a true child of God: Christ is "the 'first-born' to whom believers 'are to become like in form' (Rom. 8.29)."[63] In defending the individual's messianic destiny as *imago Christi*, Moltmann places himself again at odds with Augustine's theology, which explicitly rejected the notion that the individual is created in the image of any single person of the Trinity. While Augustine contends that the individual is created in the image of the whole Trinity, Moltmann argues that it is only by first becoming *imago Christi* that human beings can become the image of the intra-trinitarian fellowship of love:

> So as *imago Christi* human beings are gathered into his relationship
> of sonship, and in the brotherhood of Christ the Father of Jesus
> Christ becomes their Father also. . . . As God's image, human beings
> are the image of the whole Trinity in that they are "conformed" to
> the image of the Son: the Father creates, redeems and perfects hu-
> man beings through the Spirit in the image of the Son.[64]

According to this soteriological narrative, human beings only gain entrance into the trinitarian fellowship in and through the Son. The Spirit adopts human beings into the Son's relationship with the Father and thus enables them to realize their messianic destiny as *imago Trinitatis*. Although Moltmann does not develop fully here either his model of redemption or his vision of the Christian life, we can already see how he seeks to integrate his christocentric emphasis of his earlier theology within this new messianic social trinitarian pattern for God's economy.

The third and final significant aspect of Moltmann's theological anthropology is his insistence that embodiment belongs to the human likeness to God. As I noted earlier, Moltmann objects strongly to the spiritualization of theological anthropology that has dominated in both ancient and modern Western models of the human person. Its spirit-body dualism has both compromised the dignity of the body (particularly that of women) and subjected nature to humankind's domination and instrumentalization. As we have seen him argue in other contexts, Moltmann refutes this anthropological dualism on biblical grounds. He points out that at every stage of the messianic history of God with the world—in creation, redemption, and glorification—embodiment is the goal of God's works. In the original act of creation there is a movement from God's inward resolve toward expression in the Word and then into embodied reality. Similarly, God accomplishes the work of reconciliation through incarnation into the flesh: "By becoming flesh, the reconciling God assumes the sinful, sick and mortal flesh of human beings and heals it in community with himself. . . . In his taking flesh, exploited, sick and shattered human bodies experience their healing and their indestructible dignity."[65] Finally, throughout the New Testament—in Paul and in the apocalypse of Revelation—redemption ends with the "transformation of the body" and the eschatological vision of the renewal of all the earth.[66]

If we attend to the biblical images for anthropology, argues Moltmann, we must develop a more holistic approach to the soul's relationship to the body. In the Hebrew scriptures, he looks to the concept of covenant as the best clue to the Hebrew understanding of the reciprocal relation between the inner life and the body. Just as Israel experienced and came to know its God in a covenant relationship, so, too, it understands its own selfhood in terms of covenant or partnership: "The unity of soul and body, what is inward and what is outward, the centre and the periphery of the human being is to be comprehended in the forms of covenant, community, reciprocity, a mutual encircling, regard, agreement, harmony and friendship."[67] In considering the New Testament Moltmann turns again to the perichoretic pattern of mutual indwelling as his archetype of the relationship between the body and the soul. Here John 17:21 becomes his trinitarian archetype of the kind of unity in differentiation that he has in mind: "We shall therefore view the relationship between soul and body, the conscious and the unconscious, the voluntary and involuntary . . . as a perichoretic relationship of mutual interpenetration and differentiated unity."[68]

Although Moltmann does not expand much on how these biblical images might translate into contemporary anthropological terms, he does invoke the modern notion of *Gestalt* as one that corresponds well to this biblical perspective of reciprocal relationality. Moltmann defines *Gestalt* as "the configuration or total pattern of the lived life"; it includes nature, society and culture, personal history and religious value systems.[69] *Gestalt* connotes a form of exchange between an individual and his various relationships to his environment that combines unity and differentiation. Human beings gain their *Gestalt* both by relating to these various external forces and structures and by setting boundaries through their inward structures.

One final aspect of Moltmann's anthropology is distinctive: he treats sexual differentiation as an integral aspect of the image of God in humankind. Here Moltmann sides with those exegetes who interpret the differentiation of male and female in Genesis 1:26–27 as part of humankind's unique designation as *imago Dei*: "If God created his image on earth 'as man and as woman,' then this primal difference is not a subsidiary, physical difference. It is a central, personal one."[70] Given Moltmann's insistence that the *imago Dei* is a social as well as a sexual likeness, one might think that he would readily adopt the Greek church fathers' position (over and against Augustine's) that the family is the primary social trinitarian analogy in the human sphere. Moltmann, however, adopts a mediating position between the East and the West. On the one hand, he agrees with the East that there is a certain legitimacy in seeing the primal human community of man, woman, and child as a natural likeness to the trinitarian analogy of relations, since all of humankind participates in this "anthropological triangle" as the child of two parents—male and female;

therefore, "the community of sexes" between husband and wife and "the community of generations" between parent and child can be an image of "true human community" after the divine life.[71] On the other hand, Moltmann rejects a narrow prescriptive interpretation of the familial analogy for the Trinity on the same grounds that Augustine did, namely, that a person cannot only be designated as *imago Dei* if he or she is part of a family.[72]

In my view, Moltmann does not subscribe to a narrow social interpretation of the *imago Trinitatis* in humankind because he predicates his analogy of fellowship in terms of the quality of relationships among the divine persons rather than the relationships of origin that constitute the persons. The social likeness to God is not a one-to-one correspondence of divine and human persons but a correspondence between the patterns of fellowship that constitute the inner divine life with those that can be actualized in the human community. In Moltmann's words, "It is the *relations* in the Trinity which are the levels represented on earth through the *imago Trinitatis*, not the levels of the trinitarian *constitution. Just as* the three Persons of the Trinity are 'one' in a wholly unique way, so, *similarly*, human beings are *imago Trinitatis* in their personal fellowship with one another."[73] By interpreting the social analogy in this more flexible manner, Moltmann paves the way for a wealth of interpersonal relationships ranging from the personal to the political, the ecclesial to the secular, that can reflect the trinitarian fellowship. It is to these trinitarian dimensions of the Christian life that we will turn in the chapter ahead.

5

The Human Pilgrimage in the Messianic Life of Faith

In chapter 4 I laid the cornerstone for Moltmann's vision of the Christian life by analyzing the author's messianic and social trinitarian reconstruction of an *imago Dei* anthropology. There I described how Moltmann draws upon his social trinitarian theology of love to reconceive the *imago Dei* in terms of an *"analogia relationis,"* an analogy of interpersonal relationships in human community. In keeping with his Reformed tradition, Moltmann portrays the *imago Dei* not as a quality or an attribute with which human beings are permanently endowed. It signifies a relationship to God, which God graciously establishes with human beings in the act of creation and which God actualizes ever anew. Through this relationship, God establishes human beings' messianic destiny as God's counterpart, God's beloved Other in creation. The human being fulfills his or her messianic destiny as *imago Dei* by becoming an image of Christ, who incarnates for humankind what it means to be the true child of God—the beloved Other of God the Father. As *imago Christi*, human beings are called to respond to the Father's self-communication of love as the Son did—with their own finite expression of self-giving love.

This gracious relationship of God to the human being provides the foundation for the horizontal dimension of this *imago Dei* anthropology: the human being as *imago Trinitatis*, an image of God in the form of a social likeness to the inner-trinitarian being. Moltmann specifies this second horizontal dimension of his *imago Dei* anthropology according to what I termed his "social trinitarian analogy." He uses his relational and interpersonalist model of the inner-trinitarian life as a divine analogue or an archetype of right relationships among persons both in the church and in wider society. Finally, we observed that this twofold trinitarian model of the *imago Dei* has a messianic structure. Human beings were not originally created in the image of God only to distort or lose this image and have it returned through grace. Rather, human beings are created with the messianic destiny of becoming the image and the glory of God in their personal and communal history with one another. This offers a radically dynamic and "anticipatory structure" to human existence.[1] A person never becomes utterly fixed in his or her identity but remains continuously open and directed toward what Moltmann terms "*the project* of his [or her] life."[2]

Taking Moltmann's messianic and social trinitarian anthropology as our springboard, we pursue in this chapter the human being's pilgrimage toward fulfillment of its messianic destiny as *imago Dei* in the life of faith—what Moltmann depicts as life in the Spirit. We thus enter the second and third stages of the author's messianic narrative of the human being as *imago Dei*: what it means for the human being to become an *imago Christi*, and what is entailed in his or her pilgrimage toward the ultimate destiny of the Christian life, namely, becoming *gloria Dei*. In what follows we will investigate how Moltmann's social trinitarianism shapes the way of salvation and the life of discipleship with respect to both the individual's relationship to the trinitarian God and his or her social relationships, activities, or forms of life. While this sketch of the messianic life of faith will surely not be comprehensive, it will provide sufficient evidence to assess the practical significance of Moltmann's social trinitarian program at the conclusion of this chapter.

The Trinitarian Pattern of Salvation

Salvation as Participation in the Trinitarian Fellowship

Moltmann's messianic *imago Dei* anthropology provides the clue to his construal of salvation. As we saw in chapter 4, Moltmann describes human beings as having the messianic destiny of maturing into a true and full likeness to God and of becoming *gloria Dei*. Given this messianic anthropology, salvation can be defined formally as human beings' eschatological consummation of their created destiny. Salvation signifies that process of deification (*theosis*) by which human beings participate in and reflect the trinitarian life. In the author's words, salvation represents "the transfiguration of human beings in the glory of the new creation."[3]

We can begin to give some specific contours to the author's model of deification by recalling the nature of the trinitarian God, in whose image God newly creates human beings. As I argued in chapter 3, Moltmann interprets the essence of the trinitarian God as *koinonia*, an ecstatic communion or fellowship of love among the divine persons. The divine persons' relations of mutual indwelling constitute this fellowship of love. Through their eternal *perichoresis*, the Father, the Son, and the Holy Spirit illuminate or glorify one another; "they . . . express themselves and depict themselves with one another in the eternal light."[4] Moreover, this trinitarian fellowship has an ecstatic structure; it is open to and draws the whole of creation into its loving embrace.

Against this horizon of trinitarian being, Moltmann's construal of salvation as deification comes into sharper focus as humankind's acceptance and participation in this dynamic trinitarian communion of loving relations. Moltmann appeals to two of his favorite New Testament passages (as usual, one from the Pauline corpus and the other from the Johannine) to describe the goal of salvation as a coinherence of human beings in the trinitarian being of love: "Their mutual indwelling includes men and women: 'Whoever abides in love, abides in God and God in him' (I John 4.16). The indwelling is also the mystery of the new creation, 'That God may be all in all' (I Cor. 15.28)."[5] In Johannine terms, salvation is an abiding in God as love; we abide in love when God abides in us and we in God. The eschatological goal of our new creation is our permanent indwelling in a trinitarian communion of love. In terms of Paul's eschatology, this indwelling occurs when God becomes all in all.

How does this view of salvation address the human predicament of sin? Quite surprisingly, Moltmann does not address this issue at great length within the framework of his messianic anthropology. In fact, the doctrine of sin remains a *lacuna* in Moltmann's *Messianic Theology*—a critical issue to which I will return at the conclusion of this chapter. He does, however, offer a few hints about his understanding of sin in *God in Creation* that we can use to clarify the meaning of salvation. Moltmann appeals to his relational understanding of the *imago Dei* in order to interpret sin as a disruption or perversion of this primary loving relationship to God. In quite classical Reformation terms, Moltmann depicts sin as the idolatry of turning to oneself, others, or created objects as one's primary love.[6] Since God first establishes a relationship to humankind in grace, human beings cannot unilaterally abrogate their status as *imago Dei* through their sinful turning away. Despite humankind's faithlessness, God's love toward human beings is utterly steadfast, and, therefore, human beings' status as *imago Dei* remains intact. What sin does do is utterly distort or pervert a person's loving response to God, and in this sense sin separates him or her from true fellowship with God.

Against this backdrop, salvation represents a healing of this broken fellowship or communion with the God of love. As Moltmann explains in the following passage, salvation means that human beings are accepted into the inner-trinitarian life of love as the adopted sons and daughters of God the Father. Through this participation in the divine life the separation of sin is overcome:

> If the misery of creation lies in sin as separation from God, then salvation consists in the gracious acceptance of the creature into communion with God. Salvation lies in this union. The union with God of what is separated is not just an external union. It takes place by the Son accepting human beings into his relationship with the Father and making them children, sons and daughters, of the Father. It takes place by the Holy Spirit accepting human beings into his relationship with the Son and the Father and letting them participate in his eternal love and his eternal song of praise.[7]

This passage offers a snapshot of the trinitarian pattern of activity that consummates human salvation. Through the indwelling Spirit human beings enter first into fellowship with the Son and become Christ's brothers and sisters. In this way human beings are adopted into the Son's exclusive loving relationship to God the Father and are gradually conformed into the *imago Christi* or into true children of God. To become an *imago Christi* is to be transfigured into a visible image of the self-giving love of God. With this transfiguration human beings attain their messianic destiny; they glorify God the Father with the Son and the Holy Spirit, and become themselves the glory of God. In Moltmann's words, "In glorifying God, the creatures created to be the image of God themselves arrive at the fulfillment of what they are intended to be."[8]

Let us turn now to examine the distinctive roles that the Son and the Holy Spirit play in this eschatological process of new creation. Moltmann takes issue with the long-accepted distinction in Protestant theology between the objective work of redemption accomplished in Christ and its subjective appropriation through the Holy Spirit in Word and sacrament. Moltmann contests the classical Reformed notion of Christ as the sole agent of human redemption on the grounds that it equates redemption with the forgiveness of sins—a forgiveness that was accomplished exclusively through Jesus' death on the cross and independently of his resurrection from the dead and the *parousia* to come. This meant that the "redemptive work could be objectivized"[9] in Christ, and that the Spirit's work could be restricted to the efficacy of Christ's justification in human beings.

Moltmann revises this classical Reformation soteriological pattern in the christological and pneumatological volumes of his *Messianic Theology* so as to reflect the Son's and Spirit's interdependent roles in salvation. Here he follows the lead of the Eastern Orthodox tradition that emphasizes the reciprocal interaction of the Holy Spirit and the Son that accomplishes human salvation.[10] This means, for example, that in *The Way of Jesus Christ* Moltmann develops what he calls a *"pneumatological christology"* that emphasizes the Spirit's ongoing agency throughout the ministry, death, and resurrection of Christ.[11] Similarly, in *The Spirit of Life*, Moltmann proposes *"a christological doctrine of the*

Spirit,"[12] in which he configures Christian life in the Spirit in terms of being conformed to the way of Christ.

In the interest of systematizing Moltmann's soteriology, I will look first at its foundation in the life, death, and resurrection of Jesus as the Christ, and then turn to the Spirit's role in the rebirth of human beings into a new life of righteousness. Although I treat the Son's and the Spirit's redemptive work here as if they are successive stages, I am actually describing one unified process in which both the Son and the Spirit are at all times involved.

The Foundation of Salvation in Christ

In keeping with the christological pattern he established in *The Crucified God*, Moltmann addresses the soteriological question via the christological one in *The Way of Jesus Christ* and in his other recent christological essays.[13] He unfolds the meaning and the means of salvation in terms of a twofold description of Jesus' identity: his exclusive divine identity as "the only-begotten Son of God" and his inclusive identity as the representative of true humanity or, in Moltmann's preferred Pauline expression, as "the firstborn among many brothers."[14]

Moltmann defines Jesus' divine status as the only-begotten Son in terms of Jesus' relationship with God the Father as it came to be expressed in Jesus' message and earthly ministry. What distinguishes Jesus as the only-begotten or messianic child of God is the loving intimacy that Jesus experiences in his relationship with God the Father. In Moltmann's words, "God is as close to him in space—as much 'at hand'—as the kingdom of God is now, through him, close, or 'at hand,' in time."[15] Jesus' *Abba* prayer epitomizes this incomparable fellowship with God, his Father. Moltmann follows the Spirit-christology of the synoptic gospels in arguing that Jesus first comes to know and love the Father as *Abba* through his anointing by the Spirit in his baptism. Here the Spirit descended upon him and "found its Shekinah, its permanent indwelling in him."[16] Through the Spirit's indwelling, the Father establishes a loving intimacy with Jesus. This sets the stage for the Spirit's functioning in an analogous role in human redemption. Just as the Spirit mediates the loving relationship of the Father and the Son, so, too, the Spirit is the one who joins the believer into the fellowship of Father and Son. Through the gift of the Spirit, human beings become the adopted children of God and participate in Jesus' "cry 'Abba, beloved Father' (Rom. 8.15)."[17]

Now Moltmann had already emphasized Jesus' unique communion with the Father in *The Trinity and the Kingdom*. What is different here is how Jesus' ministry and his interactions with others become central to his identity as the messianic child of God. Moltmann describes this new approach as a "social Christology," that is, one that attends to the social interactions and relationships of Jesus as clues to his identity.[18] In the mutual relationships that Jesus has with the poor, the outcast, and the sick, he manifests the creative love that he receives from the Father in the "life-giving mercy"[19] he offers to others. For example, in the open fellowship that Jesus offers to the tax collectors and the sinners in Luke's gospel, he demonstrates "in his own person what acceptance by the merciful God and the forgiveness of sins means."[20] Through his ministry and his proclamation of the kingdom, Jesus provides human beings with a prototype of what it means to be the true child of God.

Although Jesus' earthly life represents the consummation of humankind's messianic destiny, salvation does not rest solely in his being an exemplar of what it means to be a child of God. Through his merciful self-giving Jesus also provides the means of grace through which human beings can enter into this relationship with God. This offer of divine mercy occurs uniquely in and through Christ's sufferings in the passion and his resurrection into new life. Only through the cross and resurrection does the trinitarian God of love open to human beings the possibility of partaking in this relationship of loving intimacy with God the Father and of sharing this fellowship with others.

We have already seen Moltmann's exegesis of the cross-event as an act of divine surrender in the discussions of *The Crucified God* and *The Trinity and the Kingdom* in chapters 2 and 3. In *The Way of Jesus Christ*, Moltmann incorporates this earlier soteriological account into his messianic christology and again emphasizes the mutual self-giving and active suffering that both Father and Son undergo through the cross-event.[21] He takes this argument one step further, however, by including the sufferings of the Spirit into this earlier theology of mutual surrender of Father and Son. At the cross the Spirit (whom Moltmann had characterized as the creative power in Jesus' life) also enacts a surrender or *kenosis* of her life-giving power. The Spirit suffers, too, as "the dying Jesus 'breathes him out' and 'yields him up' (Mark 15.37; stronger John 19.30)."[22]

In *The Way of Jesus Christ* and in his subsequent essay on the doctrine of justification, "Justice for Victims and Perpetrators," Moltmann develops most fully the soteriological significance of this trinitarian act of divine surrender. First and foremost, he describes the divine suffering at the cross as an act of divine solidarity with the victims of injustice or evil, a suffering in "solidarity with human beings and his whole creation everywhere: *God is with us.*"[23] God not only identifies with the victims of injustice and violence in history, but in the person of the Son, God in God's self becomes the victim of the violent and the unjust. This act of solidarity is salvific, suggests Moltmann, because it takes away the victim's existential despair and godforsakenness and replaces them with God's loving presence: "Christ brings eternal communion with God and God's life-giving righteousness through his passion into the passion story of this world."[24]

While the sufferings of Christ provide God's vicarious atonement for the perpetrators of violence and injustice in the world, Moltmann vigorously objects to the notion that such atonement is an expiatory offering or a penal sacrifice on behalf of human sin. The surrender of the cross and the resurrection, he cautions, are not "an emergency measure made necessary by the predicament of human sin."[25] Instead, Moltmann describes Christ's atonement in the language of personal representation—as a divine bearing with the guilt and pain of human injustice. This divine suffering does away with human sin by accepting its pain into itself. In the author's words, "God reconciles this world in conflict by the way in which he suffers the contradiction, not by contradicting the contradiction, i.e. through judgment. He turns the pain of his love into atonement for sinners."[26] By taking the whole range of sin's consequences upon God's self, God transmutes the guilt and the pain of an individual's sin into liberty.

For both victims and perpetrators, the soteriological significance of the cross is inseparable from the resurrection of Jesus from the dead. As Moltmann argued in his earlier christology, the raising of Christ is not just a divine confirmation of what has already transpired through the cross. Nor is it a symbolic promise of a future victory over the death-dealing forces of the world. Rather, Christ's resurrection from the dead initiates the whole of creation into an eschatological process of new creation—a new creation of all things through the Spirit into an image of God's glory. Moltmann writes, "The Christ who is bodily risen is the beginning of the new creation of mortal life in this world. In his body the bodily risen Christ leads human nature into the kingdom of God."[27] With the transfiguration of Jesus from a mortal into a glorified body, the life-giving Spirit begins an ontological transformation of the very conditions of all mortal life and the cosmos itself.

Although Moltmann's emphasis on the resurrection as an unfinished event is certainly not new in *The Way of Jesus Christ*, what is different is his attention to the physical as well as cosmological dimensions of salvation. Just as Moltmann proposed a more holistic approach to his theological anthropology that privileges neither soul over body nor human history over nature, so, too, he emphasizes the embodied and cosmological dimensions of the promised transfiguration in his doctrine of redemption. In elucidating the soteriological significance of cross and resurrection for believers, Moltmann appeals to the traditional Reformation category of justification for sins or "justifying righteousness,"[28] but then expands its meaning to integrate his model of new creation. Beginning with several key Pauline texts, Moltmann develops four interwoven "horizons of purpose and meaning" with respect to this justifying righteousness; each of these represents integral aspects of the messianic process of new creation that has begun in Christ.[29]

The most immediate soteriological horizon is humankind's justification or liberation from sin. Here Romans 4:25 ("Christ was put to death for our trespasses and raised for our justification") serves as Moltmann's biblical cue for this model of "justifying faith."[30] If sin is the separation or closing off of human beings from the source of life in God, then justification represents the process by which we return into open fellowship with this source of life: "Through *the justification of sinners*, the gospel brings men and women who are closed in upon themselves into the open love of God. Through *rebirth from the Spirit*, it brings people who have been subject to death into touch with the eternal source of life."[31] Despite his traditional (Augustinian!) language about sin and human beings' conversion, Moltmann does stretch the Reformation notion of justification to include the rebirth of human beings into righteousness. He argues that the message of justification is bound up with the raising of the crucified Jesus, and that Jesus' resurrection offers a surplus of grace that takes the individual beyond the forgiveness of past sins and initiates him or her into a process of new creation.

By linking the rebirth into righteousness with the moment of justification, Moltmann parts ways with the Reformers, who confine justification to the divine forgiveness of sins. Moltmann takes issue with Barth's and Bultmann's models of justification as reconciliation for the same reason. They assume an original state of perfection that requires restoration, and in this sense, reconciliation becomes in Moltmann's view "a backward-looking act."[32] Moltmann counters that justifying faith in the resurrection is not just a restoration of former things but also a " 'new creation' which is more than 'the first creation.' "[33] The grace of cross and resurrection offers an eschatological hope for a new creation, a hope that in turn empowers humankind to resist the structures of injustice and suffering in the world.

The second and third interpretative horizons of the cross and resurrection signify Christ's eschatological victory on behalf of the dead and over the forces of death itself. Here God addresses in the cross and resurrection not just humankind's present sinful condition but also the universal condition of suffering unto death. Following Romans 14:9, Moltmann sees in Christ's resurrection a new eschatological future opened up for the dead as well as the living. Although Moltmann admits that the biblical metaphors with which we explain Christ's fellowship with the dead are mythological, he upholds the truth they communicate, namely, that God's suffering and creative love, poured forth in the cross and the resurrection, mysteriously break the power of death. Christ's resurrection from the dead affirms that the universal and unconditional love of God proves greater than the power of death itself.[34]

Moltmann appeals to Philippians 2:9–11 to cast his final soteriological horizon of cross and resurrection in terms of the "glorification of God": "All created beings find their bliss in participation in his glory."[35] Here we are reminded that the ultimate goal of Christ's rising from the dead is not anthropological but theological, not just human liberation but the doxological celebration of God. The ultimate victory of divine love over the forces of death and suffering occurs with God's homecoming to the world in which God's radiance will be revealed fully in the world.

Taken together, these four horizons of interpretation reveal how Moltmann's view of salvation in Christ coheres with, indeed, consummates his messianic doctrine of creation. I mean by this most simply that redemption has the same anticipatory and cosmological structure as that of creation. The resurrection of Christ initiates a process of new creation that stretches from the present experience of justification for the individual believer to the eschatological annihilation of all death-dealing forces. "It is a process," writes Moltmann, "which begins in the individual heart through faith, and leads to the just new world. The process begins with the forgiveness of sins and ends with the wiping away of all tears."[36] Just as we saw in his doctrine of creation, redemption does not perfect the world but prepares it for its ultimate glorification in God.

Now that we have a clearer picture of how Moltmann's trinitarian theology revises traditional Protestant models of justification (and reconciliation), we still need to consider how human beings come to participate in this eschatological salvation in Christ. To do so we need to return to the *inclusive* dimension of Jesus' identity, that is, to his status as the representative of true humanity or what Moltmann describes in Paul's terms as "firstborn among many brothers" (Rom. 8:29).[37] If the former title "only-begotten Son" refers to what is utterly unique about Jesus' identity, this latter title describes what Jesus shares with the rest of humanity. The ontological foundation for Jesus' inclusive identity was already set in Moltmann's trinitarian theology of creation and incarnation explored in the previous chapter. There we saw how the act of creation results from the Father's overflowing creative love for the Son. In their exchange of divine love there was room for humanity in communion with the Son to respond and fulfill the joy of the Father. Within this exchange of creative and responsive love, the Son functions as both the mediator and the prototype of human creation. That is to say, the incarnation of the Son consummates the act of creation, because Jesus fulfills the human being's true messianic destiny—to be an *imago Dei*: "In him we have the fulfillment of the promise made to man that he will be 'the image of the invisible God.' Christ is the 'true man' in this perverted and inhumane world."[38] In essence, this means that Jesus embodies in his life and death what it means to live truly as the child of God. As the firstborn from the dead, the resurrected Christ fulfills the messianic promise of human beings' original creation; he fulfills what it means to be transfigured and glorified in God.

For their part, believers consummate their messianic destiny as *imago Dei* through fellowship with the incarnate Christ in the form of the Spirit. Through the Spirit we "receive 'Sonship' and are taken up into the relationship of Jesus with the Father."[39] Here Moltmann emphasizes that the human being's relationship to Christ is one of brotherhood, and not that of a servant to a lord. The believer enters into a communion with Jesus that is patterned after the dynamic relations among the divine persons; it is "a social mutuality of deep fellowship rather than obedience and subordination."[40]

Integral to Moltmann's vision of the Christian life is that the believer's fellowship with Christ is both mystical and ethical. It is mystical, insofar as the believer is actually introduced into a loving union or indwelling with Christ. It is ethical, insofar as human beings are simultaneously drawn into his messianic way of life and his passion, a way of life that entails creative and suffering love. Human beings "take part in his messianic mission to liberate the poor, justify sinners and heal the sick. So they also take part in the apocalyptic 'suffering of Christ,' suffering for Christ's sake, suffering for the sake of the kingdom of God, and suffering for the least of his brothers and sisters."[41] For Moltmann, the mystical and the ethical are inseparable dimensions of the believer's fellowship with Christ. Only through the mystical fellowship with Jesus does the believer receive the creative love that turns into life-giving mercy for others.

To conclude, I would like to emphasize that Moltmann's model of salvation uniquely, if at times uneasily, blends the soteriological traditions of the Eastern and Western church traditions. On my reading of the later volumes of his *Messianic Theology*, the Greek patristic model of salvation as deification (*theosis*) provides his dominant soteriological pattern. Here Christ serves as the paradigm of true humanity and thus provides the archetype of humankind's messianic destiny as *imago Dei*. The process of salvation entails our being gradually conformed through grace into a more perfect image of God through fellowship with Christ; the human being becomes *imago Christi*, and as such participates in the glory of God. Moreover, through our indwelling in this divine fellowship, human being's patterns of fellowship with one another are transformed in accordance with this divine way of life.

Within this primary model of salvation as deification, Moltmann introduces his own amplified liberationist version of the Western model of salvation as forgiveness and righteousness in the sight of God. Taking a step explicitly beyond the Reformers, Moltmann addresses the problem of righteousness before God in terms of both the perpetrators of sin and their victims; salvation includes both the forgiveness of sins and the execution of justice on behalf of the victims of human sin and evil. In this twofold model of justification, Christ serves two distinct soteriological functions. He offers vicarious atonement for the sinner, specifically liberating him or her from guilt. At the same time he offers solidarity with the victims of injustice, thus liberating them from godforsakenness and promising an eschatological victory over all death-dealing forces.

The Spirit of Life

Given this dynamic model of salvation, the Holy Spirit assumes an amplified role in the process of salvation. The biblical hermeneutical key to the Spirit's role is its life-giving power in resurrecting Jesus from the dead. Moltmann directs his readers to the Easter appearances of the crucified Jesus as chief witness to this life-giving power of the Holy Spirit. The disciples, the women, Paul, and John all experienced the "quickening power of the Spirit," or what Moltmann calls "the Spirit of life," in their apprehension of the resurrected Christ.[42] Citing 1 Corinthians 15:45, Moltmann argues that the risen Christ is so permeated by the life-giving Spirit that one can speak of a reciprocal indwelling of the risen Christ and the Spirit of God: in his words, "The risen Christ lives from, and in, the eternal Spirit, and . . . the divine Spirit of life acts in and through him."[43]

As we saw in the discussion of salvation in Christ, Moltmann describes the believers' experience of the risen Christ as nothing short of the beginning of the eschaton—the new creation of all things in which death will be no more. Human beings participate in this new creation through the gift of the Holy Spirit, in whom the risen Christ now lives. Following Romans 8:11, Moltmann argues that the Holy Spirit mediates the presence and knowledge of the risen Christ to human beings. The Spirit unites the believer to the historical event of the resurrection and, in so doing, unites him or her to the "anticipation of eternal life for mortal beings."[44]

Although the resurrection of Christ is the historical anchor for the believer's experience of the Spirit, Moltmann does not define the Holy Spirit exclusively as the Spirit of Christ. He invokes a more comprehensive paradigm for the Holy Spirit as "the Spirit of life," in order to underscore the continuity between the Old Testament Spirit of creation (*ruach*) and the New Testament Spirit of resurrection.[45] As we saw in *God in Creation*, Moltmann describes *ruach* in *The Spirit of Life* as the "creative power of God" and "the divine energy of life"; it is the immanent divine presence in the world that "keeps all things in being and in life."[46] The Spirit of redemption does not supersede the Spirit of creation but rather intensifies it. Believers experience a more intimate communion with God than that given with their created relation. In a bold interpretation of Romans 5:8, Moltmann portrays the Holy Spirit's intimate fellowship with human beings as analogous to the *perichoresis* that exists among the trinitarian persons: "In the love of God which is 'poured out' in our hearts through the Holy Spirit, God himself is 'in us' and we ourselves are 'in God' . . . we experience the reciprocal perichoresis of God and ourselves."[47] Just as the divine persons dwell in one another through their reciprocal acts of self-giving love, so, too, human beings through the gift of the Holy Spirit can be said to dwell in the midst of this life-giving love. The Spirit imbues each believer with a "vitality" or "love of life."[48] He or she participates in God's unconditional love of all living things and discovers a "passion for life" and "a new delight in living in the joy of God."[49]

Moltmann juxtaposes this vitality or unconditional love of life with a disembodied and otherworldly spirituality. We have already seen in earlier writings how Moltmann goes to great lengths to criticize the spirituality that developed in Christian antiquity (particularly that of Augustine) as gnostic and antithetical to that of the Hebrew and Christian scriptures. In his *Messianic Theology*, Moltmann continues to contest ascetic spiritualities as a fundamental misunderstanding of life in the Spirit. Any such ascetic model of the Christian life defies the Old Testament picture of the Creator Spirit as the life force in all created things.[50] Moreover, such ascetic spiritualities contradict the New Testament's claim that the gift of the Spirit is being "'poured out on all flesh.'"[51] The living hope born of the resurrection is not directed toward a separation of the soul from the trappings of the body but toward a holistic transfiguration of body and soul. Rather than turning the individual away from the body, from nature, or from one's network of social relationships in the world, the Spirit infuses human beings with a love of all life, a "new sensuousness"[52] that delights in all things.

At this point we can pause to see how the Spirit of life lends a creative and liberating dynamic to the Christian life. The Holy Spirit knits human beings into the most intimate fellowship with the Trinity, a fellowship in which human beings are gathered into the midst of the life-giving and freeing love of God. In Moltmann's words, "People are raised above earth and heaven, life and death, present and future, to God himself, and participate in his creative freedom. . . . [The believer] lives in the free space of God's creative possibilities, and partakes of them."[53] Through this gift of the Spirit, human beings are granted that very same creative freedom that poured forth in the Trinity's original creation of the world. In an uncharacteristically positive appeal to the term "lordship," Moltmann argues that it is in the Lordship of the Spirit that the believer discovers a new freedom: "'Now the Lord is the Spirit, and where the Spirit of the Lord is, there is freedom' (II Cor. 3.17)."[54] This newly found freedom unfolds in the cardinal fruits of the Spirit, in faith, love, and hope, to each of which Moltmann gives a distinctive interpretation.

Moltmann describes the first aspect of human freedom as "liberating faith" or "freedom as subjectivity."[55] If in modernity the freedom of the individual has largely meant self-possession, the "'right to self-determination,'" faith's freedom represents exactly the opposite—possession by God's Spirit, or what Moltmann calls being "possessed by the divine energy of life."[56] Being possessed by this Spirit of the Lord has nothing whatsoever to do with enslavement, for it marks the beginning of the individual's participation in the creative freedom of God. Faith signals openness to the future of creation: "*Faith leads to a creative life which is life-giving through love,* in places where death rules and people resign themselves, and surrender to it. . . . So faith means crossing the frontiers of the reality which is existent now, and has been determined by the past, and seeking the potentialities for life which have not yet come into be-ing."[57] In other words, the individual believer experiences him- or herself as no longer determined by or in bondage to the past, but free to actualize new possibilities in his or her life. Here faith's freedom presses beyond liberation from sin; it represents new agency—the liberation for new life.

The second dimension of freedom in the Spirit is "liberating love" or "free-dom as sociality," the freedom that is enjoyed by persons through their rela-tionship to one another.[58] Here the gift of creative freedom transcends the boundaries of the individual to create fellowship between persons through their mutual love for one another: "Life is communion in communication. We give one another life, and come alive from one another. In mutual participation in life, individuals become free beyond the borders of their individuality."[59] In keeping with his social trinitarian anthropology, Moltmann views loving par-ticipation in the life of one another as essential to the individual's life in the Spirit. Just as the trinitarian persons consummate their freedom through their love for one another, so, too, human beings consummate their personal free-dom through mutual love for one another.

As he had previously in *The Trinity and the Kingdom*, Moltmann juxtaposes his concept of freedom as sociality with that of freedom as lordship that has often prevailed in theological and political history. In the lordship model, in-dividual freedom is identified with domination over another; it is attained only at the expense of the other. By contrast, in Moltmann's model of freedom as sociality, freedom is attained in and with another person. Individuals are no longer perceived as rivals in my "struggle for power and possessions,"[60] but become the source of my own freedom.

Moltmann sketches only with the broadest of strokes his third dimension of human freedom as "liberating hope" or "freedom as future."[61] In language strongly reminiscent of *Theology of Hope*, he describes how the Spirit infuses human beings with a messianic hope, what Moltmann terms "*the creative pas-sion for the possible*. . . . It is directed towards the future, the future of the coming God."[62] Here Moltmann affirms the eschatological character of human free-dom in the Spirit: freedom is not only a present experience but also a dynamic process toward a not yet realized future possibility. Human beings enjoy the promise and foretaste of the fellowship of the coming kingdom. Although there is joy at the coming of the trinitarian kingdom, there is at the same time restlessness over the broken character of this world. This dialectical experience of already and not yet awakens in believers a messianic impulse toward trans-formation of the present state of human relations and social structures. In-spired with hope for the coming kingdom, human beings envision creative possibilities for trinitarian fellowship in the world and are empowered to work for their consummation.

To conclude, I would like to point out that these three gifts of the Spirit, faith, love, and hope mirror different aspects of the trinitarian life. In faith's freedom, the human being enjoys the same creative freedom, the same life-giving energy that characterizes God's creative love toward human beings. In love as sociality, human beings participate in relationships of mutual indwelling, relationships that correspond to those among the trinitarian persons. Finally, in hope's freedom, the human community partakes of the same power of the future that characterizes the coming God of the kingdom. As we will see ahead, this analogy between the gifts of the Spirit and the trinitarian life will become even more pronounced in the actual forms of relationships and practices that Moltmann envisions as part of the Christian life.

The Gift of Life and the Order of Salvation

The Spirit as the gift of life serves as Moltmann's basic paradigm for the workings of grace in the Christian life. In *The Spirit of Life* he reformulates the entire traditional Protestant order of salvation as stages in this messianic gift of new life: "the liberation and justification of life, life's regeneration and endowment, as well as its development, in the living space of the Spirit."[63] These different stages do not result from successive gifts of the Spirit; they all proceed from the single gift of grace that continually draws humankind toward the eschatological goal of fellowship in God.

As I noted earlier, Moltmann pointedly refuses to separate the divine act of justification from that of regeneration; the human being is simultaneously justified and regenerated with the initial gift of grace. In discussing the foundation of salvation in Christ, we have already encountered Moltmann's model of justification. There I pointed to how Moltmann revises the classical model of justification as forgiveness of sins in order to address the soteriological situation of both the perpetrator and the victim of sin and evil; in both cases, the goal of justification remains the same—the restoration of fellowship with God through our acceptance as his children in Christ.

In *The Spirit of Life*, Moltmann presents essentially the same model of justification but attends specifically to the Spirit's role in the process. He redoubles his efforts to modify the Protestant model of justification so that it addresses not only the forgiveness of personal sins but also the concrete sufferings of the victims of sin, as well as the structural aspects of sin. To do so, Moltmann differentiates how we understand the believer's reception of the Spirit's gift of righteousness. For example, the sinner experiences the Spirit's gift of righteousness as liberation from the guilt and the pain of sin; here the Spirit of God appears as "*the atoning power* of Christ's substitution among and in the perpetrators."[64] By contrast, sin's victims experience the Spirit's gift of righteousness as liberation from the pain and suffering of the experience of abandonment by God; here the Spirit of life conveys Christ's brotherly fellowship, "Christ's solidarity with them."[65] Finally, the Spirit's gift of righteousness addresses the suprahuman structures of sin—the unjust systems of power and social relations. Here Moltmann depicts the Spirit's agency only in the most general terms as creating hospitable social structures that protect the personal dignity and the rights of all their members. The Spirit's gift of life manifests itself as a "rectifying" righteousness that "destabilizes" unjust and violent social structures and re-creates them into patterns of fellowship.[66]

Moltmann forges his model of rebirth in the Spirit as a via media between that of Karl Barth and his pupil and Moltmann's own teacher, Otto Weber. Barth depicts the rebirth of all men and women as having already occurred in Christ on the cross; the gift of the Spirit to the individual is only a subjective recognition of what has already objectively transpired in Christ. In contrast to Barth's stance, Weber adopts an entirely eschatological view of regeneration. He treats the individual's rebirth in the Spirit as a purely eschatological hope. The Christian does not live with a present experience of rebirth but "from what is coming to meet him."[67] For his part, Moltmann straddles Barth's and Weber's two positions by describing regeneration as joining the believer simultaneously to the past and to her eschatological future. The Spirit makes present the risen Christ, in whom the eschatological future has already been fully anticipated. The Spirit of the resurrection enters human beings, so that they experience in the here and now the rebirth into new life. In the experience of the risen Christ, believers become "born again to a well-founded hope for eternal life."[68]

The believer's experience of this rebirth in the Spirit is full of messianic tension. On the one hand, rebirth in the Spirit is experienced as a "rapturous joy" and as a "tremendous *affirmation of life*."[69] Through the gift of the Spirit, human beings come to engage the world with the same ecstatic love with which God has already addressed them. Moltmann describes this experience of joy as accompanied by a sense of peace or "*shalom*," a holistic "*happiness* of both body and soul."[70] On the other hand, such positive experiences of rebirth in the Spirit are inseparable from the human being's restlessness over the yet unfulfilled expectation of the new creation. Believers experience the difference between their eschatological hope and the present reality "and begin to suffer, and to contradict, and to resist."[71] This means that the Spirit of life is at work in negative experiences as well, for example, in prayers of lament and outcries against God. In such circumstances, the Spirit of life empowers active resistance against all life-denying forces. It leads the believer to what Moltmann calls a "determined negation of the negative,"[72] that is, to take action against all forces of violence and death.

In keeping with his messianic trajectory of the human process of redemption, Moltmann depicts the individual's regeneration in the Spirit as an ongoing process rather than a once-and-for-all conversion that occurs at a given point in time. An individual's renewal in the Spirit always makes a fresh beginning: "We are still involved in the experience of renewal, and the becoming-new travels with us."[73] This does not mean, however, that the believer does not gain a measure of certitude or assurance in his or her faith. Believers do experience an underlying "certainty of preservation," but here again this rests on God's faithfulness, not on the strength of one's faith.[74]

Moltmann describes sanctification as an ongoing process by which human beings gradually become *imago Christi* on the way toward their eschatological glorification. He patterns it in Pauline terms as " 'putting on the new human being, created after the likeness of God' (Eph. 4.24; cf. also Col. 3.10)."[75] Although Moltmann explicitly allows for growth toward becoming *imago Dei* in the Christian life, he insists that such progress rests entirely on God's graciousness to humankind and not on a heightened goodness of the human being. Just as he did previously with the notion of *imago Dei*, Moltmann argues here, too, that our new creation through the Spirit is not a permanent disposition or habitual grace in the individual. Rather, it is "a relationship and an affiliation" that God institutes always anew with the believer.[76]

Note that Moltmann's emphasis on the gratuitous nature of sanctification does not in any sense diminish human agency in the Christian life. On the contrary, human beings are charged to respond to this gift of grace "as determining subjects of their own lives."[77] The fellowship of the Spirit grants believers the very freedom to become God's counterpart in love, and they are called to respond by entering into Jesus' messianic way of life. In this way, the believer fulfills his or her messianic destiny—what Moltmann describes as "the life corresponding to God."[78]

Before we consider what this messianic way of life entails, I would like to return to one of the critical questions that I raised in the opening chapter of this study, namely, Allan Torrance's contention that Moltmann overplays the human being's role in salvation. To recall, Torrance raised the specter of "Pelagian tendencies" in how Moltmann construes the believer's "doxological participation in the transcendent triune life."[79] He argues that Moltmann presents the act of worship more as a human task to be achieved rather than "an event of grace" and questions whether this is not indicative of how the central mediatory role of Christ is compromised in Moltmann's theology.[80]

Given my foregoing analysis of the trinitarian structure of salvation, there is little evidence in my view to support either of Torrance's criticisms, namely, that Moltmann compromises the gratuity of grace in the Christian life or the centrality of Christ as the source of that grace. As I have argued earlier, the consummation of the human being's messianic destiny is mediated through the reciprocal agency of Christ and the Spirit. Whatever correspondences to the trinitarian life do develop among human beings, these are always and everywhere Spirit-filled works of love. They are born of the fellowship of the Spirit who joins the human being into the intimate fellowship of Christ; only in this way is humankind graced with the capacity to respond in love to God and to one another. In this light, such correspondences to the trinitarian life are not merely human works, as Torrance charges, "a natural human response or innate capacity."[81] Rather, such glimmers of divine fellowship in the human life are "analogies of grace," that is, fruits of the Holy Spirit's work in the life of faith.

The Messianic Praxis of Trinitarian Fellowship

Let us turn now to consider some of these trinitarian analogies of grace in the life of faith. What might this messianic way of life look like today? What forms of human relationships, ecclesial practices, and social structures belong to life in the Spirit? And, most important, does this social trinitarian theology live up to Moltmann's wager that it will become a source of prophetic critique and of messianic hope for the transformation of this world into the coming kingdom?

The reader who pores over the six volumes of Moltmann's *Messianic Theology* anticipating a detailed social trinitarian program is bound for disappointment. Nowhere does Moltmann prescribe a set of distinctive trinitarian practices for the Christian life. Instead of devoting an entire volume to theological anthropology or to his proposed messianic ethics, Moltmann discusses only certain dimensions of the Christian life, and these discussions are interspersed throughout the six volumes of his work or in separate essays. For example, he gives immediate attention to the political and ecclesial implications of his social trinitarianism in the opening volume of the series, *The Trinity and the Kingdom*. But readers must wait until the fourth volume of the series, *The Spirit of Life*, before Moltmann develops the implications of his social trinitarian theology for the more intimate sphere of human friendship and love.

Moltmann's ad hoc approach to questions of the Christian life and ethics has been a vexing issue for his interpreters. Especially given Moltmann's avowed commitment to being a pastoral as well as a political theologian, one would have expected a lengthy treatment of Christian discipleship in the *Messianic Theology*. In his recent book, *The Kingdom and the Power: The Theology of Jürgen Moltmann*, Geiko Müller-Fahrenholz offers the most helpful insight into Moltmann's reluctance to write such a comprehensive volume on the Christian life. Müller-Fahrenholz points to Moltmann's comments in his 1997 essay "How I Have Changed?" in which he describes his failed attempt to write an *Ethics of Hope* as a companion volume to his *Theology of Hope*. Moltmann explained that he had been in the midst of writing such an ethics with the twofold strategy of describing "the great alternative" and "the many little alternatives," that is, describing an ideal Christian vision and addressing it to a series of concrete problems confronting the world today.[82] He found himself, however, without the requisite knowledge in the various disciplines and spheres of life to fulfill his ambitious agenda. For this reason, Moltmann abandoned his large volume on Christian ethics, electing instead to continue his ad hoc approach to addressing concrete ethical issues throughout his career. While Moltmann elucidates "the great alternative in outline form" in his major works, he chooses to address specific issues confronting his church and society only in his occasional writings.[83] For Müller-Fahrenholz, Moltmann's great alternative is the concept of a kingdom of freedom that the author developed in his early writings. This "kingdom of freedom" translates into a Christian "praxis of liberation" that seeks to overcome all forms of alienation in history— be it in the sphere of economics (poverty), politics (totalitarianism), or culture and society (sexism, racism).[84]

Although I agree that the notion of freedom or liberation from various forms of social alienation is at the heart of Moltmann's theological agenda, in my view, the concept of trinitarian fellowship provides a better key to the au- thor's mature theological vision of what norms the Christian life than the notion of the kingdom of freedom. Trinitarian fellowship not only provides a theological critical principle for evaluating various liberation movements in history but also illuminates the overall graced dynamic of the Christian life, that is, how an individual believer's fellowship with God becomes active in fellowship with others. Moreover, the notion of trinitarian fellowship helps us to link the contemplative and the active, the doxological and the political aspects of this messianic way of life.[85] Participation in the trinitarian fellowship is the messianic goal of the individual's communion both with Christ and with his fellow brother and sister.

This is not to suggest that Moltmann appeals straightforwardly to trinitar- ian fellowship in his brief discussions of the Christian life. Most often he invokes his trinitarian theology only indirectly, by transposing it into a norm or rule of faith for guiding human relationships. Most generally, Moltmann's social trinitarian rule prescribes that true human relationships involve recip- rocal self-giving and acceptance of others. In the author's words, true fellow- ship is founded on "openness to one another, sharing with one another and respect for one another. It is the reciprocal communication of all that one has and is."[86] Furthermore, true human fellowship unites persons in community, all the while guaranteeing their particularity. Just as we discovered the dialectic of unity in personal differentiation in trinitarian communion, so, too, all true human relationships are based on a dynamic of self-donation and self- differentiation. They involve giving oneself fully to others in order to form bonds of community, all the while creating the free space in which individual identity both is recognized and flourishes. In other words, trinitarian fellow- ship does not commend homogeneous human communities that erase per- sonal differences. It fosters human fellowships of "diversity in unity," in which individual potentials are realized and differences may abound.[87]

In the following let us turn briefly to three different spheres of human life, the political, the ecclesial, and the interpersonal, to see how Moltmann constructs his analogy of trinitarian fellowship in each of them. These various analogues to trinitarian fellowship will provide a basis from which to see how Moltmann's social trinitarian theology is realized in the life of faith and to evaluate the practical significance of his proposals.

Incarnating Trinitarian Fellowship in the World

Let us turn first to the political sphere for what it means to incarnate trinitarian fellowship in the world. In *The Trinity and the Kingdom*, Moltmann deduces two principles from his model of trinitarian fellowship that he applies to the political arena. First, he contends that trinitarian fellowship finds its earthly reflection only in those political orders that are built on relationships of reciprocity and absolute equality of all members: a "community of men and women, without privileges and without subjugation."[88] Just as the three divine persons share a common and equal rule of fellowship in the Godhead, so, too, human beings as *imago Trinitatis* are called to join together in egalitarian structures of political rule.

The second principle that Moltmann derives from his trinitarian fellowship is the interdependence of personal and communal identity. Just as personal and communal identity prove inseparable in the trinitarian Godhead, so, too, they are in the political order: "So the Trinity corresponds to a community in which people are defined through their relations with one another and in their significance for one another, not in opposition to one another, in terms of power and possession."[89] Given the interdependence of personal and communal identity, Moltmann concludes that in the political sphere one cannot divorce the pursuit of individual rights from those of the community and vice versa.

Moltmann does not advance a full-scale political agenda on the basis of these two principles and in fact warns his readers against a forced transposition of theological ideals into the political sphere. Nonetheless, he does single out democratic or personalist socialism as the political option within the European context that most closely corresponds to trinitarian rule: "If we take our bearings from the Christian doctrine of the Trinity, personalism and socialism cease to be antitheses and are seen to be derived from a common foundation. The Christian doctrine of the Trinity *compels* us to develop social personalism or personal socialism."[90] For Moltmann, democratic or personalist socialism overcomes the antithesis between individualism and socialism that plagued the East-West political debates of his day. His social doctrine of the Trinity, with its interlocking notions of personhood and community, supports such a political order of democratic socialism that similarly balances the rights of the individual and those of society in an egalitarian framework. Personalist or democratic socialism provides the needed corrective to both the excessive individualism in Western democracies and the homogenizing impulses of Eastern socialism.

Moltmann wagers an even more direct correlation between his trinitarian theology and ecclesiology than that in the political sphere because he views the church community as springing forth directly from the trinitarian fellowship. Citing John 17:20–21 as his biblical support, Moltmann not only models the church after the trinitarian fellowship but also anchors its very being in the trinitarian fellowship: "It [i.e., the unity of the Christian community] *corresponds* to the indwelling of the Father in the Son, and of the Son in the Father. It *participates* in the divine triunity, since the community of believers is not only fellowship *with* God but *in* God too."[91] Since the church participates in this trinitarian fellowship, Moltmann reasons that the relationships among its individual members as well as its church structures are meant to correspond most closely to those of the trinitarian communion. The church is to be "the 'lived out' Trinity," where "mutual love is practised which corresponds to the eternal love of the Trinity."[92]

On the basis of this divine archetype of fellowship, Moltmann challenges the traditional locus of church authority in the monarchical episcopate. He represents this as a form of "clerical monotheism," which reflects the monarchianism that has accompanied the Western doctrine of God.[93] In particular, Moltmann objects to the church's identity being grounded in the office of ministry, which in turn relegates the community of believers into obedient and passive recipients of word and sacrament. Moltmann calls instead for the church to exist as a reciprocal fellowship of sisters and brothers in Christ— " 'a community free of dominion.' "[94] Here Moltmann's sympathies clearly lie with the radical wing of the Reformation and with the idea that church authority should rest ultimately in the congregation, in the gathered fellowship of believers. In *The Trinity and the Kingdom*, he argues, therefore, that the "presbyterial and synodal church order"[95] corresponds most readily to the life of the Trinity.

Let us turn finally to the sphere of personal relations to explore two final expressions of trinitarian fellowship: the human experiences of friendship and of love. Moltmann's lengthiest discussion of these relationships appears in *The Spirit of Life* under the rubric of "the theology of social experience of God."[96] Here he argues for the central role that such social experiences of God should play in the life of faith over and against Western theology's tendency to focus on the individual's experience of God. As we saw in the previous chapter, Moltmann attributes the introspective cast of Western spirituality largely to Augustine's pivotal influence. On Moltmann's reading, by identifying the *imago Dei* with the rational soul, Augustine's theology had the deleterious effect of withdrawing the human being from its web of interpersonal relations in the world and rendering one's relationship to one's neighbors secondary to one's love of God.

On the basis of his social model of the *imago Dei*, Moltmann describes one's self-relation and relationship to one's neighbor as inseparable dimensions of the experience of God in the life of faith. "In fact they are two sides

of the same experience of life, in which we experience others and ourselves."[97]
Just as personal identity and sociality prove inseparable within Moltmann's
theological anthropology, so, too, the individual's experience of divine love and
the friendship or love experienced among human beings are inextricable in
the Christian life.

Moltmann develops his theology of love over and against two other theologies of love that he characterizes as representative of the patristic and the
medieval traditions.[98] In the first model, the "physical conception of love," the
love of God is already present in the soul of all human beings and needs only
to be perfected by grace. Here each person is charged to love others not in and
for themselves but insofar as they serve as a rung on the ladder upward toward
the love of God: "Everything which God loves, will also become an object of
human love for God, simply because God loves it. Everything is loved for God,
and for God's sake."[99] In the medieval "'ecstatic conception' of love," true
human love is also directed only toward God, but it is identified with the total
divestiture of self and with the human being's disengagement from others:
"The person who loves God perfectly is the person who is totally forgetful of
himself and indifferent towards the world."[100]

Moltmann challenges these two theologies of love on soteriological
grounds. They did not take God's love for us in Christ and our experience of
being loved as the basis for interpreting persons' love for one another. Citing
1 John 4:9 as his biblical support, he argues that the human experience of
God's love in Christ must be the starting point and the archetype for human
beings' love of one another. In Moltmann's words, "We live through him because through him we are reconciled with God. . . . Because of the incarnation
of God's love in the sending and self-surrender of Christ, *the love of God is
realized in love of our neighbor, and realized in such a way that the neighbor is
loved for himself, not as means to a higher end*."[101] Here Moltmann's mandate to
love the neighbor rests firmly on his messianic *imago Dei* anthropology and
his understanding of salvation as new creation. Just as God's love for humankind takes incarnate form in the life, death, and resurrection of Christ, so, too,
human beings are called to incarnate this same love toward the neighbor. In
keeping with the terms of Moltmann's messianic anthropology, human beings
are called to fulfill their destiny as *imago Dei* by conforming themselves to the
messianic way of Christ, that is, by loving other human beings just as God has
loved them in Christ. In this way they become with one another a realization
of the *imago Trinitatis*.

On a superficial reading, Moltmann's proposed models of Christian friendship and love do not appear to be intrinsically related to his trinitarian theology.
Unlike our previous examples of fellowship in the spheres of politics and the
church, he does not spell out for his readers any direct correspondences between the trinitarian life and these most personal forms of human relationships. In fact, Moltmann alerts his readers to his theological approach to these

human relations only in the most general terms, by describing them as "carry[ing] over the Christian concept of love—the liberating and redeeming concept—into the different levels of social relationships."[102] Despite Moltmann's methodological unclarity, careful analysis reveals the family resemblances among these personal relationships and his trinitarian ontology. Let us turn first to his discussion of open friendship.

Open friendship is essentially Moltmann's model of Christian hospitality; it recurs throughout his works as the ideal for how Christians should engage others in the world. Moltmann initially borrows his definition of friendship from Kantian moral theory—hardly a trinitarian source. Friendship, he explains in Kant's terms, is a personal relationship that combines "respect for the other person's freedom with deep affection for him or her as a person."[103] Despite the nontrinitarian origin of this definition, Moltmann develops its meaning in such a way that it actually corresponds to the personal relations that constitute the trinitarian life of fellowship. Open friendship depends equally on the desire to share oneself fully in the life of another individual and on the recognition of the other person's difference or individuality. Furthermore, open friendship is predicated upon perfect reciprocity and equality among human beings. A person neither appropriates nor possesses another, nor do the two become subject to one another. Rather, each creates the space for the other person's freedom to emerge. In Moltmann's more poetic terms, "Friends throw open the free spaces of life for one another, and accompany one another in sympathy and immense interest."[104]

Though Moltmann fails to make this point explicit, the person and the work of Jesus Christ secure the link between trinitarian fellowship and open friendship. As we recall from the discussion of the trinitarian pattern of salvation, human beings come to know the essence of trinitarian fellowship, the infinite self-giving love of the Other, uniquely through the person of Jesus Christ. Through his ministry and his message, human beings discover what it means to be a true child of God. When Moltmann describes how this self-giving love takes visible form, he speaks of the "open friendship" that Jesus extends to all persons, especially those at the margins of society—the sinners, the poor, and the outcast:

> [Jesus] celebrated the messianic feast with the people who had been thrust out of society. In inviting joy, he opened himself for them, and respected both them and the poor, as the first children of the divine grace that creates everything afresh. He recognized their dignity as people. He bridged the gulf of their self-isolation, and did away with the social prejudice under which they suffered. Through speech and gesture, the divine "friend of sinners and tax collectors" spread the encouraging and supportive atmosphere of open friendship among men and women.[105]

For Moltmann, Jesus' ministry exemplifies perfectly the reciprocal dynamic of affection and respect, self-giving and self-distinction that characterize open friendship. Jesus gives fully of himself by entering with compassion and active solidarity into others' situations; he creates the free space to accept others' differences and to respect their unique dignity. He offers this open friendship to all persons he encounters, not out of moral duty but out of overflowing love, the very same infinite generosity that constitutes the trinitarian life of fellowship.

Jesus is more than a perfect exemplar of open friendship in his ministry. He incarnates God's friendship with all human beings in his self-giving love at the cross. Building on John 15:13–15, Moltmann describes this act of divine love toward human beings as the means of human friendship with God in the Spirit.[106] Ultimately, the believer's personal experience of open friendship with God through Christ and in the Spirit empowers his or her practice of open friendship toward others. Just as the trinitarian God has opened his kingdom to all human beings who are profoundly other from God's self and invites them into friendship, so, too, Christians are called to be conformed to Christ— to open and welcome other human beings into their " 'society of friends.' "[107]

Let us turn finally to Moltmann's description of human love and its roots in trinitarian fellowship. Here Moltmann is far more explicit about how he envisions the relationship between divine and human loves. He objects to the various terminological distinctions that have been drawn in the theological tradition between divine and human loves, most notably *eros* versus *agape*, as severing the unity that is given in the double commandment of love. Citing 1 John 4:16, Moltmann describes divine and human loves as intersecting spheres of experience; they are experiences that "deepen and shelter one another mutually."[108] This does not mean that the two are indistinguishable from one another, but that we can genuinely experience the love of God in and through human expressions of love.

Appealing to the Greek church fathers (particularly Maximus the Confessor), Moltmann uses the single term *eros* to describe both divine and human loves. *Eros* signifies both God's fellowship with humankind and the force that joins human beings into community with one another. "The community of love is an *erotic community*: God's loving community with his beloved creation is erotic; the force which differentiates and unites all his creatures is erotic; the rapturous delight of lovers in one another is erotic."[109] Moltmann identifies *eros* with the creative Spirit of life who infuses love—an affirmation of life— into all of creation. *Eros* imparts to human beings a share in the divine life and enables them to reflect this same love in the sphere of earthly relations.

Although once again Moltmann does not spell out the correspondences to his trinitarian theology of love, they are there for the careful reader to uncover. For one, his model of true human love mirrors the dialectic of union in personal freedom that characterizes the trinitarian life. On the one side, human love is a desire for union with the other. True erotic desire does not wish to subjugate or possess another but rather "to participate in the life of the other person, and to communicate his or her own life."[110] On the other, human love offers the gift of freedom. True human love, for Moltmann, is "generous," insofar as it delights in the freedom of the other person: "Like friendship, love unfolds only in the fragile and vulnerable sphere of freedom—indeed it is love itself which in the personal sense opens up freedom in the free spaces of life. . . . It sounds paradoxical, but in the experience of love it is no contradiction to say that to desire and to liberate are one and the same thing.[111] Just as I described Moltmann's vision of God as one who frees in love, so, too, we discover here that true human love enjoins the freedom of the other.

Moltmann alerts us to the intrinsic connection between divine and human loves by using parallel terminology to describe the two experiences. For example, he depicts human lovers as being a counterpart and presence for one another. Lovers are each other's counterpart, insofar as they respond in concert to one another: "The inclination of the Thou awakens a responding movement in the I, and vice versa."[112] Beyond enjoying this I-thou relationship with one another, lovers become an "encompassing presence" for one another; "they begin to live in each other."[113] When Moltmann describes the intimate communion that human beings enjoy with God through the fellowship of the Spirit, he employs the same terms: "In the experience of the Spirit, God is primal, all-embracing presence, not a detached counterpart."[114] Just as the Spirit and human beings dwell in one another, so, too, lovers are called to dwell reciprocally in one another.

In sum, despite Moltmann's often opaque argumentations on behalf of his theology of the social experiences of God, careful reading of *The Spirit of Life* uncovers the numerous ways in which his trinitarian rule of faith norms the sphere of human interpersonal relations. Like trinitarian fellowship, friendship and love are interpersonal relationships of self-giving that combine affection and respect. They are both forms of unity in differentiation; they involve a genuine participation or indwelling in the life of another that engenders mutual freedom. Finally, both friendship and love are grounded in the experience of trinitarian love as it is directed toward human beings. In the friendship extended toward the stranger and in the love of the neighbor, human beings reflect the Trinity's gift of love that has been first offered with infinite generosity to humankind.

The Promise of Trinitarian Fellowship as a Rule of Faith

We would need to analyze other aspects of Moltmann's political theology and his ecclesiology to see fully how his trinitarian theology shapes his ideals for the Christian life. Nonetheless, we can draw some important conclusions about the practical dimensions of Moltmann's social trinitarian theology from the examples that I have provided here. To do so, I would like to return to one practice of the Christian faith—that of open friendship—as illustrative of the prophetic and transformative possibilities inherent in Moltmann's trinitarian fellowship as a rule of faith. The category of open friendship provides an excellent vantage point from which to evaluate how trinitarian fellowship norms human action, since Moltmann appeals to it throughout his works as the distinctive ethos of the Christian life of faith.

First and foremost, open friendship recasts the notion of true human freedom in communal terms as a freedom for and with another person. In so doing, this social trinitarian model of human freedom contests the modern (and some would argue postmodern) ideal of freedom as individual liberty or the "right to self-determination."[115] Moltmann criticizes this modern notion of human freedom as autonomy by pointing to how it atomizes human society into a collection of solitary and competing individuals. In modernity's social contract, each individual is perceived as the limit to another's freedom. At its best, such a model of freedom isolates individuals from one another by engendering fierce competition for common resources and property. At its worst, it leads to the subjugation of the weak by the dominant and the dissolution of all true bonds of community.[116]

Open friendship provides a powerful antidote to the concept of human freedom as "self-constitution" that triumphed in much modern theological anthropology.[117] In contrast to this modern concept, the freedom of open friendship is found in the ties that bind diverse persons together as a community. To borrow Moltmann's words, it is "a communicative freedom":[118] a freedom that emerges in reciprocal giving and receiving, in mutual recognition and acceptance. In such open friendship, personal identity flourishes rather than being sacrificed to that of another. Here the antinomy between the freedom of the person and that of one's neighbor is overcome in a life of mutual participation; other persons become the source as well as the complement to one's own freedom. Just as in the individual's fellowship with the Holy Spirit, so, too, in open friendship there coexists "both *the love* that binds and *the freedom* which allows everything to arrive at itself, in its own unique nature."[119]

A second promising dimension of open friendship lies in its charge to practice a self-giving love toward the Other. As I have argued earlier, this self-giving love is essentially christological praxis; it is patterned after the ministry and proclamation, the life and self-donation of Christ. In this messianic way of life, such self-giving love can manifest itself in a variety of concrete relationships and forms of action toward others. For example, a believer may express open friendship through compassionate fellowship, that is, by participating so fully in the trials and joys of others that she provides companionship in their midst. In other situations, self-giving love of the Other takes the form of active solidarity with persons on the margins of society. Here open friendship might mean welcoming the stranger, the outsider, into the midst of the

Christian assembly. Or else it might mean active resistance against unjust structures that create social exclusion in the first place; it may mean risking spiritual or physical suffering on behalf of others. Finally, self-giving love of the Other may take the form of a restorative forgiveness that heals the brokenness of human relationships and welcomes the person who becomes imprisoned by either personal or collective guilt back into community with others.

What joins all these forms of self-giving love of the Other is their movement toward inclusivity, their acceptance of all others in their diversity. Moltmann underscores this radical inclusivity by juxtaposing his proposal for open friendship with the Greek concept of friendship (*philia*), in which friendship is restricted to those who are identical in nature or rank, for example, in gender, race, or social status. In contrast, the practice of open friendship reaches specifically beyond those who are like us out toward those who are radically "Other." Just as Jesus welcomes all persons regardless of their situation, gender, or station in life with the boundless mercy and life-giving love of the kingdom's fellowship, so, too, the Christian is charged to embody such open friendship in the world.

Wherein lies the emancipatory potential in these diverse expressions of open friendship? Through acts of creative and passionate fellowship, open friendship breaks the bondage of human exclusion and weaves new bonds of community in its place. Regardless of an individual's situation, whether she or he is the victim or the perpetrator of broken fellowship, the practice of open friendship restores an individual to the embrace of community. In so doing, such self-giving love of the Other dramatically transforms human economies of even exchange into ones of infinite generosity and creative possibility. In open friendship, human love is neither just returned in kind nor meted out in equal portions. Rather, self-giving love of the Other expresses itself with the same overflowing abundance that characterizes the life-giving love of trinitarian fellowship. With trinitarian fellowship as its measure, the circle of open friendship widens to include all persons and not just those who resemble one another in social status, gender, or ethnicity. It is truly a boundless self-giving that is without reserve or conditions.

To conclude the discussion of the promising aspects of trinitarian fellowship as a rule of faith, let us revisit the critical debate over the practical significance of Moltmann's social trinitarian theology raised in the first chapter of this study. There I pointed out how Moltmann has been caught in the crossfire between critics who think that his trinitarian theology promises too much and others who think it delivers too little. On the one hand, contemporary theologians such as Werner Jeanrond and Karen Kilby charge Moltmann with overfreighting his trinitarian doctrine by applying it too readily to human beings' relationships and their social structures. On the other, critics such as David Cunningham applaud Moltmann's efforts to use his trinitarian theology to address political and social concerns, but they think he falls short of achieving this aim by offering too few concrete suggestions about what it might mean to put his theology into practice.

In light of my foregoing analysis, let me suggest that a more nuanced evaluation of Moltmann's social trinitarian program is needed. Against the backdrop of the author's creation-redemption schema, I have suggested that an implicit doctrinal logic unites the doctrine of the Trinity to that of the life of faith. More specifically, I have argued that Moltmann employs a social trinitarian analogy to guide the Christian life, one in which the specific patterns of divine relations that constitute divine fellowship provide the archetype for different practices and forms of relationships in the human community. This does not mean that he superimposes trinitarian categories onto the created order but that he translates these categories into what I have termed a trinitarian rule of faith, which he then uses to norm diverse human relations. This divine analogy of fellowship may not provide prescriptive rules for the Christian life. Nor does it legislate a particular course of action in any given situation. Nonetheless, in my view, this social trinitarian analogy does demonstrate the theological cohesion between Moltmann's concept of God and the concrete practices of individual believers and their communities. It demonstrates what Amy Plantinga Pauw has helpfully described elsewhere as the "flexible integrity" that should exist between doctrines and practices of the Christian life.[120]

Finally, Moltmann's trinitarian pattern of salvation gives rise to a distinctive understanding of the cardinal fruits of the Spirit—of faith, love, and hope—through which human beings come to enjoy a graced participation and transfiguration into the life of trinitarian fellowship. These gifts of the Spirit provide a broad but sturdy theological framework for the Christian life that is built upon the inseparable pillars of love of God and love of one's neighbor. The deeper one's fellowship with the triune God, the more freely and generously one goes out into the world to share this fellowship with others. As one concrete expression of these intertwined loves, open friendship leads believers into the way of Jesus Christ—toward imitating the boundless hospitality that Jesus shared with all those he encountered and particularly with those on the margins of society. The fellowship of the Spirit infuses believers with the creative freedom to engage in acts of compassionate solidarity, to resist situations of injustice and violence, and to offer restorative forgiveness to others. Moltmann's trinitarian theology thus offers a robust theology of grace that empowers individuals to engage in the transformation of the world into the kingdom of fellowship.

Speaking about Sin against the Spirit of Trinitarian Fellowship

Although my constructive interpretation of Moltmann's views of the Christian life and his social and political ethics counters many of the criticisms that have been raised against his social trinitarian theology, it does not still all my disquietude about Moltmann's social trinitarian program. In the conclusion of this study, I will press again the issue of Moltmann's ad hoc theological methodology and how it ultimately detracts from his praxiological trinitarian agenda. At this point, I would like to take up again David Cunningham's criticism of the utopian character of Moltmann's social trinitarian theology, but redirect this criticism to a theological gap in his *Messianic Theology* that has been thus far overlooked by Moltmann's interpreters, namely, the lack of a fully developed theology of sin. As one recalls, Cunningham challenges the practical relevance of Moltmann's social trinitarian theology on the grounds that it never actually touches the ground, that is, provides sufficient guidelines for human agency in particular situations. While I agree that Moltmann's rhetoric about the Christian life may at times sound optimistic, the problem, in my view, lies elsewhere than Cunningham suspects, namely, in Moltmann's failure to develop an adequate doctrine of sin, one that coincides with his mature trinitarian analysis of the Christian life.

Now the notion of sin does not disappear altogether from the *Messianic Theology*. As we saw earlier in this chapter, Moltmann does briefly discuss the human predicament of sin at the conclusion of his *imago Dei* anthropology in *God in Creation*. There I showed how Moltmann interprets sin in quite classical terms as a disruption or perversion of one's primary loving relationship to God due to the idolatry of turning to oneself, others, or created objects as one's primary love. Moltmann returns again to the theme of sin in his later volume *The Spirit of Life*, in which he introduces a broader cosmological concept of sin. Here sin represents all the death-dealing forces that deny the Spirit as the wellspring of life; sin negates or quenches the Spirit of creation and of new creation—its "vitality" and "love of life."[121]

Moltmann explains this notion of sin most fully in his discussion of the doctrine of justification. There he is set on reforming the classical Reformed understanding of God's righteousness that justifies all sinners, on the grounds that such "a universal concept of sin" can too easily become an "excuse for specific, practical guilt."[122] In place of a generic imputation of all persons as justified sinners, Moltmann introduces a differentiated view of God's righteousness that offers justification for the perpetrators of sin and justice to its victims. The Spirit of life frees the perpetrators of sin from the bondage of their guilt and repression at the same time that she liberates sin's victims by creating possibilities for new life.[123] Finally, Moltmann calls for an expansion in the classical doctrine's focus on personal sin to include structural sin—those institutionalized forms of injustice in which individuals experience themselves as both caught and complicit. Here the Spirit of life manifests itself as a "rectifying" righteousness that "destabilizes" these unjust and violent social structures and transforms them into patterns of fellowship.[124]

While these innovations in the doctrine are significant, Moltmann's sketch of his doctrine of sin still does not correspond well to his social trinitarian framework of the Christian life. He depicts sin largely as a cosmic force against the Spirit of life rather than developing it in terms of being either personal or systemic distortions of trinitarian fellowship. Symptomatic of this disjunction is that Moltmann does not draw upon his social trinitarian categories to analyze either individual or corporate sins, for example, as expressions of un-faith, un-hope, and un-love in the Christian life. For example, we do not discover how distorted patterns of fellowship manifest themselves either in structures of domination or else in dissolution of the necessary boundaries between the self and the other. Missing as well is an in-depth reflection of the debilitating and ongoing effects of sin upon human beings' relationships and how these might be passed on and distort either the community of generations or the fellowship with creation that the author espouses in his messianic doctrine of creation. Finally, Moltmann pays little attention to how Christians seek to heal such broken fellowship, for example, through corporate acts of confession and lamentation or individual acts of forgiveness and repentance.

In my view, these underdeveloped aspects of the Christian doctrine of sin go a long way toward explaining the gap that Cunningham points to between Moltmann's trinitarian principles and his concrete proposals for the Christian life. Without a robust theological notion of sin, Moltmann's claims on behalf of his practical theory and concrete doctrine of the Trinity appear overly optimistic, as if to suggest that once persons of faith know these trinitarian norms, their fulfillment lies close at hand. The absence of a robust theology of sin also lends credence to what critics such as Torrance identify as the Pelagian tendencies in Moltmann's mature theology, as if salvation might be achieved through persons of faith practicing these trinitarian norms. Finally, by not including a robust doctrine of sin in his trinitarian theology of grace, Moltmann sacrifices the distinctive Reformed dialectic of sin and grace in his social trinitarian analogy for the Christian faith. This Reformed dialectic reminds believers that they remain forever bound to the gift of grace to justify and to free them from sin's bondage. Furthermore, this dialectic serves a prophetic-critical function in the life of faith, for it reminds the Christian community of its ongoing susceptibility to self-deception and the always broken character of its witness in the world. The dialectic of sin and grace inspires the Christian community to ongoing critical examination of the integrity of its theological and praxiological commitments.

To conclude this discussion, I would like to take a step further and suggest what Moltmann's social trintarian theology might gain from developing a doctrine of sin in social trinitarian terms. First of all, speaking of sin as a distortion or separation from trinitarian fellowship draws into sharp relief that sin is a *theological* problem. At its deepest level sin is more than a transgression against a moral or social code. It is a fundamental breach of our fellowship with God the Father through the Son in the Spirit. Sin puts us at odds with God's being and eternal purpose in creating humankind—the will to fellowship with humankind. Sin cuts at the heart of who we are called to be, creatures whose messianic destiny is to flourish as *imago Trinitatis.*

Once we recall that the Spirit of fellowship is the creative passion that creates and sustains all of creation in existence, the dire consequences of such a rupture or falling out of divine fellowship become strikingly evident. Sin amounts to an unraveling of our personal identity—a turning away from the life-giving energy that holds all things in life. Placed within the horizon of divine fellowship, sin emerges in all its violence and its destructive potential as an ontological problem—what British theologian Mary Grey has aptly called our "structural de-creation" or "unmaking of the world."[125] It not only diminishes or strips away our particular vocation in life but also has corrosive effects on the relationships, structures, and institutions in which we participate.

Speaking about sin as distorted or broken fellowship not only highlights the destructiveness of sin but also provides an elastic metaphor with which one can describe distinct manifestations of sin among human beings. For example, broken fellowship can helpfully redescribe both the classical notion of sin as pride and contemporary feminist reconstructions of sin as "self-loss" or "lack of self-esteem."[126] In the former case, the egotistic self who instrumentalizes or dominates over others distorts the dynamic of self-giving that is intrinsic to trinitarian fellowship. In the latter, the self who threatens to dissolve in and through relationships with others also distorts the gift of trinitarian fellowship that calls one to proper self-relation as well as self-giving.

To take another example, broken fellowship can help describe the sin that lies beneath racial or ethnic conflict, in which the Other is violently excluded from rather than welcomed into one's community. Here sin takes the form of fear-driven desire for homogeneity among the members of a community and the rejection of diversity as integral to the flourishing of fellowship.[127] Finally, speaking about sin as broken fellowship has the potential to speak out against those various betrayals of the human body and the nonhuman creation, be they through sexual abuse, torture, world hunger, or exploitative environmental practices, all of which are too-regular features of our global culture. All these are profound distortions of the embodied fellowship that the Spirit seeks to foster among individuals and in the community of creation.

In all these examples, speaking of sin as a fall from fellowship joins together the ethical and the mystical, the political and the doxological dimensions of the Christian life. It highlights how distortions of true human fellowship are intrinsically related to the loss of personal fellowship with the Trinity. Just as faith's freedom and the gift of freedom to others are intertwined gifts of the Spirit, so, too, sin as ruptured fellowship can be understood as the simultaneous rupture of one's relationship with God and with one's fellow human beings.

On a superficial reading, my proposal to develop a more differentiated trinitarian theology of sin might appear to contradict the messianic trajectory of Moltmann's vision of life in the Spirit, a life aimed toward the regeneration of the human being as *imago Trinitatis*. And yet, my point in calling for such a robust notion of sin is not to cast a pessimistic gloom over the human condition that would rob either the individual believer or the Christian community of the freedom and, even more, the responsibility for emancipatory action. I am not suggesting that sin creates such an undertow in human existence that it becomes fruitless to offer resistance and to seek transformation in the Christian life. On the contrary! Such sin-talk is intended to strengthen one's faith in the fellowship that is offered through the Spirit, and in this way to inspire believers with the passion and the creative vision to mend the broken fellowships in their midst. On this point, I agree with Rebecca Chopp, who reminds us that when properly understood a large doctrine of sin can be an "act of grace": "A discourse about sin is in itself a resistance to injustice and the expression of the desire for human flourishing, for correcting all that is false, distorted, depraved."[128] In other words, speaking about sin against the Spirit of trinitarian fellowship encourages believers to identify and rout out the systemic distortions and the forces of destruction that stand in the way of true fellowship between God and human beings. In this way, speaking robustly about sin in the midst of grace can advance Moltmann's praxiological agenda— of encouraging believers to engage in the messianic praxis of trinitarian fellowship, and of transfiguring all things into a fuller and more glorious image of the coming kingdom of fellowship.

6

Conclusion

Toward a Contemporary Trinitarian Theology of Love

This study has engaged one of the liveliest theological debates at the turn of the twenty-first century: the significance of the doctrine of the Trinity to the Christian concept of God and to its life of faith. I have entered this debate by offering a critical and constructive interpretation of its most far-reaching Protestant contribution to date, Jürgen Moltmann's social trinitarian theology. For more than thirty years Moltmann has sought to re-vision a doctrine of the Trinity that reflects the dynamic and passionate love of God revealed in the scriptures. At the same time, he has sought to respond creatively to the intellectual, political, and pastoral challenges of the day. Along the way Moltmann's proposals have never failed to provoke controversy but also to renew dialogue across confessional traditions and cultural expanses.

To conclude this study, I propose to revisit the various conclusions that I have reached about Moltmann's ambitious trinitarian agenda. I do so with two aims in mind. First, I seek to recall the interpretative issues raised by Moltmann's evolving trinitarian theology and to situate my reading of his *Messianic Theology* within these current debates. Now that Moltmann has drawn his *Messianic Theology* to a close, such a comprehensive interpretation of his work is at once possible and urgently needed in contemporary theology. Second, and more important, I seek to identify the distinctive contributions that Moltmann has made toward a contemporary trinitarian theology of love and to advance a constructive agenda for its further development. Here I seek to highlight those points at which his theology begs further clarification and at the same time recognize its "openness" to ongoing development.

Discerning the Development of a Doctrine and the Nature of Divine Love

I have pursued both a hermeneutical and a systematic-theological agenda in analyzing Moltmann's trinitarian theology. On the hermeneutical side, I sought an answer to one of the most vexing problems in reading Moltmann's extensive body of work: How best to make sense of the evolution of his trinitarian theology and his shifting understanding of divine love? In response to this question, I took as my interpretive key to Moltmann's doctrinal development its unfolding soteriological content. From the first to the last, Moltmann's doctrine of the Trinity is an account of God's identity that is anchored in God's reconciling and liberating agency on behalf of humankind as witnessed to in the scriptures. It is the story of God's infinite passion for the world—for its creation, salvation, and ultimate glorification. For Moltmann, this soteriological root is more than an epistemological claim about the source of human knowledge about the Trinity. It is an ontological claim about the significance of the history of the trinitarian persons' loving relations to the world for the divine life itself.

As we saw in chapter 2 of this study, Moltmann at first limits the soteriological content of his doctrine to the cross-event. As a result, his initial proposal for a doctrine of the Trinity is quite rudimentary and in many respects resembles the Augustinian version of the doctrine that he will later sharply criticize. Essentially it is a trinitarian theology of the cross in which the Father and Son enact a mutual *kenosis*, or reciprocal acts of self-surrender. Here the Holy Spirit appears only in a highly subordinated role—first as the bond of love that unites the Father and the Son in the midst of their separation, and again as the gift of new life that reconciles the world to God. These different works of love lend a dialectical structure to Moltmann's trinitarian history of God: this history traces an ontological division in God's being that is ultimately overcome in the eschaton through the uniting work of the Spirit.

Based on my reading of Moltmann's trinitarian theology of the cross in *The Crucified God* (along with some hints gathered from his theology of the resurrection in *Theology of Hope*), I interpreted his early concept of divine love (*agape*) as a dialectic of crucified and creative love. Divine love manifests itself primarily as crucified love: an unconditional suffering for the Other, in which the Father and Son mutually suffer the grief of abandonment both in personal representation of and in solidarity with creation. Creative love represents notably a minor key in Moltmann's early works. It, too, is a form of unconditional love for the Other, but this love manifests itself in the work of the Holy Spirit who creates new possibilities for humankind and, in so doing, returns humankind to the embrace of divine love.

As I argued in chapter 3 of this study, Moltmann never deviates from this soteriological norm for his doctrine of the Trinity, but he does significantly augment his account of the divine economy from *The Trinity and the Kingdom* onward. While the cross- and resurrection-events remain the fulcrum of his trinitarian history of God, this history now reaches back to the sending of the Son and the Spirit into the world in the act of creation and extends forward to the eschatological glorification of all of creation in the divine fellowship. To capture the various dimensions of this divine pilgrimage of love into the world, Moltmann develops what I described as a narrative approach to trinitarian doctrine. He identifies different plotlines within the biblical text that trace the Father, the Son, and the Holy Spirit's changing relations and works in this economy of creation, redemption, and glorification; Moltmann synthesizes these into a complex narrative that he calls the trinitarian history of God. For Moltmann, we come to know the identity of the triune God only by immersing ourselves in this narrative, that is, by following the divine pilgrimage of love in the world.

Based on my reading of *The Trinity and the Kingdom*, I proposed that there are two distinct, if intrinsically related, concepts of divine love in Moltmann's mature trinitarian theology: the concept of divine passion as the self-communication of the good and the concept of fellowship or communion (*koinonia*) of Father, Son, and Spirit. These two concepts frame the author's trinitarian history of God—the former as the eternal condition for its possibility and the latter as its messianic goal. I argued further that Moltmann's concept of divine passion as the self-communication of the good is a reworking of his earlier concept of divine love. Although divine passion still takes the conceptual form of self-giving to the Other, its essence shifts from *kenosis* to *ecstasis*—to the passionate longing for the Other and the overflowing passion for life. Formulated differently, we can say that the locus of divine revelation shifts from the event of the cross to that of creation, and its meaning shifts accordingly from suffering love to creative love and the gift of life and freedom to love. This does not mean that suffering love disappears from Moltmann's work; on the contrary, it remains the paramount expression of God's passionate engagement on behalf of God's beloved creation in order to grant it ultimate freedom.

In conclusion, let me propose two related ways in which Moltmann's ecstatic concept of divine passion in *The Trinity and the Kingdom* surpasses his earlier one. First, it succeeds at uniting the two sides of the earlier dialectic of crucified and creative love into a single concept of God's being as love. This new ecstatic concept of divine passion contains *in nuce* the entire trajectory of the trinitarian history of God with the world from its creation to its eschatological consummation. Divine passion unfolds as the ecstatic love of the Father

for his eternal counterpart, his Son, a love that in its infinite generosity over-
flows through the Spirit in the creation, redemption, and eschatological glorification of the world. Second, this ecstatic concept of divine passion is a
teleological concept of divine love that corresponds to the messianic trajectory
of Moltmann's entire work. It announces from the outset the messianic goal
of this trinitarian history of God, namely, the gift of freedom to humankind
through fellowship with the Trinity.

If this ecstatic concept is the beginning and the end of the divine pilgrimage of love, Moltmann's other model of divine love as fellowship (*koinonia*) is
the centerpiece of his social trinitarian theology. Throughout this study I have
argued that trinitarian fellowship is more than just a recurring rhetorical figure
that threads throughout Moltmann's works. It represents the doctrinal structuring principle for his entire theology. Fellowship describes at once the nature
of the divine kingdom, the abiding character of God's relationship to creation,
and the messianic destiny of all human beings.

In chapter 3 I identified the christological root of Moltmann's concept of
trinitarian fellowship in the intimate relationship that Jesus shares with his
Abba Father. Here divine fellowship appears as a life-giving compassion—a
mutual self-giving out of which springs forth ever-greater life. The nature of
divine fellowship emerged ever more vividly as we widened our perspective
from the personal communion between the Father and the Son to Moltmann's
entire history of the Son and the corresponding history of the Spirit. Without
recounting the various plotlines in this complex narrative, let me call into view
three characteristics of trinitarian fellowship that prove essential to the other
doctrines of his theology.

First and foremost, trinitarian fellowship is a communal property of the
three divine persons. It is neither the attribute of any single divine person nor
a reality distinct from their personal relations. Rather, trinitarian fellowship
signifies the social unity constituted by the reciprocal self-giving relations
among Father, Son, and Spirit. Moltmann appeals to the ancient christological
notion of *perichoresis* to describe this unique communion shared among the
divine persons. *Perichoresis* signifies the circling movement that occurs through
the three persons' eternal acts of self-donation to one another. This circling
movement creates a dynamic form of unity (at-oneness), in which the divine
persons dwell in and through one another. Through their interanimation the
divine persons realize not only their unity but also their personal distinctions
from one another.

Radical equality is the second key feature of true fellowship. This may not
appear to be a terribly unique claim of Moltmann's theology, since trinitarian
orthodoxy has always affirmed that all three persons are of one being and,
therefore, of equal rank. In Moltmann's view, however, the Western trinitarian
doctrine has seriously imperiled this equality with its processional model of
the intra-divine relations, in which the Father serves as the source of all divinity,

the Son as the mediator between the Father and humankind, and the Spirit as the power of the other two. To remedy what Moltmann judges to be a monarchical structure, he proposes an entirely different doctrinal construction: different forms of the Trinity, each of these illustrating a different pattern of relationships among Father, Son, and Spirit, which appear in the divine economy. Together these trinitarian forms manifest the perfect equality and mutual interdependence of the three divine persons. This kaleidoscope of changing patterns reveals the trinitarian fellowship to be free from all traces of domination and subjugation—a kingdom governed by reciprocal friendship and a spirit of mercy and liberty.

The third and final key feature of trinitarian fellowship is what I term its infinite generosity. I use this term to emphasize that the divine fellowship bestows itself freely and without reserve upon creation. It is an utterly bountiful and boundless love that passionately desires to include all of creation in its midst. Moltmann most often describes the infinite generosity of trinitarian fellowship in figurative terms. He depicts the trinitarian life not as a closed circle, a life sufficient unto itself, but as an open and inviting communion that summons all of creation into joyful participation in its dynamic movement.

Before I turn to the implications of Moltmann's concept of trinitarian fellowship for the other doctrines in his theology, let me draw a couple of final conclusions about his doctrine of God. First, Moltmann mounts, in my view, a highly compelling biblical argument for refiguring divine love in terms of fellowship. I do not mean that his concept of trinitarian fellowship can be readily identified in the biblical text but that it represents a persuasive interpretation of divine love as it is revealed in the works of the Son and the Holy Spirit. Admittedly, Moltmann begins in *The Trinity and the Kingdom* with a slim biblical foundation for his notion of divine fellowship, namely, his interpretation of Jesus' relationship with his Father as described in a few texts that the author gathers from the Gospel of Matthew and the Johannine corpus. Over the course of writing his *Messianic Theology*, Moltmann succeeds, however, at weaving more and more narrative threads from both the Old and New Testaments into his depiction of the kingdom of fellowship. In *The Way of Jesus Christ*, for example, Moltmann interprets different acts in Jesus' ministry as a living out of this divine fellowship, and he draws on all of the synoptic Gospels as well as the Johannine corpus for scriptural support. In *God in Creation* and *The Spirit of Life*, Moltmann complements this christological account with a corresponding pneumatological perspective on fellowship. Here he links the Old Testament notion of *ruach*, the breath of life, to the Pauline notion of the Spirit of Christ to depict the Spirit's gift of life in terms of God's ever-deepening fellowship with human beings.

Having said this in favor of Moltmann's biblical sources for his concept of trinitarian fellowship, what is missing from his works is a fuller explication of the hermeneutical principles that guide his interpretation of biblical texts.

Although Moltmann assembles a broad canon of scriptural texts to support his social trinitarian theology, he does so usually without clarifying either his hermeneutical presuppositions or the various exegetical tensions that arise from individual texts' disparate historical, literary, or rhetorical contexts.[1] By not directly addressing these hermeneutical and canonical questions in his earlier writings, Moltmann exposes himself to the charge of assuming an uncritical approach to the scriptures and, even more, of imposing a false doctrinal unity onto the biblical witness.

A second major contribution of Moltmann's trinitarian theology is that it secures a model of God's being as fellowship that is indivisible from the relationships among the three divine persons. Recall that one of Moltmann's chief objections to the Western trinitarian doctrine (and especially its preference for a psychological analogy) is that it devolves into a form of modalism or monarchical monotheism that privileges the divine unity to the specificity of the divine persons. For this reason, Moltmann adopts an alternative approach in constructing his social doctrine, namely, beginning with the three divine persons' agency and subsequently considering the nature of their unity with one another. In my estimation, he overcomes these monadic tendencies with his notion of a divine fellowship that is built on personal relations of mutual indwelling. In this divine fellowship the divine persons, their relations, and dynamic unity are mutually constitutive of one another and come into being together. Furthermore, Moltmann's concept of trinitarian fellowship eliminates any hint of monarchianism from the divine kingdom. Trinitarian fellowship represents a nonhierarchical form of divine rule in which there can be no domination and subjugation of one another; here love and freedom coincide insofar as each person exists for and with the others.

This is not to suggest that Moltmann's trinitarian ontology is free of conceptual tensions. As I argued in chapter 3, when one presses his concept of divine fellowship, it cannot eliminate the threat of tritheism from his social trinitarian doctrine. Moltmann's highly anthropomorphic depictions of the three divine persons incarnating distinct roles in his trinitarian history (roles that he insists are not appropriated to them but constitute their identity) invite the picture of three independent agents who merely act in concert with one another. Moreover, Moltmann's frequent appeal to the term "union" or "unitedness" (Einigkeit) to describe the fellowship among Father, Son, and Holy Spirit only heightens the suspicion that theirs is a volitional rather than an ontological unity. As I argued at the close of chapter 3, Moltmann, though he never explicitly admits to doing so, is forced to take recourse to the ancient idea of the Father as the source of unity to secure the ontological claim that these three are one. He thus actually holds two notions of divine unity, a protological and a doxological are, without resolving the philosolphical tensions between the two.

In chapter 3 I disclosed further conceptual tensions in how Moltmann conceives of the relationship between divine love in the origin as the self-communication of the good and his eschatological vision of divine fellowship. Are they one and the same reality, or does the essence of the divine love change over the course of this trinitarian history? As I argued in chapter 3, there are no doubt strong correspondences between these two concepts in terms of passionate self-giving and infinite generosity. And yet, the temporal structure of Moltmann's doctrinal framework, combined with his insistence that this trinitarian history has real effects on the intra-divine relations, suggests that the Trinity endures a transformation through its pilgrimage in human history. Moltmann's affirmation of an eschatological panentheism, in which all of creation will be taken up into the midst of divine being, lends further support to the view that divine fellowship is a becoming reality, one that reaches its fulfillment only with the return of creation into its midst.

In the end Moltmann does not provide his readers with a fully satisfying answer to the question of whether divine love is a becoming reality. In fact, he demurs when it comes to providing conceptual closure on this kind of issue in his works on the grounds that theological claims about the messianic nature of God's being are always fragmentary and subject to ongoing revision. As long as humankind finds itself under way toward the consummation of the kingdom, Moltmann counters that our theological constructs must tolerate this kind of epistemic openness. This is not to suggest that we are to remain agnostic about the eternal nature of God, for as we have seen throughout this study, Moltmann does not hesitate to make claims about God's eternal nature based on God's faithfulness to his promises. Rather, Moltmann argues that we can trust in the correspondences between our present experiences of divine fellowship and the kingdom. At the same time we must maintain a certain epistemic humility in assuming that the messianic reality will infinitely surpass our present understanding.

The Analogy of Trinitarian Fellowship: Will It Stretch or Will It Break?

I turn now to the other side of my systematic-theological agenda in engaging Moltmann's social trinitarian theology: whether it succeeds at becoming the kind of concrete doctrine and practical theory that can meaningfully shape the corporate identity and the individual praxis of contemporary believers. In addressing this question, I sought first an answer to a theological puzzle in Moltmann's *Messianic Theology*, namely, how the author actually links his doctrine of the Trinity to the Christian life of faith. As I pointed out in the introduction to this study, many of Moltmann's sharpest critics discover insuperable difficulties at this juncture of his trinitarian theology. Some dismiss his return to trinitarian theology as a speculative move that detracts from his earlier political theology's bold agenda for emancipatory praxis in the world. Others charge him with overtaxing the doctrine in assuming its direct relevance to the sphere of human relationships and diverse forms of communities.

Based on a comprehensive analysis of Moltmann's *Messianic Theology*, I argued that there was a coherent, if also not fully realized, theological strategy that links the doctrine of the Trinity to the author's vision of the Christian life—what I construed as a social trinitarian analogy of fellowship. With this term, I described how Moltmann appeals to his distinctive model of personal relations in the trinitarian fellowship as a divine archetype for relationships in the political, ecclesial, and personal spheres of human existence. In support of this interpretation, I demonstrated how the concept of trinitarian fellowship systematically unites his theological anthropology, his model of salvation, and the process of sanctification. Without retracing all the steps of my argument, let us recall only the skeleton of this analogy to underscore its liberatory promise, as well as its deficiencies for shaping Christian praxis.

The cornerstone of this trinitarian analogy is Moltmann's *imago Dei* anthropology, which construes human beings as created with the messianic destiny of becoming an *imago Trinitatis*. This divine image is founded on a twofold analogy of relations: the individual person's correspondence to God's loving relationship to creation, and a corporate correspondence to God's inner-trinitarian relations. In other words, human beings fulfill their messianic destiny through two intertwined forms of fellowship: an individual believer's participation in the communion among Father, Son, and Holy Spirit, and his or her transfiguration into an image of this communion with other human beings. To trade on the terms that I coined with respect to Moltmann's doctrine of God, human beings consummate their messianic destiny in becoming free in love to the Other (God) and in becoming those who free others (their fellow creatures) in love.

One of the chief issues that we have wrestled with in assessing Moltmann's trinitarian theology is whether it overestimates the human being's role in her own salvation at the expense of the mediating and atoning work of Christ. The suspicion lingers, especially among Moltmann's Reformed critics, that his social trinitarian theology results in a Pelagianist program for redemption—a kind of moral exemplarism that compromises the Reformed tenets of *sola gratia* and *sola fide* in the Christian life. In response to this doctrinal question, I drew forth several crucial aspects of Moltmann's *imago Dei* anthropology and his view of salvation that reveal such criticisms to be unfounded.

First, I demonstrated how Moltmann's trinitarian analogy of relations is rooted in an "analogy of grace." Our acts of self-giving always occur as a response to God's prior act of self-giving, that is, through God's initiating and preserving a relationship with us through the indwelling fellowship of the Spirit. For this reason, whatever likeness or correspondences to the trinitarian life appear in and among human beings can never be treated as the human being's innate capacity or fixed possession. True human community remains always and everywhere a gift that the trinitarian fellowship bestows freely and that human beings receive in gratitude ever anew.

Second, I drew attention to the fact that human beings consummate their messianic destiny as *imago Trinitatis* only through the reciprocal and continuous work of the Son and the Holy Spirit. If we follow Moltmann's pattern of redemption closely, we discover that human beings must first be conformed to the person of Christ, that is, become *imago Christi*, before they are freed to realize their own works of fellowship in the world. In *The Way of Jesus Christ*, Moltmann goes to great lengths to develop a fully incarnational christology in which Jesus serves as both the exemplar of true humanity (lived trinitarian fellowship) and the divine representative who through cross and resurrection creates the possibility of participation in the divine fellowship. Furthermore, it is only through the Holy Spirit's gift of fellowship that human beings are adopted into the Son's exclusive fellowship with the Father and, in turn, are graced with the possibility of becoming visible images of fellowship with one another. Given this trinitarian pattern of salvation, it becomes difficult, in my view, to substantiate the claim of Moltmann's critics that he sacrifices a theology of grace in order to rely on human beings' innate capacities in the life of faith.

When it came to evaluating the praxiological significance of Moltmann's social trinitarian theology, I argued at once on behalf of its transformative potential and for its more nuanced development. On the positive side, Moltmann constructs what I interpret as a highly flexible social trinitarian analogy in the life of faith. Although his heightened rhetoric often indicates otherwise, Moltmann's social trinitarian doctrine does not narrowly dictate a set of practices, forms of life, or courses of action in the Christian life. This analogy of fellowship functions less like a program and more like an elastic rule of faith— what Miroslav Volf has elsewhere called a "social vision" that can shape a wealth of different relationships from the political to the personal.[2] When interpreted in this manner—as a flexible framework for faith—Moltmann's social trinitarian program holds much promise for contemporary theological anthropology.

First, it offers a powerful theological antidote to the individualism that has gripped most modern views of human personhood. Rather than construing human subjectivity in terms of self-relationality or transcendentality as modern theology has largely done, Moltmann's social trinitarian anthropology defines the human being wholly in interpersonal terms, that is, in terms of its participation in a complex web of social relationships. Like the divine persons, true human persons gain their self-identity in and through their relations with others. At the same time, however, Moltmann's *imago Dei* anthropology does not simply reduce the individual to the sum of her social relations; it secures a separate space for the individual's fellowship with God and for her self-differentiation from other human beings.

Second, Moltmann's social trinitarian analogy recasts the nature of human freedom in robust communal terms as freedom for and with another person. Human beings image trinitarian fellowship not simply by participating in the life of another person but in engendering the freedom of the other. As I illustrated through the practice of open friendship, Moltmann's social trinitarian theology commends a nonhierarchical ethic of social relations. Here the antinomy between the individual's freedom and that of his or her neighbor is overcome in a life of reciprocal giving and receiving, one that is built on mutual respect and acceptance.

Related to this notion of human freedom is the prophetic charge to practice an inclusive ethic of self-giving love to the other. Here the christological dimension of Moltmann's concept of trinitarian fellowship comes to the forefront: human fellowship as self-giving love to the other is patterned after Jesus' ministry and his proclamation of the messianic kingdom. While such self-giving love may take different concrete expressions, for example, as acts of hospitality, repentance, or resistance to social injustice, what unites all of these is their spirit of radical inclusivity and infinite generosity. Such works of love are infused with the same spirit of freedom and passion for life that characterize the triune fellowship.

This leads to a final promising implication of this social trinitarian rule of faith: what I term its doxological-political vision of the Christian life. In coining this term, I seek to emphasize the dynamic unity that exists between an individual's fellowship with God and that with her neighbor. For Moltmann, an individual's fellowship with the triune God, which expresses itself in gratitude and praise, empowers human beings to realize a visible image of that very same fellowship with other human beings in the world. Individuals and communities of faith participate in this doxological fellowship with the Trinity not by cordoning themselves off from the world but by engaging more deeply in its midst—by incarnating the same life-giving fellowship with others that was bountifully bestowed upon them.

Without losing sight of these promising dimensions of Moltmann's social trinitarian theology, I have also pointed to methodological and theological weaknesses in Moltmann's social trinitarian theology that jeopardize its practical relevance. Chief among the methodological concerns is Moltmann's tendency to slip into univocal predication of the same terms to the divine and human spheres, most notably the term *perichoresis*. Moltmann neither develops a theory of divine predication that helps distinguish between his literal and metaphorical use of such terms, nor qualifies in a precise manner how particular trinitarian concepts apply differently to the divine and human realms. As a result, Moltmann's analogy of trinitarian fellowship often obscures the manifold differences that separate human existence from the divine, for example, the temporal and material conditions under which human beings seek to realize their messianic destiny of fellowship with one another. In my view, once Moltmann permits these anthropological constraints to slip from clear sight, his prophetic charge to communities of faith to live out trinitarian fellowship becomes far too idealized to translate into actual praxis.

Related to this methodological concern is the primary theological shortcoming that I singled out in Moltmann's *Messianic Theology*, namely, the absence of a robust theology of sin. As I pointed out in the preceding chapter, Moltmann fails to provide an in-depth analysis of sin—in either its personal or structural forms—that corresponds fully to his social trinitarian vision of the Christian life. Without such an account, Moltmann's analogy of trinitarian fellowship appears not only to underestimate the fragility of human existence but also to obscure the destructive forces that threaten human fellowship in the world. In short, his analogy of fellowship risks falling prey to an idolatry critique, namely, of assuming too readily correspondences between the divine life and human communities. Without recalling the ever-present dialectic of sin in the midst of grace, his analogy of fellowship loses much of its prophetic potential to expose concrete evils in the world and to awaken hope for their resistance and amelioration.

While Moltmann does not develop this line of argumentation himself, his notion of trinitarian fellowship has yet untapped potential for describing various manifestations of sin in the life of faith. As I have demonstrated in the previous chapter, sin understood as a fall out of trinitarian fellowship is an elastic metaphor that encompasses both individual and collective forms of sin as well as its active and passive dimensions. Moreover, conceiving of sin as a fall out of fellowship underscores the theological root of sin, namely, separation from one's messianic destiny of fellowship with God and one's neighbor.

To conclude this assessment of Moltmann's contributions to a contemporary trinitarian theology of love, it seems most fitting to recall one of the author's statements about the nature of his theology and its highest aims. In an autobiographical reflection that he penned in 1996, Moltmann characterized his understanding of the theological task in these terms: "For me, theology is *imagination for the Kingdom of God in the world and for the world in the Kingdom of God*. As Kingdom of God theology, it is necessarily public theology and participates in the sufferings of this time, formulating the guiding memories and hopes on behalf of one's contemporaries."[3] With these words Moltmann echoes one of the classic aims of Christian theology, one that he shares with Augustine, Aquinas, Calvin, and Barth: true theology takes its cue from its divine subject. Above all, theology seeks to conform itself to the nature of the God about whom it strives to speak. For Moltmann, this means orienting his theological vision to the coming kingdom of God, a kingdom that promises joyful participation and fellowship to all of creation. It is a kingdom that stirs hope ever anew for the world's transformation and awakens restlessness and resistance to the concrete sufferings of the world.

Moltmann's vision of this coming kingdom has both chastened and inspired him throughout his career. On the one hand, it chastened him for the illusion of being able to create an unassailable theological system. Yet it also inspired him to venture a theology that is always under construction and constant revision—one that is experimental and provocative, fragmentary and provisional. At the same time that Moltmann delights in these creative possibilities of the coming kingdom, he commits to writing a theology that is responsive and responsible to the issues pressing upon the church and society in his day. Envisioning theology as imagination for the world in the kingdom of God means keeping his sights trained on this world, on identifying its sources of conflict and of suffering, and working toward their amelioration in light of God's promised renewal of all creation. Finally, kingdom of God theology means taking his theological proposals into the public square for dialogue about the future shape of the world with the hope of sparking new possibilities and engendering concrete change.

In light of his prophetic vision of theology's tasks, Moltmann's most significant contribution to contemporary theological debate lies, in my view, neither in his conceptual innovations to Christian doctrine nor in his emancipatory agenda for the Christian life. Rather, his lasting contribution lies in returning the trinitarian God to the horizon of contemporary theology and in challenging the coming generation to pursue this divine pilgrimage of love in history. His contribution lies in opening a broad theological space in which the fellowship of the kingdom might be experienced anew. To the degree that his trinitarian theology not just gives rise to thought and to action but awakens passion for the kingdom, Moltmann achieves the highest aim of theology—the true wisdom of drawing believers into the heart of trinitarian fellowship.

Notes

CHAPTER I

Epigraph from Augustine, *The Trinity*, ed. John E. Rotelle, trans. Edmund Hill (Brooklyn, NY: New City Press, 1990), 251.

1. Nicholas Lash, "Considering the Trinity," *Modern Theology* 2 (1986): 183.

2. Leonard Hodgson, *The Doctrine of the Trinity*, Croall Lectures, 1942–43 (New York: Charles Scribner's Sons, 1944), 176–177.

3. Karl Rahner, *The Trinity*, trans. Joseph Donceel (New York: Herder and Herder, 1970), 10–11.

4. Catherine Mowry LaCugna, "Re-conceiving the Trinity as the Mystery of Salvation," *Scottish Journal of Theology* 38 (1985): 1. For a comprehensive argument on the "displacement of God" in modernity, see Colin E. Gunton, *The One, the Three and the Many: God, Creation and the Culture of Modernity*, Bampton Lectures 1992 (Cambridge: Cambridge University Press, 1993), esp. 28–34. Gunton casts a sweeping indictment against Western thought by arguing that the displacement of God by human reason and will in modernity is the inevitable outcome of its nontrinitarian understanding of divine being since antiquity.

5. Cf. LaCugna, "Re-conceiving the Trinity," 16. For her part, LaCugna characterizes the reigning contemporary options in the concept of God as "unitarian" and "Christomonistic" (ibid.). See also the similar remarks on this unacknowledged nontrinitarianism in the contemporary doctrine of God, specifically with regard to the neglect of the Holy Spirit, in Werner Jeanrond, "The Question of God Today," in *The Christian Understanding of God Today*, Theological Colloquium on the Occasion of the 400th Anniversary of the Foundation of Trinity College, Dublin, ed. James M. Byrne (Dublin: Columbia Press, 1993), 13.

6. We might take Reinhold Niebuhr as a classic twentieth-century ex-

ample of a theistic perspective on divine love. Although Niebuhr specifies the love of God in christological terms as self-sacrificial love (*agape*), nonetheless he describes this love in nontrinitarian terms as the activity of the single subject, God. See, for example, his discussion of *agape* in *Human Destiny*, vol. 2 of *The Nature and Destiny of Man: A Christian Interpretation* (New York: Charles Scribner's Sons, 1943), 68–97.

7. Vincent Brümmer, *The Model of Love: A Study in Philosophical Theology* (Cambridge: Cambridge University Press, 1993), 3.

8. Except for historical references to the significance of the Trinity for Bernard of Clairvaux, Brümmer refers to trinitarian doctrine only at one other point, namely, to raise the specter of tritheism in any social doctrine of the Trinity. Cf. ibid., 71, 194, 237–238.

9. Ibid., 33.

10. Sallie McFague, *Models of God: Theology for an Ecological, Nuclear Age* (Philadelphia: Fortress Press, 1987).

11. Ibid., 184.

12. Ibid., 224 n. 5.

13. For an overview of the current diversity in the trinitarian debate, see Ronald J. Feenstra and Cornelius Plantinga Jr., eds., *Trinity, Incarnation, and Atonement: Philosophical and Theological Essays* (Notre Dame, IN: University of Notre Dame Press, 1989); David Tracy, "The Hermeneutics of Naming God," *Irish Theological Quarterly* 57 (1991): 257; Ingolf U. Dalferth, *Der auferweckte Gekreuzigte: Zur Grammatik der Christologie* (Tübingen: J. C. B. Mohr, 1994), 187–197.

14. The term "modern theism" (or Enlightenment theism) appears frequently in contemporary theological literature, but it is applied with an extremely fluid meaning. For our purposes, Elisabeth Johnson provides a good working definition of the term: "It signifies the so-called natural knowledge of God arrived at primarily through philosophical inference, or that idea of God which separates the one God from knowledge of God's Trinity, places consideration of this one God first, and views this God alone in 'himself' apart from any *kenosis*, incarnation, self-communication in grace, or other self-involving activity with the world" (Elisabeth A. Johnson, *She Who Is: The Mystery of God in Feminist Theological Discourse* [New York: Crossroad, 1992], 19). See also Herbert Vorgrimler, "Recent Critiques of Theism," in *A Personal God?* ed. Edward Schillebeeckx and Bas van Iersel (New York: Seabury Press, 1977), 23–34.

15. Immanuel Kant and Friedrich Schleiermacher are most frequently cited as representative of the Enlightenment viewpoint that the Trinity is morally and practically irrelevant to the Christian faith. See, for example, Jürgen Moltmann, *The Trinity and the Kingdom: The Doctrine of God*, trans. Margaret Kohl, 1st HarperCollins pbk. ed. (San Francisco: HarperCollins, 1991), 2–9.

16. Catherine Mowry LaCugna and Killian McDonnell, "Returning from 'The Far Country': Theses for a Contemporary Trinitarian Theology," *Scottish Journal of Theology* 41 (1988): 201.

17. Catherine Mowry LaCugna, *God for Us: The Trinity and the Christian Life* (San Francisco: HarperCollins, 1991), 1. Following Karl Rahner's lead, LaCugna traces the current defeat of the doctrine of the Trinity to its uprooting from the economy of salvation and the one-sided focus of the doctrine on God's inner life. For this argument, see ibid., esp. 8–13, 209–241.

18. Fueling these debates about trinitarian praxis is a wide-ranging debate

among systematic theologians and theological educators about the meaning of Christian praxis and the role of Christian practices in second-order theological discourse and in the catechesis of Christian believers. For an excellent overview of the history of the term "praxis" and its multiple significations in contemporary theology, see Rebecca S. Chopp, "Praxis," in *The New Dictionary of Catholic Spirituality*, ed. Michael Downey (Collegeville, MN: Liturgical Press, 1993), 756–764. See also Chopp's superb treatment of the methodological issues raised by this "turn to praxis" in political and liberation theologians in *The Praxis of Suffering: An Interpretation of Liberation and Political Theologies* (Maryknoll, NY: Orbis, 1986). For a contrasting paradigm on the relationships among Christian practices, catechesis, and doctrinal theology, see Ellen Charry, *By the Renewing of Your Minds: The Pastoral Function of Christian Doctrine* (New York: Oxford University Press, 1997).

19. For an application of the doctrine to personal ethics, see L. Gregory Jones, *Transformed Judgment: Toward a Trinitarian Account of the Moral Life* (Notre Dame, IN: University of Notre Dame Press, 1990), as well as his recent book, *Embodying Forgiveness: A Theological Analysis* (Grand Rapids, MI: Eerdmans, 1995). For a trinitarian theology of culture, see Gunton, *The One, the Three and the Many*.

20. On the implications of the doctrine of the Trinity for social ethics, see LaCugna, *God for Us*, esp. chap. 10. For a trinitarian ecclesiology, see Miroslav Volf, *After Our Likeness: The Church as the Image of the Trinity* (Grand Rapids, MI: Eerdmans, 1998).

21. Elisabeth A. Johnson, "To Let the Symbol Sing Again," *Theology Today* 53 (1997): 300. On this surprising consensus on the practical relevance of the doctrine, see Ronald J. Feenstra and Cornelius Plantinga Jr., introduction to *Trinity, Incarnation, and Atonement: Philosophical and Theological Essays*, ed. Ronald J. Feenstra and Cornelius Plantinga Jr. (Notre Dame, IN: University of Notre Dame Press, 1989), 5.

22. Jürgen Moltmann, *The Crucified God: The Cross of Christ as the Foundation and Criticism of Christian Theology*, trans. R. A. Wilson and John Bowden, preface to the pbk. edition trans. Margaret Kohl, 1st HarperCollins pbk. ed. (New York: HarperCollins, 1991), 7–31.

23. Moltmann, *Trinity and the Kingdom*, 131.

24. Ibid., 65.

25. Jürgen Moltmann, "My Theological Career," in *History and the Triune God: Contributions to Trinitarian Theology*, trans. John Bowden (New York: Crossroad, 1992), 167.

26. Jürgen Moltmann, " 'The Fellowship of the Holy Spirit': On Trinitarian Pneumatology," in *History and the Triune God: Contributions to Trinitarian Theology*, trans. John Bowden (New York: Crossroad, 1992), 60.

27. Cf. Jürgen Moltmann, *God in Creation: A New Theology of Creation and the Spirit of God*, Gifford Lectures 1984–85, trans. Margaret Kohl, 1st HarperCollins pbk. ed. (San Francisco: HarperCollins, 1985); *The Way of Jesus Christ: Christology in Messianic Dimensions*, trans. Margaret Kohl, 1st Fortress Press ed. (Minneapolis, MN: Fortress Press, 1993); *The Spirit of Life: A Universal Affirmation*, trans. Margaret Kohl (Minneapolis, MN: Fortress Press, 1992); *The Coming of God: Christian Eschatology*, trans. Margaret Kohl (Minneapolis, MN: Fortress Press, 1996); *Experiences in Theology: Ways and Forms of Christian Theology*, trans. Margaret Kohl (Minneapolis, MN: Fortress Press, 2000).

28. Most discussions of the contemporary debate in trinitarian theology present Moltmann as the most significant representative of a social doctrine of the Trinity. See, for example, Jeanrond, "Question of God Today," 14–17; John Milbank, "The Second Difference: For a Trinitarianism without Reserve," *Modern Theology* 2 (1986): 213–234; John J. O'Donnell, "The Trinity as Divine Community: A Critical Reflection upon Recent Theological Developments," *Gregorianum* 69 (1988): 5–34; Feenstra and Plantinga, introduction to *Trinity, Incarnation, and Atonement*, 6–7. Two excellent brief introductions to Moltmann's theology and its contribution to contemporary theological discussion are Richard Bauckham, "Jürgen Moltmann," in vol. 1 of *The Modern Theologians: An Introduction to Christian Theology in the Twentieth Century*, ed. David F. Ford (Oxford: Basil Blackwell, 1989), 293–310; Francis Schüssler Fiorenza, introduction to *Faith and the Future: Essays on Theology, Solidarity, and Modernity*, by Johann-Baptist Metz and Jürgen Moltmann (Maryknoll, NY: Orbis, 1995), xi–xvii. For a survey of the monographs on Moltmann's theology through 1987, see Jürgen Moltmann, *Bibliographie*, comp. Dieter Ising with the collaboration of Günther Geisthardt and Adelbert Schloz (Munich: Chr. Kaiser, 1987), 71–77.

29. One glance at the trinitarian articles and books that have been published in the last ten years demonstrates the vast impact that Moltmann's work has had on the international theological scene. Leonardo Boff, Paul Fiddes, Elisabeth Johnson, Catherine Mowry LaCugna, Alistair I. McFayden, and Miroslav Volf are only a small sampling of the authors who note their indebtedness to Moltmann's trinitarian theology.

30. McFague, *Models of God*, 223.

31. Alan J. Torrance, *Persons in Communion: An Essay on Trinitarian Description and Human Participation* (Edinburgh: T. & T. Clark, 1996), 310–313.

32. David S. Cunningham, *These Three Are One: The Practice of Trinitarian Theology* (Oxford: Basil Blackwell, 1998), 43.

33. Jeanrond, "Question of God Today," 16.

34. Karen Kilby, "Perichoresis and Projection: Problems with Social Doctrines of the Trinity," *New Blackfriars* 81, no. 956 (Oct. 2000): 432–445.

35. Moltmann, *Trinity and the Kingdom*, 192. Here I am taking up and extending Paul Ricoeur's wager on behalf of religious symbols giving rise to thought to include the critical turn to praxis. See Paul Ricoeur, *The Symbolism of Evil* (Boston: Beacon Press, 1967), 347–357.

36. For the terms "constative" and "commissive force," see Vincent Brümmer's analysis of how religious concepts and models of God function in *Model of Love*, 17.

37. Here I adapt and expand the notion of "divine analogy" as developed by the late British theologian and political theorist David Nicholls. Nicholls uses this term exclusively to refer to the correspondences between a theologian's concept of God and the structures of the political order. See David Nicholls, *Deity and Domination: Images of God and the State in the Nineteenth and Twentieth Centuries* (London: Routledge, 1989), esp. 5–30, 232–245.

38. Moltmann, *Experiences in Theology*, xv.

39. In highlighting these three motifs, I take my cue from an autobiographical essay written in 1985, in which Moltmann gave one of his few extended reflections on his theological method. There he summed up his theology this way: "I am attempting to reflect on a theology which has: –a biblical foundation, –an eschatological orientation, –a political responsibility. In and under that it is certainly a theology in pain and

joy at God himself, a theology of constant wonder" (Moltmann, "My Theological Career," 182).

40. Ibid., 167–169. For a critical discussion of Moltmann's early biblical approach, see the various contributions to Wolf-Dieter Marsch, ed., *Diskussion über die "Theologie der Hoffnung" von Jürgen Moltmann* (Munich: Chr. Kaiser, 1967); Christopher Morse, *The Logic of Promise in Moltmann's Theology* (Philadelphia: Fortress Press, 1979).

41. See Moltmann's first defense of the scriptural root of the doctrine in his "Antwort auf die Kritik an 'Der gekreuzigte Gott,' " in *Diskussion über Jürgen Moltmanns Buch "Der gekreuzigte Gott,"* ed. Michael Welker (Munich: Chr. Kaiser, 1979), 176–177.

42. For Karl Barth's scriptural root of the doctrine of the Trinity in terms of lordship, see *The Doctrine of the Word of God: Prolegomena to Church Dogmatics, Volume I/1,* trans. G. W. Bromiley, 2nd ed. (Edinburgh: T. & T. Clark, 1975), 302–347. For Moltmann's exegetical disagreement with Barth on this point, see Moltmann, *Trinity and the Kingdom,* 63–64.

43. Moltmann, *Crucified God,* 246.

44. Moltmann, *Trinity and the Kingdom,* 61–65.

45. John J. O'Donnell, *Trinity and Temporality: The Christian Doctrine of God in the Light of Process Theology and the Theology of Hope* (Oxford: Oxford University Press, 1983), 115.

46. Although Moltmann does not ally himself explicitly with the narrative theology of the Yale school, his Barthian emphasis on the realism of the scriptural witness and his suspicion of speculative concepts distorting the scriptural witness bear striking similarities to this approach. At the same time, Moltmann's use of narrative also resembles closely that of other political liberation theologies. As Rebecca Chopp notes, Moltmann appeals to narrative not only "to retrieve the Christian tradition" but also "to narrate the dangerous memories of suffering and to effect conversion and transformation" (Chopp, *Praxis of Suffering,* 141).

47. Moltmann, "Antwort auf die Kritik an 'Der gekreuzigte Gott,' " 186–187 (trans. mine): "Will man nun diesen verschiedenen Gesichtspunkten aus der trinitarischen Geschichte Gottes—der Sendung, der Hingabe, der Auferstehung und der Verherrlichung—gerecht werden, dann darf man nicht über nur einer geschichtlichen Erfahrung der Trinität eine entsprechende 'immanente Trinität' als metaphysischen Hintergrund errichten. Um die Fülle des trinitarischen Lebens Gottes umfassend zu verstehen, muß man alle geschichtlichen Erfahrungen integrieren. . . . Das ist dann eine Trinitätslehre mit—abstrakt formuliert—veränderlichen Vektoren. Ihre Entfaltung steht noch bevor."

48. Moltmann, *Spirit of Life,* 290.

49. Moltmann, *Crucified God,* 238 (emphasis added).

50. Cf. Moltmann, "My Theological Career," 166.

51. Dietrich Bonhoeffer, *Letters and Papers from Prison,* enlarged ed. (London: SCM Press, 1971), 361.

52. Moltmann, *Crucified God,* x.

53. Jürgen Moltmann, *Theology of Hope: On the Ground and the Implications of a Christian Eschatology,* trans. James W. Leitch, 10th ed. (New York: Harper and Row, 1983), 179.

54. Moltmann, "My Theological Career," 170.

55. Moltmann, *Crucified God*, 249.

56. Moltmann, *Trinity and the Kingdom*, 157 (emphasis added).

57. Ibid., 3.

58. For this point, see Richard Bauckham, *The Theology of Jürgen Moltmann* (Edinburgh: T. & T. Clark, 1995), 166–170.

59. For this criticism, see Kilby, "Perichoresis and Projection," esp. 435–436.

60. On occasion Moltmann himself makes use of this classical terminology. See, for example, *Trinity and the Kingdom*, 7. See also his "Introduction: Some Questions about the Doctrine of the Trinity Today," in *History and the Triune God: Contributions to Trinitarian Theology*, trans. John Bowden (New York: Crossroad, 1992), xiii. See as well Richard Bauckham's insightful remarks on Moltmann's fundamental orientation "to praxis and doxology" in "Jürgen Moltmann," 296.

61. Moltmann, "My Theological Career," 166.

62. Ibid., 167.

63. Moltmann, *Theology of Hope*, 304.

64. Moltmann, *Experiences in Theology*, 116. For an overview of his early political theology of the 1970s, see his essays collected in *Politische Theologie—Politische Ethik* (Munich: Chr. Kaiser, 1984). Rebecca Chopp offers an excellent interpretation of his political theology in *Praxis of Suffering*, 100–117.

65. Jürgen Moltmann, "Political Theology," *Theology Today* 28 (Apr. 1971): 7.

66. Jürgen Moltmann, "Toward a Political Hermeneutic of the Gospel," in *Religion, Revolution, and the Future*, trans. M. Douglas Meeks (New York: Charles Scribner's Sons, 1969), 98.

67. Moltmann, *Experiences in Theology*, 117. Much of these concrete proposals emerged only in the volumes of his *Messianic Theology*, where Moltmann aligned his theology with the political system of democratic socialism and in support of a human rights agenda.

68. Moltmann, *Crucified God*, 329–332.

69. Ibid., 25.

70. Moltmann, "My Theological Career," 179.

71. Jürgen Moltmann, *Theology and Joy*, trans. Reinhard Ulrich (London: SCM Press, 1973); cf. also his more recent reference to the Westminster Catechism in *Experiences in Theology*, 26.

72. See Moltmann, *Trinity and the Kingdom*, 191–193.

73. Ibid., 9. In his most recent writings, Moltmann cautiously speaks of this doxological form of trinitarian faith as mystical experience. See, for example, his remarks in *Spirit of Life*, 198–213.

74. Moltmann, *Trinity and the Kingdom*, 7.

75. Ibid., 152.

76. Ibid., 9.

77. For this "turn to praxis," see Chopp, *Praxis of Suffering*, esp. 139–142.

78. Moltmann, *Trinity and the Kingdom*, 7.

79. Moltmann, *Experiences in Theology*, 294–295.

80. Ibid., 294.

81. Ibid., 295.

82. Chopp, *Praxis of Suffering*, 139–142.

83. For examples of such an ideology critique, see in addition to Kilby, "Pericho-

resis and Projection," James Mackey's acerbic remarks in his essay "Are There Christian Alternatives to Trinitarian Thinking?" in *The Christian Understanding of God Today*, Theological Colloquium on the Occasion of the 400th Anniversary of the Foundation of Trinity College, Dublin, ed. James M. Byrne (Dublin: Columbia Press, 1993), 66–75.

84. Moltmann, *Trinity and the Kingdom*, 4.

85. Ibid., 7, 9.

86. Ibid., 9.

87. Moltmann, *Experiences in Theology*, xvi.

88. Ibid., 25.

89. An exception to this in the North American scene is Douglas Meeks, who highlights Moltmann's "restless imagination" and his desire for theology to regain such "suffering and joyful imagination." See Meeks's excellent review article, "Jürgen Moltmann's *Systematic Contributions to Theology*," *Religious Studies Review* 22, no. 2 (1996): 95–102; here 95. In the European context, see also Geiko Müller-Fahrenholz's excellent chapter on mysticism in Moltmann's theology in Müller-Fahrenholz, *The Kingdom and the Power: The Theology of Jürgen Moltmann*, trans. John Bowden (London: SCM Press, 2000), 230–244; and Richard Bauckham's similar discussion in his *Theology of Jürgen Moltmann*, 213–247.

90. Moltmann, *Experiences of Theology*, xxi.

91. Bauckham, "Jürgen Moltmann," 308. For further criticism on the lack of logical precision in Moltmann's thinking, see also Ernstpeter Maurer, "Tendenzen neuerer Trinitätslehre," *Verkündigung und Forschung* 39, no. 2 (1994): 20.

92. See Moltmann, *Bibliographie*, in which already in 1987 more than five hundred separate listings of Moltmann's essays and books had been compiled.

93. The two significant and indeed related developments in Moltmann's trinitarian theology since his publication of *The Trinity and the Kingdom* (1980) are his intensified focus on pneumatology and on a holistic consideration of nature and the role of the body in theology. See his comments to this effect in *Spirit of Life*, x–xiii, and Jürgen Moltmann, "The Adventure of Theological Ideas," *Religious Studies Review* 22 (1996): 104.

94. Moltmann, *Trinity and the Kingdom*, xii.

95. Cf. ibid., vii-ix, and his more recent remarks to that effect in his "Adventure of Theological Ideas," 103.

96. Moltmann, "Antwort auf die Kritik an 'Der gekreuzigte Gott,'" 166–167 (trans. mine and emphasis added): "Mit diesen drei Büchern habe ich in der jeweiligen geistigen, theologischen und politischen Situation etwas Bestimmtes gewollt. Sie sind aus der Zeit für die Zeit geschrieben und also als Theologie im Kontext des gegenwärtigen Lebens zu verstehen. Man hat sie darum mit Recht als eher pastoral und prophetisch denn professoral und systematisch charakterisiert."

97. Moltmann, *Experiences in Theology*, xvi.

98. Moltmann, *Spirit of Life*, 301.

99. Moltmann, "My Theological Career," 180.

100. Moltmann, "Adventure of Theological Ideas," 102–103.

101. Daniel Day Williams, *The Spirit and the Forms of Love* (New York: Harper and Row, 1968), 212.

102. See Moltmann's critical remarks about the incompatibility of process theol-

ogy's bipolar concept of God with a Christian trinitarian perspective in *Crucified God*, 255–256.

103. Moltmann, *Spirit of Life*, 301.

CHAPTER 2

1. On this shift in Moltmann's theological approach, see Richard Bauckham, *Moltmann: Messianic Theology in the Making* (Basingstoke, UK: Marshall Pickering, 1987), 2. See also Moltmann's comments in his "My Theological Career," 176, and "Adventure of Theological Ideas," 102–103.

2. For an in-depth analysis of Moltmann's sources in this early period, see M. Douglas Meeks, *Origins of the Theology of Hope*, with a foreword by Jürgen Moltmann (Philadelphia: Fortress Press, 1974); Bauckham, *Moltmann: Messianic Theology*, 3–22.

3. Bauckham, *Theology of Jürgen Moltmann*, 33; cf. ibid., 4–5.

4. Ibid., 82. On Barth's christocentrism and its influence on Moltmann's theology, cf. Moltmann's remarks in his foreword to *Origins of the Theology of Hope*, by M. Douglas Meeks (Philadelphia: Fortress Press, 1974), ix–xii, esp. xii.

5. Moltmann, "Adventure of Theological Ideas," 104.

6. Moltmann, "My Theological Career," 168.

7. For this interpretation, see Meeks's foreword to *The Experiment Hope*, by Jürgen Moltmann, ed. and trans. M. Douglas Meeks (Philadelphia: Fortress Press, 1975), xi. Although Moltmann had not planned his early trilogy to follow this biblical pattern, he agrees later with his colleague's interpretation of its biblical trajectory. See Moltmann, "My Theological Career," 176.

8. See the critical responses collected in Marsch, *Diskussion über die "Theologie der Hoffnung."*

9. See Meeks's excellent analysis of the cultural situation at the time of Moltmann's first work in Meeks, *Origins of the Theology of Hope*, 4–7.

10. Moltmann, "My Theological Career," 170.

11. See Bauckham, *Theology of Jürgen Moltmann*, 30. For an excellent overview of the "school of hope," see Walter H. Capps, *Time Invades the Cathedral: Tensions in the School of Hope*, with a foreword by Jürgen Moltmann (Philadelphia: Fortress Press, 1972).

12. Jürgen Moltmann, "Hope and History," in *Religion, Revolution, and the Future*, trans. M. Douglas Meeks (New York: Charles Scribner's Sons, 1969), 200.

13. Moltmann, *Theology of Hope*, 16. Moltmann makes this connection explicit some pages later, when he quotes approvingly one of Barth's dramatic statements from the second edition of his Romans commentary, "If Christianity be not altogether and unreservedly eschatology, there remains in it no relationship whatever to Christ" (Karl Barth, *Der Römerbrief*, 2nd ed. [(n.p.), 1922], 298 [English translation, *The Epistle to the Romans*, trans. E. C. Hoskyns ([n.p.], 1933), 314], quoted in Moltmann, *Theology of Hope*, 39).

14. See Bauckham, *Theology of Jürgen Moltmann*, 29. During this period Moltmann sought to revive the significance of dialectical theology's eschatological critique for the post–World War II theological scene by republishing a collection of these theologians' early essays. See his remarks to that effect in his foreword to *Karl Barth—*

Heinrich Barth—Emil Brunner, pt. 1 of *Anfänge der dialektischen Theologie*, ed. Jürgen Moltmann, 5th ed. (Munich: Chr. Kaiser, 1985), ix–xviii.

15. Moltmann, *Theology of Hope*, 57.

16. See Moltmann's detailed discussion of the contemporary Old Testament scholarship in ibid., 95–138.

17. Ibid., 42.

18. Ibid., 30.

19. Ibid., 103.

20. See ibid., 18.

21. Ibid, 163. Despite Moltmann's emphasis on the Jewish roots of resurrection hope, he defends the uniqueness of the resurrection promise offered in the raising of Jesus from the dead. Employing a Pauline law and gospel distinction, Moltmann contrasts the conditional promises given to Israel under the law with the resurrection as a universal and unconditional promise for the ultimate triumph over the evil and suffering of the world. For this point, see esp. ibid., 147.

22. Ibid., 196.

23. Ibid., 198.

24. Ibid., 200.

25. Ibid., 21.

26. Jürgen Moltmann, *Umkehr zur Zukunft* (Munich: Siebenstern Taschenbuch, 1970), 10. For an excellent discussion of Bloch's influence on Moltmann's work, see Meeks, *Origins of the Theology of Hope*, 16–19. For Moltmann's critical discussions of Bloch's philosophy of hope, see in particular his essays "Hope and Confidence: A Conversation with Ernst Bloch," in *Religion, Revolution, and the Future*, trans. M. Douglas Meeks (New York: Charles Scribner's Sons, 1969), 148–176; "Ernst Bloch and Hope without Faith," in *The Experiment Hope*, ed. and trans. M. Douglas Meeks (Philadelphia: Fortress Press, 1972), 30–43; and " 'Where There Is Hope, There Is Religion,' " also in *The Experiment Hope*, 15–29.

27. In my view, Richard Bauckham rightly compares Moltmann's critical appropriation of Bloch's philosophy to Augustine's use of Neoplatonist philosophy, or Aquinas's adaptation of Aristotelianism. See Bauckham, *Moltmann: Messianic Theology*, 9.

28. See Moltmann, " 'Where There Is Hope,' " 19, and "Hope and Confidence," 150–151.

29. Moltmann, "Ernst Bloch and Hope without Faith," 34.

30. Moltmann, " 'Where There Is Hope,' " 25.

31. Moltmann, "Hope and History," 209.

32. Cf. ibid., 209–210; Jürgen Moltmann, "Theology as Eschatology," in *The Future of Hope: Theology as Eschatology*, ed. Frederick Herzog (New York: Herder and Herder, 1970), 13–15.

33. See Moltmann's summary and discussion of these charges in Jürgen Moltmann, "Antwort auf die Kritik der Theologie der Hoffnung," in *Diskussion über die "Theologie der Hoffnung" von Jürgen Moltmann*, ed. Wolf-Dieter Marsch (Munich: Chr. Kaiser, 1967), 221–229.

34. See Moltmann's remarks in "Theology as Eschatology," 11–16, and his "Introduction to the 'Theology of Hope,' " in *The Experiment Hope*, ed. and trans. M. Douglas Meeks (Philadelphia: Fortress Press, 1972), 50–53.

35. Excerpted from Moltmann, "Antwort auf die Kritik der Theologie der Hoffnung," 210–211 (trans. mine): "Was sein wird, entspringt aus dem ewigen Werde- und Zeugungsprozeß des Seins. Es ist Aktualisierung von Urpotenz."

36. Moltmann, *Theology of Hope*, 34.

37. Bauckham, *Moltmann: Messianic Theology*, 91.

38. Moltmann, "Hope and History," 210.

39. See, e.g., Moltmann, *Theology of Hope*, 34. In these passing references to Christian love as the fruit of faith, Moltmann usually contrasts Christian *agape* to *philia*. Here one sees an early hint of his later concept of divine love as love for the "unlike" or opposite. See later discussion of this concept in *The Crucified God*.

40. Moltmann, "My Theological Career," 169–170.

41. On God being known through God's faithfulness to his promises in history, see especially Moltmann, *Theology of Hope*, 117–118.

42. Moltmann, "Introduction to the 'Theology of Hope,'" 47.

43. Moltmann, "Hope and History," 207.

44. Moltmann, *Theology of Hope*, 36.

45. Moltmann, *Crucified God*, 204.

46. Ibid., 5.

47. For a summary of these critical responses, see Wolf-Dieter Marsch's "Zur Einleitung: Wohin—jenseits der Alternativen," in *Diskussion über die "Theologie der Hoffnung" von Jürgen Moltmann*, ed. Wolf-Dieter Marsch (Munich: Chr. Kaiser, 1967), 7–18.

48. See Moltmann, "Antwort auf die Kritik der Theologie der Hoffnung," 225.

49. Moltmann, *Crucified God*, 2. See also Jürgen Moltmann, "Why Am I a Christian?" in *Experiences of God*, trans. Margaret Kohl (Philadelphia: Fortress Press, 1980), 13–15.

50. Moltmann, *Crucified God*, 7.

51. Ibid., 17. See also Moltmann's personal recollections of that time in his autobiographical essay, "My Theological Career," 171–172.

52. Moltmann, "My Theological Career," 165–166.

53. Moltmann, *Crucified God*, 252.

54. For these terms, see the titles of chapters 4 and 5 of *The Crucified God*, respectively.

55. For Moltmann's complete discussion of the various meanings of the cross, see ibid., 126–199.

56. Ibid., 149.

57. Ibid., 150–151 (emphasis added).

58. Ibid., 149.

59. Ibid., 184.

60. Ibid., 151–152.

61. Ibid., 181–183.

62. Ibid., 185.

63. Ibid., 192. In particular, Moltmann cites Rom. 8:32, Gal. 2:20, and 2 Cor. 5:19 on the soteriological significance of God's giving up the Son for humankind.

64. Moltmann, *Crucified God*, 192–193 (emphasis added).

65. Ibid., 193.

66. Ibid., 211.

67. Ibid., 27, with quotation from F. W. J. Schelling, *Über das Wesen der menschlichen Freiheit* ([n.p.]: Reclam, 1809), 8913–8915.

68. For this criticism, see Richard Bauckham, "Moltmanns Eschatologie des Kreuzes," in *Diskussion über Jürgen Moltmanns Buch "Der gekreuzigte Gott,"* ed. Michael Welker (Munich: Chr. Kaiser, 1979), 47. For similar criticisms of Moltmann's lack of precision in his dialectical principle of knowledge, see also Walter Kasper, "Revolution im Gottesverständnis? Zur Situation des ökumenischen Dialogs nach Jürgen Moltmanns 'Der gekreuzigte Gott,'" also in *Diskussion über Jürgen Moltmanns Buch "Der gekreuzigte Gott,"* 143–144, and Moltmann's response in "Antwort auf die Kritik an 'Der gekreuzigte Gott,'" 187–189.

69. Bauckham, *Moltmann: Messianic Theology,* 69. I agree with Bauckham's criticism that by subsuming the cross-event under this general dialectical principle, Moltmann obscures the precise meaning and the biblical source of his thinking on divine love in the cross-event. In turn, this dialectical principle contributed to the growing impression that the author was subjecting divine revelation to a predetermined schema of dialectical Hegelian philosophy. See my later discussion of this critique.

70. Moltmann, *Crucified God,* 26.

71. Ibid., 212.

72. Ibid., 28.

73. Ibid.

74. Ibid., 27–28.

75. Moltmann criticizes especially Karl Barth (as well as Karl Rahner) for interpreting the cross-event "*theo*logically" and not in a sufficiently "trinitarian direction" (ibid., 203). Although Moltmann acknowledges that Barth does integrate the cross-event into his understanding of God in the later christological sections of the *Church Dogmatics,* the author objects to Barth's distinction between God in himself and God in Christ in his doctrine of election as "a trans-christological proviso" (ibid., 280 n. 16), which protects the cross-event from having any real significance for the eternal being of God.

76. Ibid., 204.

77. Ibid., 237.

78. Cf. Rahner, *Trinity.*

79. Moltmann, *Crucified God,* 239.

80. Ibid., 237.

81. Ibid., 240. Although in his later work Moltmann distances his position from that of Rahner's, the author's early trinitarian theology reflects the unmistakable influence of Rahner's analysis of the problems besetting the doctrine in contemporary theology. Indeed, Moltmann defends his own method of procedure as a response to the problems that Rahner had already identified in the doctrine. See, for example, ibid., 245.

82. Ibid., 207.

83. In *The Trinity and the Kingdom,* Moltmann will modify this position by restoring a version of the distinction to defend the eternal nature of the trinitarian relations. Nevertheless, he never retreats from the position that the cross-event has ontological implications for the trinitarian nature of God. See my further discussion of this in chapter 3.

84. Moltmann, *Crucified God,* 205.

85. Ibid., 243.

86. Ibid., 207. Moltmann substitutes this idea of a "death in God" for the *theopaschite* expression of the "death of God," on the grounds not only that it explains the cross-event more satisfactorily but also that it also avoids the paradoxes which a purely monotheistic concept draws one into. For a criticism of this distinction (which Moltmann eventually drops in *The Trinity and the Kingdom*), see Paul S. Fiddes, *The Creative Suffering of God* (Oxford: Clarendon Press, 1988), 195–200.

87. Moltmann, *Crucified God*, 246.

88. On this issue of division within the Godhead, see Bauckham, *Theology of Jürgen Moltmann*, 55; Fiddes, *Creative Suffering of God*, 196–197, 202; Bertold Klappert, "Die Gottverlassenheit Jesu und der gekreuzigte Gott. Beobachtungen zum Problem einer theologia crucis in der Christologie der Gegenwart," and Hermannus Heiko Miskotte, "Das Leiden ist in Gott. Über Jürgen Moltmanns trinitarische Kreuzestheologie," in *Diskussion über Jürgen Moltmanns Buch"Der gekreuzigte Gott,"* ed. Michael Welker (Munich: Chr. Kaiser, 1979), 69–73 and 78–81, respectively.

89. Moltmann, *Crucified God*, 243–244. Miskotte remains unconvinced that this solves the problem of divine unity. He remarks that despite this stated unity of will, Moltmann's accent is still on the division or *statis* in God. See Miskotte, "Das Leiden ist in Gott," 79–80.

90. Moltmann, *Crucified God*, 245 (emphasis added).

91. Ibid., 248–249.

92. Moltmann did subsequently acknowledge his use of the dominant Augustinian model in his "Antwort auf die Kritik an 'Der gekreuzigte Gott,' " 185.

93. Moltmann, *Crucified God*, 255 (emphasis added).

94. Ibid., 265.

95. Ibid., 255.

96. Ibid., 246.

97. Ibid., 277.

98. Miskotte, "Das Leiden ist in Gott," 85 (trans. mine): "Aber Gott scheint am Ende der Gefangene dieser Geschichte geworden zu sein."

99. Kasper, "Revolution im Gottesverständnis?" 144.

100. Ibid., 146 (trans. mine): "Besteht hier nicht die Gefahr, daß das Wunder der Liebe Gottes, das Kreuz, aufgelöst wird in Dialektik, die umschlägt in Identität?"

101. Excerpted from Michael Welker, introduction to *Diskussion über Jürgen Moltmanns Buch "Der gekreuzigte Gott,"* ed. Michael Welker (Munich: Chr. Kaiser, 1979), 11 (trans. mine): "Doch kein einziger Theologe hat, wie Hegel, die Trinitätslehre zu einem vestigium der 'absoluten Methode' gemacht."

102. Bauckham, *Theology of Jürgen Moltmann*, 49.

103. Moltmann, *Crucified God*, 248 (emphasis added). Earlier in the book Moltmann quotes this passage from Bonhoeffer directly: "God lets himself be pushed out of the world on to the cross. . . . Only the suffering God can help" (Bonhoeffer, *Letters and Papers*, 360–361, quoted in Moltmann, *Crucified God*, 47).

104. Moltmann, *Crucified God*, 270.

105. Ibid., 274.

106. For this point, see Bauckham, *Moltmann: Messianic Theology*, 105.

107. Moltmann, *Crucified God*, 278.

108. Ibid., 215. For these various terms, cf. especially ibid., 214–216, and Molt-

mann's discussion of the concept of God in the ancient world, ibid., 267–269. It is important to note that classical theism is a highly ambiguous term in the author's writings. At times he formulates his concept of theism in terms of the ancient Hellenistic concept of God, in which he includes both Platonist and Aristotelian versions of this concept. At other times, the God of theism appears more to be the God of natural theology, who, during the Middle Ages, became divorced from the trinitarian God of revelation. At still other points, Moltmann appears to have the Enlightenment moral or modern psychological concept of God mainly in view.

109. Ibid., 222.

110. For Moltmann's appropriation of Jüngel's and Geyer's phenomenological analyses of Christ's death as the death of God, see ibid., 203–219. Moltmann strongly disagrees with how these two authors limit the significance of the death of Christ to its existential implications, thereby nullifying its social-political ramifications. He also disagrees with their judgment that the theology of the cross is "the end of metaphysics," since such a view does away with the cosmological and historical-eschatological implications of the theology of the cross (ibid., 216).

111. Ibid., 228; cf. ibid., 227–229. For a significant critique of Moltmann's simplified reading of patristic christology on the issue of suffering, cf. Bauckham, *Theology of Jürgen Moltmann*, 60–62.

112. Moltmann, *Crucified God*, 222. Bauckham wisely cautions against interpreting such statements as indicating that Moltmann derives the nature of divine love from human love. Although Moltmann readily invokes analogies between the human and divine loves, it is the cross-event that ultimately reveals the nature of God as suffering love. See Bauckham, *Theology of Jürgen Moltmann*, 49–53.

113. See Moltmann, *Crucified God*, 223–227, 251–252.

114. Ibid., 227.

115. For the following, see the discussion of the classical meaning of divine love as beneficence in Fiddes, *Creative Suffering of God*, 17–25. See also the parallel discussion in Moltmann, *Crucified God*, 268–269.

116. Moltmann, *Crucified God*, 230.

117. Ibid. (emphasis added). Here we have a precursor to Moltmann's subsequent argument on the relationship between divine love and freedom in *The Trinity and the Kingdom*. See the discussion in chapter 4 of Moltmann's development of this argument in terms of revising his concept of divine love from active suffering to overflowing goodness.

118. Moltmann, *Crucified God*, 247–248.

119. On Moltmann's reliance on this personal analogy of love, see Bauckham's astute remarks in his *Theology of Jürgen Moltmann*, 65–69.

CHAPTER 3

1. For a broad description of the crisis of the church in the late sixties and the seventies, see Jürgen Moltmann, *The Church in the Power of the Spirit: A Contribution to Messianic Ecclesiology*, trans. Margaret Kohl (New York: Harper and Row, 1977), xiii–xv.

2. Moltmann, "My Theological Career," 174–175.

3. Moltmann, *Church in the Power of the Spirit*, 35.

4. The key review essays have been gathered in Michael Welker, ed., *Diskussion über Jürgen Moltmanns Buch "Der gekreuzigte Gott"* (Munich: Chr. Kaiser, 1979).

5. Excerpted from Miskotte, "Das Leiden ist in Gott," 87 (trans. mine): "Der Sohn scheint zur 'fons deitatis' geworden zu sein, denn das Kreuz ist der Anfang der trinitarischen Geschichte Gottes. . . ." "Aber in allen diesen Aussagen hat der Geist doch mehr den Charakter einer göttlichen Kraft als den Gottes-selbst, als Seinesweise der Trinität." Although I agree that the Spirit plays a subordinate role in *The Crucified God*, I do not attribute it to Moltmann's christocentric focus on the suffering of the Son. In my view, Moltmann's christological one-sidedness results from his unusual methodology in his early trilogy and his implicit reliance on Augustine's trinitarian theology for his proposal.

6. Moltmann, "Antwort auf die Kritik an 'Der gekreuzigte Gott,' " 176–179.

7. Moltmann, "My Theological Career," 174.

8. Excerpted from Moltmann, "Antwort auf die Kritik an 'Der gekreuzigte Gott,' " 185–186 (trans. mine): "Es ist immer schwer gefallen, für dieses sächliche *vinculum amoris* Personalität anzunehmen, denn es erfolgt dann eher die Hypostatisierung einer Relation als die Entdeckung einer eigenen Personalität."

9. Ibid., 186.

10. Jürgen Moltmann, "The Trinitarian History of God," in *The Future of Creation: Collected Essays*, trans. Margaret Kohl (Philadelphia: Fortress Press, 1979), 84.

11. Ibid., 88; see also Moltmann, "Antwort auf die Kritik an 'Der gekreuzigte Gott,' " 185.

12. Moltmann, "Trinitarian History of God," 87; see also his *Church in the Power of the Spirit*, 28–30.

13. Moltmann, *Church in the Power of the Spirit*, 58. Moltmann develops his teleological interpretation of the resurrection chiefly on the basis of the "theological final clauses" of the New Testament (ibid., 29–33; quotation on 29).

14. Ibid., 59.

15. Ibid.

16. Ibid., 191.

17. For Moltmann's description of the Orthodox influences on his thought, see his "My Theological Career," 179.

18. Moltmann, *Church in the Power of the Spirit*, 36. Moltmann does challenge the Orthodox tradition's model of salvation for the opposite tendency to that of the Reformed tradition, namely, for eclipsing the essential significance of the cross-event in favor of the transfiguration of Christ in the Spirit of glory. See ibid., 36–37.

19. Moltmann, "Trinitarian History of God," 95. Moltmann had raised a similar concern about his own political theology of the late sixties and early seventies, namely, that he risked reducing Christian faith to an ethical program and thereby eliminating the joyful dimensions of the Christian life. In his short work *Theology and Joy*, Moltmann sought to recover these elements of praise and delight by appealing to the Easter event as the eschatological inbreaking of God's glory into the world. For this earlier argument, see Moltmann, *Theology and Joy*, esp. 51–54.

20. Moltmann, *Church in the Power of the Spirit*, 60.

21. Moltmann, "Trinitarian History of God," 85.

22. For Moltmann's clearest presentation of the biblical roots of his eschatologi-

cal vision, see his essay "Creation as an Open System," in *The Future of Creation: Collected Essays*, trans. Margaret Kohl (Philadelphia: Fortress Press, 1979), 125.

23. Bauckham, *Moltmann: Messianic Theology*, 113.

24. Moltmann, *Church in the Power of the Spirit*, 63.

25. Ibid., 56.

26. Ibid., 63.

27. Ibid., 64.

28. Ibid.

29. Ibid., 61. Moltmann qualifies this criticism in *The Trinity and the Kingdom*, where he appeals in a limited way to the Father as the source of divine unity.

30. Moltmann, "Trinitarian History of God," 91–92.

31. Moltmann, *Church in the Power of the Spirit*, 61. He does mention in passing here what will later become his mature concept of unity as divine fellowship (*koinonia*).

32. Franz Rosenzweig, *Der Stern der Erlösung* (Heidelberg: [n.p.], 1954), book 3, 192; quoted in Moltmann, *Church in the Power of the Spirit*, 61.

33. Moltmann, *Church in the Power of the Spirit*, 61–62.

34. Excerpted from Moltmann, "Antwort auf die Kritik an 'Der gekreuzigte Gott,'" 186–187 (trans. mine): "Um die Fülle des trinitarischen Lebens umfassend zu verstehen, muß man alle geschichtlichen Erfahrungen integrieren und also von den Personen, ihren Relationen und den Veränderungen ihrer Relationen, also ihrer Geschichte, reden. Das ist dann eine Trinitätslehre mit—abstrakt formuliert—veränderlichen Vektoren."

35. Excerpted from ibid., 168 (trans. mine): "Aber das Ziel jener drei Bücher, . . . ist eine Neuordnung des theologischen Systems zu einer messianischen Dogmatik, in der unter dem leitenden Gesichtspunkt der Trinität und des Reiches Gottes der Weg von der Geschichte zur Freiheit eingeschlagen wird."

36. Moltmann, *Trinity and the Kingdom*, 16–20, 129–150.

37. Ibid., 192.

38. Ibid., 19.

39. Ibid., 94.

40. Ibid., 19.

41. Ibid., 65.

42. Ibid., xiv.

43. Ibid., 2–9.

44. Ibid., 10, 13.

45. Ibid., 25.

46. Ibid., 21.

47. Ibid., 24.

48. Ibid.

49. Ibid., 23.

50. Ibid., 30.

51. Ibid., 41–42. Moltmann does criticize Unamuno's one-sided emphasis on the sorrow of the Father and his neglect of "the redeeming *joy of God*" (ibid., 42).

52. Ibid., 43.

53. Ibid., 57.

54. Ibid.

55. Ibid., 58.

56. Ibid., 59 (emphasis added).

57. Ibid., 60.

58. Ibid.

59. On this question, see, for example, Hans-Georg Link, "Gegenwärtige Probleme einer Kreuzestheologie: Ein Bericht," *Evangelische Theologie* 33 (1973): 337–345.

60. For an earlier version of this same argument, see Moltmann's "Antwort auf die Kritik an 'Der gekreuzigte Gott,'" 168–174.

61. Moltmann, *Trinity and the Kingdom*, 53.

62. Ibid., 52.

63. Ibid., 54.

64. Ibid., 53.

65. Ibid., 56.

66. Karl Barth, *Church Dogmatics*, 4 vols. (Edinburgh: T. & T. Clark, 1936–69), vol. II/1, § 28, quoted in Moltmann, *Trinity and the Kingdom*, 55.

67. Moltmann, *Trinity and the Kingdom*, 55.

68. Ibid.

69. Ibid., 58.

70. Ibid., 56.

71. Ibid.

72. Ibid., 94.

73. Ibid., 63–64. It is important to note that Moltmann's critique is based exclusively on Barth's initial presentation of the Trinity within his doctrine of revelation in volume I/1 of the *Church Dogmatics*. This leaves open the question of whether or not Barth developed a more nuanced account of the inner-trinitarian relations in the later christological sections of the *Church Dogmatics*.

74. Moltmann, *Trinity and the Kingdom*, 70.

75. Ibid.

76. Ibid., 67.

77. Ibid., 73.

78. For this argument, see ibid., 94–95.

79. Moltmann also draws on Phil. 2:9–11 in support of his interpretation. See *Trinity and the Kingdom*, 91–93.

80. Moltmann, *Trinity and the Kingdom*, 92.

81. Ibid.

82. Ibid., 95.

83. Ibid., 99.

84. Ibid.

85. Ibid., 98.

86. Ibid.

87. Ibid., 101.

88. Ibid., 102.

89. Cf. ibid., 104.

90. Ibid., 111–112.

91. Ibid., 112.

92. Ibid., 107. On this point he takes the speculative theology of the nineteenth

century to task for having identified the creation of the world with the begetting of the Son of God.

93. Ibid., 113.

94. Cf. ibid. Although Moltmann retreats here from describing creation as an emanation of the divine being, he hints nonetheless that the language of emanation does have its rightful place in pneumatology.

95. Ibid., 109.

96. Ibid., 111.

97. Ibid.

98. Ibid., 116.

99. Ibid., 117.

100. Ibid., 117–118.

101. Ibid., 120.

102. Ibid., 119.

103. Ibid., 118.

104. Ibid., 119.

105. Ibid., 125.

106. Ibid., 127.

107. Ibid., 128.

108. Ibid., 131 and 129, respectively.

109. Ibid., 240 n. 7.

110. Moltmann relies primarily on secondary sources for his critique of the monarchical shape of Western trinitarian doctrine, most notably F[erdinand] C[hristian] Baur, *Die christliche Lehre von der Dreieinigkeit und Menschwerdung Gottes in ihrer geschichtlichen Entwicklung*, 3 vols. (Tübingen: [n.p.], 1843), referred to in Moltmann, *Trinity and the Kingdom*, 225 n. 21; Erik Peterson, "Monotheismus als politisches Problem," in *Theologische Traktate* (Munich: [n.p.], 1951), 48–147, referred to in Moltmann, *Trinity and the Kingdom*, 248 n. 2. Of late, patristic scholars and historians of trinitarian doctrine have questioned Moltmann's and other contemporary theologians' critiques of the monarchical or modalist trajectory in Western doctrine for being vastly oversimplified and ahistorical readings of this doctrinal development. Most notably, Michel René Barnes points to the Hegelian idealism latent in contemporary interpretations of trinitarian development in the patristic period, for example, in the presumed neat division of Eastern and Western trinitarianism in terms of their starting point in the three persons or the unity of the Godhead. Furthermore, Barnes challenges contemporary theologians (including Moltmann) for reading the problems of the modern Cartesian subject back into the patristic and medieval sources so as to create a springboard for their constructive projects. For this well-founded critique, see Michel René Barnes, "Augustine in Contemporary Trinitarian Theology," *Theological Studies* 56 (1995): 237–250. For my critique of Moltmann's one-sided reading of Augustine, see the next chapter's discussion of his *imago Dei* anthropology.

111. Moltmann, *Trinity and the Kingdom*, 137–139.

112. For this argument, see ibid., 16–17, 190. Moltmann's critique of the trajectory of Western thought from Aquinas onward follows closely that of Karl Rahner in "Remarks on the Dogmatic Treatise 'De Trinitate,'" in *More Recent Writings*, vol. 4 of *Theological Investigations*, trans. Kevin Smyth (London: Darton, Longman and Todd, 1966), 77–87.

113. Moltmann, *Trinity and the Kingdom*, 17.

114. Ibid., 139.

115. Moltmann also includes in this critique Friedrich Schleiermacher, who explicitly advocated a Sabellian form of the trinitarian doctrine. For this argument, see ibid., 136–137. Moltmann is not alone in criticizing such Idealistic tendencies in Barth's and Rahner's trinitarian schemas. For a similar critique, see Wolfhart Pannenberg, *Systematic Theology*, trans. Geoffrey W. Bromiley, 3 vols. (Grand Rapids, MI: Eerdmans, 1991–98), 1:295–296, 307–308, 319–320 n. 184.

116. Moltmann, *Trinity and the Kingdom*, 140–142. Although Barth develops subsequently a christological root for his doctrine in the *Church Dogmatics*, Moltmann charges that the doctrine's structure never becomes truly rooted in biblical revelation. As noted in the earlier discussion, Moltmann traces Barth's notion of absolute lordship to modern notions of ownership and autonomy rather than to the scriptural witness to the kingdom.

117. Moltmann, *Trinity and the Kingdom*, 142.

118. Ibid., 143.

119. Ibid., 144.

120. Ibid., 145.

121. Ibid., 147.

122. Ibid., 146.

123. Karl Rahner, *Grundkurs des Glaubens* (Freiburg: [Herder], 1976), 141, quoted in Moltmann, *Trinity and the Kingdom*, 147. In light of this critique of Rahner as an emanationist, it becomes clear why Moltmann is anxious in his own description of creation as the self-communication of divine love to avoid presenting the world as an emanation of the inner-trinitarian process. In distinction from Rahner, Moltmann claims that creation arises from the mutual and differentiated intra-trinitarian love between the Father and the Son, and that the Holy Spirit's presence in humankind is the indwelling of its own life. See the earlier discussion of Moltmann's trinitarian interpretation of creation as the self-communication of love.

124. Moltmann, *Trinity and the Kingdom*, 148.

125. See the earlier critical discussion about this dialectical structure of trinitarian love in the origin.

126. Moltmann rejects the psychological doctrine for the Trinity here with a further theological argument, namely, that an isolated individual is not the *imago Dei*: "A person is only God's image in fellowship with other people: 'In the image of God he created him; male and female he created them' (Gen. 1.27). . . . It is not the completed and fulfilled individual personality that can already be called the image of God on earth; it is only the completed community of persons" (ibid., 155–156). The next chapter on trinitarian anthropology will explore in depth Moltmann's argument for the exclusively social nature of the *imago Dei*.

127. Ibid., 150.

128. Ibid., 153.

129. Ibid., 154 (emphasis in the original).

130. Ibid., 161.

131. Ibid., 162.

132. Ibid., 163.

133. Ibid., 164.

134. Ibid., 165.

135. Ibid.

136. Ibid.

137. Ibid., 166–167.

138. Ibid., 167–168.

139. Ibid., 168.

140. Ibid., 169.

141. Cf. ibid., 170.

142. Ibid., 183.

143. Ibid.

144. Ibid., 184.

145. Ibid.

146. Cf. ibid., 186.

147. Ibid., 187.

148. Ibid. (emphasis in the original).

149. Ibid., 171.

150. Ibid.

151. Ibid., 172.

152. Moltmann does not charge Augustine with such a reduction of persons to sheer relations but rather points critically to Aquinas's reception of Augustine's position, and then to Barth's Neoscholastic version of it (ibid., 147).

153. Ibid., 173.

154. Ibid.

155. Ibid., 173–174.

156. Ibid., 174–175.

157. Ibid., 175.

158. See, for example, James Mackey's acerbic criticism of the implicit tritheism in Moltmann's highly anthropomorphic analogy in Mackey, "Are There Christian Alternatives?" esp. 68–70. For an earlier version of this criticism, cf. George Hunsinger, "The Crucified God and the Political Theology of Violence," *Heythrop Journal* 14 (1973): 278.

159. Moltmann, *Trinity and the Kingdom*, 175.

CHAPTER 4

1. Moltmann borrows the term "possessive individualism" from C. B. Macpherson, who argues that the Enlightenment notion of human freedom is "a function of possession" that serves to radically individualize people. For this argument, see C. B. Macpherson, *The Political Theory of Possessive Individualism* (Oxford: [n.p.], 1962), 3, quoted in Moltmann, *Trinity and the Kingdom*, 252 n. 47.

2. Moltmann, *Trinity and the Kingdom*, 193. For how religious monotheism translates into political monotheism, Moltmann relies primarily on Erik Peterson's influential treatise "Monotheismus als politisches Problem" (1935). See Moltmann, *Trinity and the Kingdom*, 192–195.

3. Moltmann, *Trinity and the Kingdom*, 191–192.

4. Ibid., 198.

5. Ibid., 195.

6. Ibid., 196.

7. Moltmann, *God in Creation*, 252. See Moltmann's broader discussion of these tendencies in Western anthropological theory, ibid., 244–255.

8. Ibid., 254 (emphasis added). Moltmann does admit that Barth develops his theological anthropology within the context of a christological analogy to the human being Jesus Christ, on the one hand, and the experience of God's Spirit, on the other. Moltmann argues, however, that this christological connection only enhances the monarchical character of Barth's theological anthropology, since Barth models the human being Jesus Christ on a hierarchical structure of an ordered unity of soul over body.

9. Ibid.

10. See ibid., 162. For similar criticisms, see Moltmann's later discussion of Barth's doctrine of creation in Moltmann's 1987 essay "Creation, Covenant and Glory: A Conversation on Karl Barth's Doctrine of Creation," in *History and the Triune God: Contributions to Trinitarian Theology*, trans. John Bowden (New York: Crossroad, 1992), 125–142, esp. 132–133.

11. Moltmann, *God in Creation*, 235.

12. Ibid., 237. It is important to note that Moltmann relies on two secondary sources for his interpretation of Augustine's psychological analogy: Michael Schmaus's *Die psychologische Trinitätslehre des Heiligen Augustinus* (Münster: [n.p.], 1927), from which he draws most of his citations from Augustine's *De Trinitate* (see Moltmann, *God in Creation*, 350 n. 34), and Aquinas's presentation of Augustine's intellectual analogy in the former's *Summa Theologica*, I, qu. 93, art. 4–8 (see Moltmann, *God in Creation*, 350 n. 37). Moltmann's dependence on these two secondary sources helps explain how it is that he does not differentiate among the various mental triads that Augustine explores in books 9–14 of his *De Trinitate*. Nor does Moltmann seem aware of the degree to which Augustine presents his own various mental triads as unsatisfactory analogies for the Trinity, and for this reason severely qualifies the knowledge of the Trinity that is gained through such psychological explorations by human (fallen) intelligences. As recent Augustine interpreters have pointed out, a close analysis of the original text might have led Moltmann to draw different conclusions. For a nuanced interpretation of Augustine's trinitarian theology and his contemporary critics, see Barnes, "Augustine in Contemporary Trinitarian Theology."

13. Moltmann, *God in Creation*, 239.

14. Ibid., 240.

15. See ibid., 236.

16. Ibid., 238–239. Here Moltmann offers a highly simplified interpretation of Augustine's trinitarian theology by overlooking the significance of Augustine's exploration of the social image of the Trinity based on the love of neighbor in book 8 of his *De Trinitate*.

17. Moltmann goes so far as to suggest that there is a link between the divergent trajectories of trinitarian thought in the East and West and the political alternatives of Eastern European socialism and Western personalism or individualism. For this argument, see *Trinity and the Kingdom*, 199–200.

18. Moltmann, *Spirit of Life*, 90.

19. Ibid. Moltmann does not reject altogether the contemplative path as a basis for experiencing or knowing God. However, he remains concerned about its misuse

as an escape from social responsibilities in this world and thus insists upon the inextricable link between action and contemplation in the Christian life of faith. For Moltmann's discussion of this link in dialogue with Thomas Merton, see Jürgen Moltmann, "The Theology of Mystical Experience: Contemplation in a World of Action," in *Experiences of God*, trans. Margaret Kohl (Philadelphia: Fortress Press, 1980), 55–80.

20. For a much more positive reading of Barth's anthropology in the *Church Dogmatics*, see Wolf Krötke, "The Humanity of the Human Person in Karl Barth's Anthropology," in *The Cambridge Companion to Karl Barth*, ed. John Webster (Cambridge: Cambridge University Press, 2000), 159–176, esp. 163–166, 168–170.

21. For his full argument, see Cunningham, *These Three Are One*, 31–35.

22. Moltmann, *God in Creation*, 26–27.

23. For an earlier sketch of his doctrine of creation, see Moltmann's essay "Creation as an Open System." For an excellent overview of Moltmann's ecological doctrine of creation, see Bauckham, *Theology of Jürgen Moltmann*, 183–198.

24. See Moltmann, *God in Creation*, 9–10.

25. Ibid., 11.

26. Ibid., 14.

27. Ibid., 100.

28. Ibid.

29. Ibid.

30. Ibid., 16.

31. Moltmann, "Creation, Covenant and Glory," 133.

32. For example, see Christian Link's criticism of Moltmann's imprecision in describing the relationship between God and the world in Link's "Schöpfung im messianischen Licht," *Evangelische Theologie* 47 (1987): 88–89.

33. See Moltmann, *God in Creation*, 102–103; Moltmann, "Creation, Covenant and Glory," 133–134.

34. Moltmann, *God in Creation*, 98. Despite her criticisms of his position, McFague's proposal of the world as God's body resembles Moltmann's, insofar as she also advocates a form of panentheism that combines a radical transcendence with a radical immanence. For a concise summary of her ecological theology of creation, see McFague's essay "Is God in Charge?" in *Essentials of Christian Theology*, ed. William C. Placher (Louisville, KY: Westminster John Knox Press, 2003), 101–116.

35. Kathryn Tanner, *God and Creation in Christian Theology: Tyranny or Empowerment?* (Oxford: Basil Blackwell, 1988), 89, quoted in William Placher, *The Domestication of Transcendence: How Modern Thinking about God Went Wrong* (Louisville, KY: Westminster John Knox Press, 1996), 111.

36. In Tanner's words, "[Such] a radical transcendence does not exclude God's positive fellowship with the world or presence in it. . . . God's transcendence alone is one that may be properly exercised in the radical immanence by which God is said to be nearer to us than we are to ourselves" (Tanner, *God and Creation*, 79, quoted in Placher, *The Domestication of Transcendence*, 112).

37. Moltmann, *God in Creation*, 5; see also ibid., 276–296.

38. Ibid., 5.

39. For this connection between Moltmann's understanding of economy (*oikos*) and his ecological doctrine, see Müller-Fahrenholz, *Kingdom and the Power*, 154.

40. In support of this ongoing process of creation, Moltmann emphasizes the continuity between the depiction of the Old Testament's *ruach* as the source of life in the original act of creation and the New Testament's depiction of the Holy Spirit as the breath of life in the renewal of creation. For this argument, see Moltmann, *God in Creation*, 67.

41. Ibid.

42. Ibid, 7. See also Moltmann's more detailed criticism of Barth's creation-covenant schema in Moltmann's "Creation, Covenant and Glory," 127–132.

43. Moltmann criticizes Barth's twofold model of creation and covenant because it treats the reconciliation in Christ as itself the "triumph of . . . glory" (Karl Barth, *Church Dogmatics*, 4 vols. [Edinburgh: T. & T. Clark, 1936–69], IV/3:157, quoted in Moltmann, *God in Creation*, 62).

44. Moltmann, *God in Creation*, 8 (trans. mine): "*gratia non perfecit, sed praeparat naturam ad gloriam aeternam; gratia non est perfectio naturae, sed praeparatio messianica mundi ad regnum Dei.*"

45. Bauckham, *Theology of Jürgen Moltmann*, 197.

46. Moltmann, *God in Creation*, 56. It is important to note that Moltmann portrays creation as an eschatological sign of the kingdom in response to Barth's notion of creation as an earthly parable for the kingdom of heaven. Moltmann objects to Barth's schema on the grounds that it treats creation as a mere cipher for God's reality, and not as a promise and anticipation of its own future. For this discussion, see ibid., 60–65.

47. See ibid., 187.

48. Ibid.

49. Ibid., 188.

50. Ibid., 186.

51. Ibid., 190.

52. Ibid., 227.

53. Ibid.

54. See ibid., 215.

55. Ibid., 220.

56. Ibid., 77–78. For this notion of human beings as the counterpart of God the Father, see the discussion in chapter 3.

57. Moltmann, *God in Creation*, 219–220. See Bonhoeffer's earlier discussion of this analogy of relations in Dietrich Bonhoeffer, *Creation and Fall: A Theological Interpretation of Genesis 1–3*, trans. J. C. Fletcher (London: SCM Press, 1959), 36–37.

58. Moltmann, *God in Creation*, 77.

59. Ibid., 218. Although Moltmann relies here on a literalistic reading of the Genesis account to support his social interpretation of the image of the Trinity in human community, elsewhere he objects to using biblical texts as a direct revelation of the Trinity. Such inconsistencies in his theological appeals to the scriptures have led Richard Bauckham, among others, to criticize Moltmann for his failure to explain his biblical hermeneutics in his later work. I will return to this issue in the conclusion of this study.

60. Ibid., 223.

61. Such a bare identification of the individual with her social relations would in

fact amount to a form of modalism that violates Moltmann's social trinitarian theology and the corresponding *analogia relationis* in the human sphere. Just as the divine persons cannot be reduced to modes of being of the one God in Moltmann's trinitarian theology, so, too, human persons cannot be reduced to communal modes of being in his theological anthropology.

62. Moltmann does tend in his writing to accent the sociality of human existence, but he does so, in my view, to counterbalance modern anthropology's focus on the individual and her self-transcendence.

63. Ibid., 218.

64. Ibid., 242–243.

65. Ibid., 245–246.

66. Ibid., 246.

67. Ibid., 258.

68. Ibid., 259.

69. Ibid.

70. Ibid., 240.

71. Ibid., 241.

72. Ibid.

73. Ibid.

CHAPTER 5

1. Moltmann, *God in Creation*, 265.

2. Ibid.

3. Ibid., 229.

4. Jürgen Moltmann, "The Inviting Unity of the Triune God," in *History and the Triune God: Contributions to Trinitarian Theology*, trans. John Bowden (New York: Crossroad, 1992), 86.

5. Ibid., 87.

6. Moltmann, *God in Creation*, 233–234. Despite Moltmann's frequent criticisms of Augustine's anthropology, one can hardly fail to note that his concept of sin resembles closely Augustine's concept of disordered loves.

7. Moltmann, "Inviting Unity," 87.

8. Moltmann, *God in Creation*, 228.

9. Moltmann, *Spirit of Life*, 81.

10. Moltmann, "Inviting Unity," 84.

11. Moltmann, *Way of Jesus Christ*, 73.

12. Moltmann, *Spirit of Life*, 58.

13. See especially Jürgen Moltmann, " 'I Believe in Jesus Christ, the Only-Begotten Son of God': Brotherly Talk of Christ," in *History and the Triune God: Contributions to Trinitarian Theology*, trans. John Bowden (New York: Crossroad, 1992), 31–43; and "Justice for Victims and Perpetrators," also in *History and the Triune God*, 44–56. The latter essay appears with slight additions as a chapter in Moltmann, *Spirit of Life*, 123–143.

14. For these terms, see Moltmann, " 'I Believe in Jesus Christ,' " 36–37. For an earlier version of this same argument, see his *Trinity and the Kingdom*, 120–121.

15. Moltmann, *Way of Jesus Christ*, 142.

16. Moltmann, " 'I Believe in Jesus Christ,' " 33. Moltmann defends the compatibility of the so-called adoptionist christology of the synoptic Gospels and the preexistence christology of the Gospel of John. Jesus' historical experience of the Spirit in his baptism need not contradict the essential nature of his relationship to the Father as his only-begotten Son. On this point, see ibid., 34–35; Moltmann, *Way of Jesus Christ*, 143.

17. Moltmann, " 'I Believe in Jesus Christ,' " 33.

18. Moltmann, *Way of Jesus Christ*, 71–72.

19. Moltmann, " 'I Believe in Jesus Christ,' " 35.

20. Moltmann, *Way of Jesus Christ*, 115.

21. Ibid., 173.

22. Moltmann, *Spirit of Life*, 64.

23. Moltmann, *Way of Jesus Christ*, 181.

24. Moltmann, "Justice for Victims and Perpetrators," 48.

25. Moltmann, *Way of Jesus Christ*, 178.

26. Moltmann, "Justice for Victims and Perpetrators," 52.

27. Moltmann, *Way of Jesus Christ*, 257.

28. Ibid., 181; cf. ibid., 181–196. An earlier treatment of the same doctrine of justification can be found in Jürgen Moltmann, "Justification and New Creation," in *The Future of Creation: Collected Essays*, trans. Margaret Kohl (Philadelphia: Fortress Press, 1979), 149–171.

29. Moltmann, *Way of Jesus Christ*, 183.

30. Ibid., 182.

31. Ibid., 185.

32. Ibid., 188.

33. Ibid.

34. See ibid., 190.

35. Ibid., 182.

36. Ibid., 183.

37. Moltmann, " 'I Believe in Jesus Christ,' " 40.

38. Moltmann, *Trinity and the Kingdom*, 116.

39. Moltmann, "Inviting Unity," 83.

40. Moltmann, " 'I Believe in Jesus Christ,' " 41.

41. Ibid., 37.

42. Moltmann, *Spirit of Life*, 66.

43. Ibid., 67.

44. Moltmann, *Way of Jesus Christ*, 242.

45. Moltmann, *Spirit of Life*, 83; see ibid., 83–98.

46. Ibid., 42.

47. Ibid., 195. This is one of those passages on which I agree fully with Karen Kilby's criticism of Moltmann's appeal to the term *perichoresis* to describe the divine-human relationship. Here as in other places in his writing, Moltmann fails to specify how this term applies differently to the relationship between God and human beings than it does to the relationships among the divine persons. For a full critical assessment of Moltmann's use of this term *perichoresis* as an analogy for the God-human relationship, see Joy Ann McDougall, "A Room of One's Own? Trinitarian Pericho-

resis as Analogy for the God-Human Relationship," in *Wo ist Gott? Gottesräume—Lebensräume*, ed. Jürgen Moltmann and Carmen Rivuzumwami (Neukirchen-Vluyn: Neukirchener Verlag, 2002), 133–141.

48. Moltmann, *Spirit of Life*, 86. See also Moltmann, *God in Creation*, 268–270.

49. Moltmann, *Spirit of Life*, 178.

50. See ibid., 84.

51. Ibid.

52. Jürgen Moltmann, *The Source of Life: The Holy Spirit and the Theology of Life*, trans. Margaret Kohl (London: SCM Press, 1997), 85.

53. Moltmann, *Spirit of Life*, 121.

54. Ibid., 99. Moltmann's interpretation of the Spirit as the experience of freedom does not rest solely on this text. He also draws from the experience of God as liberator in the Exodus account and varied experiences of freedom that are reported in fellowship with Jesus. For these biblical interpretations, see ibid., 99–102.

55. Ibid., 114.

56. Ibid., 115.

57. Ibid. (emphasis added).

58. Ibid., 117.

59. Ibid., 118.

60. Ibid.

61. Ibid., 119.

62. Ibid.

63. Ibid., 82.

64. Ibid., 143.

65. Ibid.

66. Ibid.

67. O[tto] Weber, *Grundlagen der Dogmatik*, 2 vols. (Neukirchen-Vluyn: [n.p.], [1955]–1962), 2:401, quoted in Moltmann, *Spirit of Life*, 151.

68. Moltmann, *Spirit of Life*, 153.

69. Ibid.

70. Ibid., 154.

71. Ibid., 75.

72. Ibid., 76.

73. Ibid., 155.

74. Ibid., 157.

75. Moltmann, *God in Creation*, 227.

76. Moltmann, *Spirit of Life*, 174.

77. Ibid., 175.

78. Ibid.

79. Torrance, *Persons in Communion*, 313.

80. Ibid.

81. Ibid.

82. Jürgen Moltmann, "How I Have Changed? Reflections on Thirty Years of Theology," in *How I Have Changed*, ed. Jürgen Moltmann, trans. John Bowden (Harrisburg, PA: Trinity Press International, 1997), 27, quoted in Müller-Fahrenholz, *Kingdom and the Power*, 107.

83. Müller-Fahrenholz, *Kingdom and the Power*, 107.

84. Ibid., 111–112.

85. To his credit, Müller-Fahrenholz is one of the few interpreters of Moltmann's work who emphasizes the centrality of spirituality and, indeed, mysticism, to Moltmann's theology, but he tends to treat these elements as separate from Moltmann's political-liberationist agenda. For Müller-Fahrenholz's discussion of mysticism in Moltmann's work, see ibid., 116–118, 230–244.

86. Moltmann, " 'Fellowship of the Holy Spirit,' " 57.

87. Moltmann, *Spirit of Life*, 219.

88. Moltmann, *Trinity and the Kingdom*, 198.

89. Ibid.

90. Ibid., 199 (emphasis added).

91. Ibid., 202.

92. Moltmann, " 'Fellowship of the Holy Spirit,' " 64.

93. Moltmann, *Trinity and the Kingdom*, 200.

94. Ibid., 202, quoting the title of G. Hasenhüttl, *Herrschaftsfreie Kirche, Sozio-theologische Grundlegung* (Düsseldorf: [n.p.], 1974).

95. Moltmann, *Trinity and the Kingdom*, 202.

96. Moltmann, *Spirit of Life*, 248.

97. Ibid., 221.

98. See ibid., 249. Moltmann borrows this typology of the patristic and medieval traditions' understandings of Christian love from the article "Liebe," written by Joseph Ratzinger for the *Lexikon für Theologie und Kirche*, ed. Michael Buchberger et al., 2nd ed., 10 vols. (Freiburg: Herder, 1957), 6:1031–1036. As has been the case in other places in his writings, Moltmann's dependence on this secondary source leads him to make sweeping criticisms about the theological tradition that lack nuance and sufficient textual warrant to support his claims.

99. Moltmann, *Spirit of Life*, 249.

100. Ibid.

101. Ibid., 250 (emphasis added).

102. Ibid., 248.

103. Ibid., 255. Although Moltmann does not cite Kant as his source for this definition in *The Spirit of Life*, he does so in his earlier discussions of "open friendship." See, for example, Jürgen Moltmann, "Open Friendship: Aristotelian and Christian Concepts of Friendship," in *The Changing Face of Friendship*, ed. Leroy S. Rouner (Notre Dame, IN: University of Notre Dame Press, 1994), 30.

104. Moltmann, *Spirit of Life*, 256.

105. Ibid., 258.

106. Ibid.

107. Ibid., 259.

108. Ibid., 260.

109. Ibid., 261.

110. Ibid.

111. Ibid., 262.

112. Ibid.

113. Ibid.

114. Ibid., 195.

115. Ibid., 115.

116. Jürgen Moltmann, *God for a Secular Society: The Public Relevance of Theology*, trans. Margaret Kohl (Minneapolis, MN: Fortress Press, 1999), 156.

117. For a powerful critique of modernity's ideal of freedom as absolute self-constitution, one that parallels Moltmann's, see Christoph Schwöbel, "Imago Libertatis: Human and Divine Freedom," in *God and Freedom: Essays in Historical and Systematic Theology*, ed. Colin E. Gunton (Edinburgh: T. & T. Clark, 1995), 57–81. Schwöbel charges that the modern notion of freedom as absolute self-constitution is a form of self-deification, in which human beings claim a freedom for themselves that is in the image of the divine attributes, e.g., divine omnipotence and omniscience.

118. Moltmann, *Spirit of Life*, 118.

119. Ibid., 220.

120. For this term, see Amy Plantinga Pauw, "Attending to the Gaps between Beliefs and Practices," in *Practicing Theology: Beliefs and Practices in Christian Life*, ed. Miroslav Volf and Dorothy C. Bass (Grand Rapids, MI: Eerdmans, 2002), 33–48. In this essay Pauw argues persuasively that theologians and Christian communities alike should expect a "flexible integrity" rather than an "unbending rigidity" between Christian doctrines and practices (ibid., 42). Along a similar vein, Kathryn Tanner in her essay "Theological Reflection and Christian Practices," also in *Practicing Theology*, 228–242, cautions theologians against expecting too tight a fit between doctrines and practices because this can mask a community's distortions of its practices and belies the "improvisional and ad hoc" nature of social practices (quotation at 230).

121. Moltmann, *Spirit of Life*, 86.

122. Ibid., 126.

123. See ibid., 129–138.

124. Ibid., 143.

125. Mary Grey, "Falling into Freedom: Searching for New Interpretations of Sin in a Secular Society," *Scottish Journal of Theology* 47, (1994): 241.

126. For an excellent discussion of the feminist critique and reconstruction of the category of sin, see Serene Jones, *Feminist Theory and Theology: Cartographies of Grace* (Philadelphia: Fortress Press, 2000), 99–125, esp. 110–111.

127. Serene Jones describes the social sins of racism and sexism in similar terms as a "refusal to celebrate difference" and an "obsessive valorization of sameness," although she does not appeal to trinitarian theology in support of her interpretation. For the details of her argument, see Jones's essay "What's Wrong with Us?" in *Essentials of Christian Theology*, ed. William C. Placher (Louisville, KY: Westminster John Knox Press, 2003), 141–158; here, 151.

128. Rebecca S. Chopp, "Anointed to Preach: Speaking of Sin in the Midst of Grace," in *The Portion of the Poor: Good News to the Poor in the Wesleyan Tradition*, ed. M. Douglas Meeks (Nashville, TN: Kingswood Books, 1995), 105.

CONCLUSION

1. For similar criticisms of Moltmann's unclear biblical hermeneutics in his later work, see the comments of New Testament scholar Richard Bauckham, *Theology of Jürgen Moltmann*, 25–26; see also Jeanrond, "Question of God Today," 16. To his credit, Moltmann acknowledges these deficiencies in his biblical hermeneutics in his 1996 autobiographical remarks: "When I ask myself what I would like to have done

differently and at which points I have to admit that my critics are right, then I have to name exegesis first" (Moltmann, "Adventure of Theological Ideas," 104). Since making these remarks, Moltmann has elaborated further on his hermeneutical approach to the scriptures in his recent work, *Experiences in Theology*, 125–150. There he highlights the significance of the Bible's "promissory history" for his messianic interpretation of Christianity, and reiterates the basis for "his trinitarian hermeneutics" in the New Testament's narration of the relationships of Father, the Son, and Spirit as "relationships of fellowship." Although this discussion does clarify Moltmann's overarching biblical hermenuetical principles, it does not put to rest the numerous exegetical concerns raised by his appropriation of highly diverse scriptures to his dogmatic ends.

2. For Miroslav Volf's use of this term, see his excellent article "The Trinity Is Our Social Program? The Doctrine of the Trinity and the Shape of Social Engagement," *Modern Theology* 14 (July 1998): 403–423. Here Volf makes a compelling argument for replacing the idea of a "social trinitarian program," which Moltmann adopts from Russian theologian Nicholas Federov, with that of a "social vision." With this term, Volf argues that trinitarian theology provides a theological framework of values that can norm Christian discipleship. Although he does not apply this term to the works of his former teacher Moltmann, in my view it captures well the sense of how Moltmann actually appeals to his trinitarian theology in making proposals for Christian praxis.

3. Moltmann, "Adventure of Theological Ideas," 103.

Bibliography

WORKS BY JÜRGEN MOLTMANN

"The Adventure of Theological Ideas." *Religious Studies Review* 22 (1996): 102–105.

"Antwort auf die Kritik an 'Der gekreuzigte Gott.'" In *Diskussion über Jürgen Moltmanns Buch "Der gekreuzigte Gott,"* ed. Michael Welker, 165–190. Munich: Chr. Kaiser, 1979.

"Antwort auf die Kritik der Theologie der Hoffnung." In *Diskussion über die "Theologie der Hoffnung" von Jürgen Moltmann*, ed. Wolf-Dieter Marsch, 201–238. Munich: Chr. Kaiser, 1967.

Bibliographie. Comp. Dieter Ising with the collaboration of Günther Geisthardt and Adelbert Schloz. Munich: Chr. Kaiser, 1987.

The Church in the Power of the Spirit: A Contribution to Messianic Ecclesiology. Trans. Margaret Kohl. New York: Harper and Row, 1977.

The Coming of God: Christian Eschatology. Trans. Margaret Kohl. Minneapolis, MN: Fortress Press, 1996.

"Creation as an Open System." In Jürgen Moltmann, *The Future of Creation: Collected Essays*, trans. Margaret Kohl, 115–130. Philadelphia: Fortress Press, 1979.

"Creation, Covenant and Glory: A Conversation on Karl Barth's Doctrine of Creation." In Jürgen Moltmann, *History and the Triune God: Contributions to Trinitarian Theology*, trans. John Bowden, 125–142. New York: Crossroad, 1992.

The Crucified God: The Cross of Christ as the Foundation and Criticism of Christian Theology. Trans. R. A. Wilson and John Bowden. Preface to the pbk. ed. trans. Margaret Kohl. 1st HarperCollins pbk. ed. New York: HarperCollins, 1991.

"Ernst Bloch and Hope without Faith." In Jürgen Moltmann, *The Experiment*

Hope, ed. and trans. M. Douglas Meeks, 30–43. Philadelphia: Fortress Press, 1972.

Experiences in Theology: Ways and Forms of Christian Theology. Trans. Margaret Kohl. Minneapolis, MN: Fortress Press, 2000.

" 'The Fellowship of the Holy Spirit': On Trinitarian Pneumatology." In Jürgen Moltmann, *History and the Triune God: Contributions to Trinitarian Theology*, trans. John Bowden, 57–69. New York: Crossroad, 1992.

Foreword to *Karl Barth—Heinrich Barth—Emil Brunner*, pt. 1 of *Anfänge der dialektischen Theologie*, ed. Jürgen Moltmann, ix–xviii. 5th ed. Munich: Chr. Kaiser, 1985.

Foreword to *Origins of the Theology of Hope*, by M. Douglas Meeks, ix–xii. Philadelphia: Fortress Press, 1974.

God for a Secular Society: The Public Relevance of Theology. Trans. Margaret Kohl. Minneapolis: Fortress Press, 1999.

God in Creation: A New Theology of Creation and the Spirit of God. Gifford Lectures 1984–85. Trans. Margaret Kohl. 1st HarperCollins pbk. ed. San Francisco: HarperCollins, 1985.

"Hope and Confidence: A Conversation with Ernst Bloch." In Jürgen Moltmann, *Religion, Revolution, and the Future*, trans. M. Douglas Meeks, 148–176. New York: Charles Scribner's Sons, 1969.

"Hope and History." In Jürgen Moltmann, *Religion, Revolution, and the Future*, trans. M. Douglas Meeks, 200–220. New York: Charles Scribner's Sons, 1969.

"How I Have Changed? Reflections on Thirty Years of Theology," 27. In *How I Have Changed*, ed. Jürgen Moltmann, trans. John Bowden, 13–21. Harrisburg, PA: Trinity Press International, 1997. Quoted in Geiko Müller-Fahrenholz, *The Kingdom and the Power: The Theology of Jürgen Moltmann*, trans. John Bowden (London: SCM Press, 2000), 107.

" 'I Believe in Jesus Christ, the Only-Begotten Son of God': Brotherly Talk of Christ." In Jürgen Moltmann, *History and the Triune God: Contributions to Trinitarian Theology*, trans. John Bowden, 31–43. New York: Crossroad, 1992.

"Introduction: Some Questions about the Doctrine of the Trinity Today." In Jürgen Moltmann, *History and the Triune God: Contributions to Trinitarian Theology*, trans. John Bowden, xi–xix. New York: Crossroad, 1992.

"Introduction to the 'Theology of Hope.' " In Jürgen Moltmann, *The Experiment Hope*, ed. and trans. M. Douglas Meeks, 44–59. Philadelphia: Fortress Press, 1972.

"The Inviting Unity of the Triune God." In Jürgen Moltmann, *History and the Triune God: Contributions to Trinitarian Theology*, trans. John Bowden, 80–89. New York: Crossroad, 1992.

"Justice for Victims and Perpetrators." In Jürgen Moltmann, *History and the Triune God: Contributions to Trinitarian Theology*, trans. John Bowden, 44–56. New York: Crossroad, 1992.

"Justification and New Creation." In Jürgen Moltmann, *The Future of Creation: Collected Essays*, trans. Margaret Kohl, 149–171. Philadelphia: Fortress Press, 1979.

"My Theological Career." In Jürgen Moltmann, *History and the Triune God: Contributions to Trinitarian Theology*, trans. John Bowden, 165–182. New York: Crossroad, 1992.

"Open Friendship: Aristotelian and Christian Concepts of Friendship." In *The Chang-

ing Face of Friendship, ed. Leroy S. Rouner, 29–42. Notre Dame, IN: University of Notre Dame Press, 1994.

"Political Theology." *Theology Today* 28 (Apr. 1971): 6–23.

Politische Theologie—Politische Ethik. Munich: Chr. Kaiser, 1984.

The Source of Life: The Holy Spirit and the Theology of Life. Trans. Margaret Kohl. London: SCM Press, 1997.

The Spirit of Life: A Universal Affirmation. Trans. Margaret Kohl. Minneapolis, MN: Fortress Press, 1992.

Theology and Joy. Trans. Reinhard Ulrich. London: SCM Press, 1973.

"Theology as Eschatology." In *The Future of Hope: Theology as Eschatology*, ed. Frederick Herzog, 1–50. New York: Herder and Herder, 1970.

Theology of Hope: On the Ground and the Implications of a Christian Eschatology. Trans. James W. Leitch. 10th ed. New York: Harper and Row, 1983.

"The Theology of Mystical Experience: Contemplation in a World of Action." In Jürgen Moltmann, *Experiences of God*, trans. Margaret Kohl, 55–80. Philadelphia: Fortress Press, 1980.

"Toward a Political Hermeneutic of the Gospel." In Jürgen Moltmann, *Religion, Revolution, and the Future*, trans. M. Douglas Meeks, 83–107. New York: Charles Scribner's Sons, 1969.

"The Trinitarian History of God." In Jürgen Moltmann, *The Future of Creation: Collected Essays*, trans. Margaret Kohl, 80–96. Philadelphia: Fortress Press, 1979.

The Trinity and the Kingdom: The Doctrine of God. Trans. Margaret Kohl. 1st HarperCollins pbk. ed. San Francisco: HarperCollins, 1991.

Umkehr zur Zukunft. Munich: Siebenstern Taschenbuch, 1970.

The Way of Jesus Christ: Christology in Messianic Dimensions. Trans. Margaret Kohl. 1st Fortress Press ed. Minneapolis, MN: Fortress Press, 1993.

" 'Where There Is Hope, There Is Religion.' " In Jürgen Moltmann, *The Experiment Hope*, ed. and trans. M. Douglas Meeks, 15–29. Philadelphia: Fortress Press, 1972.

"Why Am I a Christian?" In Jürgen Moltmann, *Experiences of God*, trans. Margaret Kohl, 1–18. Philadelphia: Fortress Press, 1980.

SECONDARY SOURCES

Aquinas, Thomas. *Summa Theologica*, I, qu. 93, art. 4–8.

Augustine. *The Trinity*. Ed. John E. Rotelle. Trans. Edmund Hill. Brooklyn, NY: New City Press, 1990.

Barnes, Michel René. "Augustine in Contemporary Trinitarian Theology." *Theological Studies* 56 (1995): 237–250.

Barth, Karl. *Church Dogmatics*. Vol. II/1 § 28. 4 vols. Edinburgh: T. & T. Clark, 1936–69.

———. *Church Dogmatics*. Vol. IV/4 vols. Edinburgh: T. & T. Clark, 1936–69.

———. *The Doctrine of the Word of God: Prolegomena to Church Dogmatics, being Volume I/1*. Trans. G. W. Bromiley. 2nd ed. Edinburgh: T. & T. Clark, 1975.

———. *Der Römerbrief*. 2nd ed. [N.p.], 1922 (English translation, *The Epistle to the Romans*. Trans. E. C. Hoskyns. [N.p.], 1933).

Bauckham, Richard. "Jürgen Moltmann." In vol. 1 of *The Modern Theologians: An In-*

troduction to Christian Theology in the Twentieth Century, ed. David F. Ford, 293–310. Oxford: Basil Blackwell, 1989.

———. Moltmann: Messianic Theology in the Making. Basingstoke, UK: Marshall Pickering, 1987.

———. "Moltmanns Eschatologie des Kreuzes." In Diskussion über Jürgen Moltmanns Buch "Der gekreuzigte Gott," ed. Michael Welker, 43–53. Munich: Chr. Kaiser, 1979.

———. The Theology of Jürgen Moltmann. Edinburgh: T. & T. Clark, 1995.

Baur, F[erdinand] C[hristian]. Die christliche Lehre von der Dreieinigkeit und Menschwerdung Gottes in ihrer geschichtlichen Entwicklung. 3 vols. Tübingen: [n.p.], 1843.

Bonhoeffer, Dietrich. Creation and Fall: A Theological Interpretation of Genesis 1–3. Trans. J. C. Fletcher. London: SCM Press, 1959.

———. Letters and Papers from Prison. Enlarged ed. London: SCM Press, 1971.

Brümmer, Vincent. The Model of Love: A Study in Philosophical Theology. Cambridge: Cambridge University Press, 1993.

Capps, Walter H. Time Invades the Cathedral: Tensions in the School of Hope. With a foreword by Jürgen Moltmann. Philadelphia: Fortress Press, 1972.

Charry, Ellen. By the Renewing of Your Minds: The Pastoral Function of Christian Doctrine. New York: Oxford University Press, 1997.

Chopp, Rebecca S. "Anointed to Preach: Speaking of Sin in the Midst of Grace." In The Portion of the Poor: Good News to the Poor in the Wesleyan Tradition, ed. M. Douglas Meeks, 97–111. Nashville, TN: Kingswood Books, 1995.

———. "Praxis." In The New Dictionary of Catholic Spirituality, ed. Michael Downey, 756–764. Collegeville, MN: Liturgical Press, 1993.

———. The Praxis of Suffering: An Interpretation of Liberation and Political Theologies. Maryknoll, NY: Orbis, 1986.

Cunningham, David S. These Three Are One: The Practice of Trinitarian Theology. Oxford: Basil Blackwell, 1998.

Dalferth, Ingolf U. Der auferweckte Gekreuzigte: Zur Grammatik der Christologie. Tübingen: J. C. B. Mohr, 1994.

Feenstra, Ronald J., and Cornelius Plantinga Jr., eds. Trinity, Incarnation, and Atonement: Philosophical and Theological Essays. Notre Dame, IN: University of Notre Dame Press, 1989.

Fiddes, Paul S. The Creative Suffering of God. Oxford: Clarendon Press, 1988.

Grey, Mary. "Falling into Freedom: Searching for New Interpretations of Sin in a Secular Society." Scottish Journal of Theology 47, (1994): 223–243.

Gunton, Colin E. The One, the Three and the Many: God, Creation and the Culture of Modernity. Bampton Lectures 1992. Cambridge: Cambridge University Press, 1993.

Hodgson, Leonard. The Doctrine of the Trinity. Croall Lectures, 1942–43. New York: Charles Scribner's Sons, 1944.

Hunsinger, George. "The Crucified God and the Political Theology of Violence." Heythrop Journal 14 (1973): 266–279.

Jeanrond, Werner. "The Question of God Today." In The Christian Understanding of God Today, ed. James M. Byrne, 14–17. Theological Colloquium on the Occasion of the 400th Anniversary of the Foundation of Trinity College, Dublin. Dublin: Columbia Press, 1993.

Johnson, Elisabeth A. *She Who Is: The Mystery of God in Feminist Theological Discourse.* New York: Crossroad, 1992.

———. "To Let the Symbol Sing Again." *Theology Today* 53 (1997): 299–311.

Jones, L. Gregory. *Embodying Forgiveness: A Theological Analysis.* Grand Rapids, MI: Eerdmans, 1995.

———. *Transformed Judgment: Toward a Trinitarian Account of the Moral Life.* Notre Dame, IN: University of Notre Dame Press, 1990.

Jones, Serene. *Feminist Theory and Theology: Cartographies of Grace.* Philadelphia: Fortress Press, 2000.

———. "What's Wrong with Us?" In *Essentials of Christian Theology,* ed. William C. Placher, 141–158. Louisville, KY: Westminster John Knox Press, 2003.

Kasper, Walter. "Revolution im Gottesverständnis? Zur Situation des ökumenischen Dialogs nach Jürgen Moltmanns 'Der gekreuzigte Gott.'" In *Diskussion über Jürgen Moltmanns Buch "Der gekreuzigte Gott,"* ed. Michael Welker, 140–148. Munich: Chr. Kaiser, 1979.

Kilby, Karen. "Perichoresis and Projection: Problems with Social Doctrines of the Trinity." *New Blackfriars* 81, no. 956 (Oct. 2000): 432–445.

Klappert, Bertold. "Die Gottverlassenheit Jesu und der gekreuzigte Gott. Beobachtungen zum Problem einer theologia crucis in der Christologie der Gegenwart." In *Diskussion über Jürgen Moltmanns Buch "Der gekreuzigte Gott,"* ed. Michael Welker, 57–73. Munich: Chr. Kaiser, 1979.

Krötke, Wolf. "The Humanity of the Human Person in Karl Barth's Anthropology." In *The Cambridge Companion to Karl Barth,* ed. John Webster, 159–176. Cambridge: Cambridge University Press, 2000.

LaCugna, Catherine Mowry. *God for Us: The Trinity and the Christian Life.* San Francisco: HarperCollins, 1991.

———. "Re-conceiving the Trinity as the Mystery of Salvation." *Scottish Journal of Theology* 38 (1985): 1–23.

LaCugna, Catherine Mowry, and Killian McDonnell. "Returning from 'The Far Country': Theses for a Contemporary Trinitarian Theology." *Scottish Journal of Theology* 41 (1988): 191–215.

Lash, Nicholas. "Considering the Trinity." *Modern Theology* 2 (1986): 183–196.

Link, Christian. "Schöpfung im messianischen Licht." *Evangelische Theologie* 47 (1987): 83–92.

Link, Hans-Georg. "Gegenwärtige Probleme einer Kreuzestheologie: Ein Bericht." *Evangelische Theologie* 33 (1973): 337–345.

Mackey, James. "Are There Christian Alternatives to Trinitarian Thinking?" In *The Christian Understanding of God Today,* ed. James M. Byrne, 66–75. Theological Colloquium on the Occasion of the 400th Anniversary of the Foundation of Trinity College, Dublin. Dublin: Columbia Press, 1993.

Macpherson, C. B. *The Political Theory of Possessive Individualism.* Oxford: [n.p.], 1962.

Marsch, Wolf-Dieter, ed. *Diskussion über die "Theologie der Hoffnung" von Jürgen Moltmann.* Munich: Chr. Kaiser, 1967.

———. "Zur Einleitung: Wohin—jenseits der Alternativen." In *Diskussion über die "Theologie der Hoffnung" von Jürgen Moltmann,* ed. Wolf-Dieter Marsch, 7–18. Munich: Chr. Kaiser, 1967.

Maurer, Ernstpeter. "Tendenzen neuerer Trinitätslehre." *Verkündigung und Forschung* 39, no. 2 (1994): 3–24.

McDougall, Joy Ann. "A Room of One's Own? Trinitarian Perichoresis as Analogy for the God-Human Relationship." In *Wo ist Gott? Gottesräume—Lebensräume*, ed. Jürgen Moltmann and Carmen Rivuzumwami, 133–141. Neukirchen-Vluyn: Neukirchener Verlag, 2002.

McFague, Sallie. "Is God in Charge?" In *Essentials of Christian Theology*, ed. William C. Placher, 101–116. Louisville, KY: Westminster John Knox Press, 2003.

———. *Models of God: Theology for an Ecological, Nuclear Age.* Philadelphia: Fortress Press, 1987.

Meeks, M. Douglas. Foreword to *The Experiment Hope*, by Jürgen Moltmann, ed. and trans. M. Douglas Meeks, ix–xvii. Philadelphia: Fortress Press, 1975.

———. "Jürgen Moltmann's *Systematic Contributions to Theology.*" *Religious Studies Review* 22, no. 2 (Apr. 1996): 95–102.

———. *Origins of the Theology of Hope.* With a foreword by Jürgen Moltmann. Philadelphia: Fortress Press, 1974.

Milbank, John. "The Second Difference: For a Trinitarianism without Reserve." *Modern Theology* 2 (1986): 213–234.

Miskotte, Hermannus Heiko. "Das Leiden ist in Gott. Über Jürgen Moltmanns trinitarische Kreuzestheologie." In *Diskussion über Jürgen Moltmanns Buch "Der gekreuzigte Gott,"* ed. Michael Welker, 74–93. Munich: Chr. Kaiser, 1979.

Morse, Christopher. *The Logic of Promise in Moltmann's Theology.* Philadelphia: Fortress Press, 1979.

Müller-Fahrenholz, Geiko. *The Kingdom and the Power: The Theology of Jürgen Moltmann.* Trans. John Bowden. London: SCM Press, 2000.

Nicholls, David. *Deity and Domination: Images of God and the State in the Nineteenth and Twentieth Centuries.* London: Routledge, 1989.

Niebuhr, Reinhold. *Human Destiny.* Vol. 2 of *The Nature and Destiny of Man: A Christian Interpretation.* New York: Charles Scribner's Sons, 1943.

O'Donnell, John J. *Trinity and Temporality: The Christian Doctrine of God in the Light of Process Theology and the Theology of Hope.* Oxford: Oxford University Press, 1983.

———. "The Trinity as Divine Community: A Critical Reflection upon Recent Theological Developments." *Gregorianum* 69 (1988): 5–34.

Pannenberg, Wolfhart. *Systematic Theology.* Trans. Geoffrey W. Bromiley. 3 vols. Grand Rapids, MI: Eerdmans, 1991–98.

Pauw, Amy Plantinga. "Attending to the Gaps between Beliefs and Practices." In *Practicing Theology: Beliefs and Practices in Christian Life*, ed. Miroslav Volf and Dorothy C. Bass, 33–48. Grand Rapids, MI: Eerdmans, 2002.

Peterson, Erik. "Monotheismus als politisches Problem." In Erik Peterson, *Theologische Traktate.* Munich: [n.p.], 1951.

Rahner, Karl. *Grundkurs des Glaubens.* Freiburg: [Herder], 1976.

———. "Remarks on the Dogmatic Treatise 'De Trinitate.'" In Karl Rahner, *More Recent Writings*, vol. 4 of *Theological Investigations*, trans. Kevin Smyth, 77–102. London: Darton, Longman and Todd, 1966.

———. *The Trinity.* Trans. Joseph Donceel. New York: Herder and Herder, 1970.

Ratzinger, Joseph. "Liebe." In vol. 6 of *Lexikon für Theologie und Kirche*, ed. Michael Buchberger et al., 2nd ed., 1031–1036. Freiburg: Herder, 1957.

Ricoeur, Paul. *The Symbolism of Evil*. Boston: Beacon Press, 1967.

Rosenzweig, Franz. *Der Stern der Erlösung*. Heidelberg: [n.p.], 1954.

Schmaus, M[ichael]. *Die psychologische Trinitätslehre des Heiligen Augustinus*. Münster: [n.p.], 1927.

Schüssler Fiorenza, Francis. Introduction to *Faith and the Future: Essays on Theology, Solidarity, and Modernity*, by Johann-Baptist Metz and Jürgen Moltmann, xi–xvii. Maryknoll, NY: Orbis, 1995.

Schwöbel, Christoph. "Imago Libertatis: Human and Divine Freedom." In *God and Freedom: Essays in Historical and Systematic Theology*, ed. Colin E. Gunton, 57–81. Edinburgh: T. & T. Clark, 1995.

Tanner, Kathryn. *God and Creation in Christian Theology: Tyranny or Empowerment?* Oxford: Basil Blackwell, 1988.

———. "Theological Reflection and Christian Practices." In *Practicing Theology: Beliefs and Practices in Christian Life*, ed. Miroslav Volf and Dorothy C. Bass, 228–242. Grand Rapids, MI: Eerdmans, 2002.

Torrance, Alan J. *Persons in Communion: An Essay on Trinitarian Description and Human Participation*. Edinburgh: T. & T. Clark, 1996.

Tracy, David. "The Hermeneutics of Naming God." *Irish Theological Quarterly* 57 (1991): 253–264.

Volf, Miroslav. *After Our Likeness: The Church as the Image of the Trinity*. Grand Rapids, MI: Eerdmans, 1998.

———. "The Trinity Is Our Social Program? The Doctrine of the Trinity and the Shape of Social Engagement." *Modern Theology* 14 (1998): 403–423.

Vorgrimler, Herbert. "Recent Critiques of Theism." In *A Personal God?* ed. Edward Schillebeeckx and Bas van Iersel, 23–34. New York: Seabury Press, 1977.

Weber, O[tto]. *Grundlagen der Dogmatik*. 2 vols. Neukirchen-Vluyn: [n.p.], [1955]–62.

Welker, Michael. ed. *Diskussion über Jürgen Moltmanns Buch "Der gekreuzigte Gott."* Munich: Chr. Kaiser, 1979.

Williams, Daniel Day. *The Spirit and the Forms of Love*. New York: Harper and Row, 1968.

Index

adventus, 35–36, 49
    See also eschatology; *futurum*
agape, 25, 56, 66
    as creative love of the other, 48
    as crucified or kenotic love, 72,
        75, 154
    vs. *eros*, 143–144
    Moltmann's early dialectical
        concept of, 44, 55, 57–58, 75,
        154
    vs. *philia*, 44
    See also divine love
analogy of relations (*analogia
    relationis*), 26, 102, 115–119, 121
    as analogy of grace, 136–137
    vs. analogy of substance, 115
    *See also imago Dei; imago
        Trinitatis*
anthropology, theological
    concept of sin in, 148
    modern individualism (atomism)
        in, 102, 161
    Moltmann's critique of
        Augustine's, 104–107, 117
    Moltmann's critique of Barth's,
        103–104, 106
    Moltmann's critique of Western,
        102–107

Moltmann's reconstruction of, 113–
    119, 141, 160–161
    See also imago Dei
appropriations, doctrine of, 78
Aquinas, 54, 88, 105, 110, 163
Augustine, 54, 70, 95, 110, 132, 163
    appropriations and, 78
    concept of freedom in, 77
    interiorization of the *imago Dei*
        and, 106
    love analogy for the Trinity and,
        48, 61, 74, 90
    model of the *imago Dei* and, 104–
        107, 116
    monarchical monotheism and,
        88, 103–104
    psychological analogy for the
        Trinity and, 104–105, 117, 182
        n.126, 184 n.12
    relational concept of personhood
        and, 96
    subordination of the Spirit in, 62,
        90
    See also imago Dei

Barth, Karl, 11, 15, 163
    biblical root of the Trinity as
        Lordship, 11, 79, 182 n.116

Barth, Karl (*continued*)
　　Church Dogmatics, 29–30, 77
　　divine freedom and, 76–78, 104
　　God as absolute subject and, 88–89
　　modalism and, 88–89
　　model of revelation and, 32
　　monarchical monotheism and, 70, 103–
　　　104
　　re-birth of the Spirit and, 138
　　theological anthropology and, 103–104,
　　　106
Bauckham, Richard, 44, 51, 112
Berdyaev, Nikolai, 72–73
biblical-narrative approach to the Trinity,
　　12–13, 155
Bloch, Ernst, 17, 34–36
Boethius, 70, 95
Bonhoeffer, Dietrich, 13, 17, 51
Brümmer, Vincent, 4–5
Bultmann, Rudolph, 31–32

Calvin, John, 108, 110, 163
Camus, Albert, 39, 53
Cappadocian Fathers, 70, 108
Chalcedon, Council of, 53
Chopp, Rebecca, 21, 151
Christian life, 121–151 (esp. 137–144),
　　167
Christian monotheism. *See* monarchical
　　monotheism
christology, dialectical, 26, 29, 37–38, 55–
　　58
christology, pneumatological, 124–125
christology, social, 125–130
Clerical monotheism, 140
Constantinople, Council of, 53
Creation
　　consummation of, in Christ, 129
　　divine love and, 74–75
　　pneumatological and messianic
　　　theology of, 107–113
　　Spirit of (*ruach*), 131
　　theological anthropology and, 113–
　　　119
　　as trinitarian act, 83–85, 87
critical praxis correlation, 21

cross-event, 65, 126
　　as act of divine surrender, 40–43, 46–
　　　48, 126, 154
　　as open-event, 56, 64
　　soteriological significance of, 40–43,
　　　56, 125–130
　　as starting-point for the doctrine of the
　　　Trinity, 12–13, 56, 61
　　as trinitarian dialectic of love, 43–50,
　　　56–57, 62, 154–155
　　See also divine passion; divine
　　　suffering
Cunningham, David, 8, 106–107, 146,
　　148

deification, 63, 130
democratic socialism, 139
dialectical theology, 17, 23
divine freedom
　　as free choice vs. freedom for the
　　　good, 76–77
　　and freedom of creation, 8, 73–75
　　as friendship (fellowship), 76–78
　　in relationship to history, 50
divine lordship 11, 77, 79
divine love, 30, 36, 153–159
　　cross-event and, 43–50
　　as dialectic of crucified and creative
　　　love, 55–58, 75, 154
　　divine freedom and, 76–78
　　as ecstatic self-communication of the
　　　good, 72–78
　　as *eros* vs. *agape*, 143–144
　　as freedom from suffering vs. freedom
　　　for suffering, 54–55
　　and relationship to human loves, 58,
　　　141–144
　　and *Shekinah*, 51–52
　　as trinitarian fellowship (*koinonia*), 26,
　　　155–157
　　trinitarian history of God and, 25, 64,
　　　71
　　as unconditional suffering with the
　　　other, 51
　　See also divine passion; trinitarian
　　　fellowship

divine passion, 67, 72–75, 155–156
   See also divine love; divine suffering;
     pathos, divine
divine rule. *See* divine lordship;
   trinitarian fellowship
divine suffering, 40–50 (esp. 40–43), 50–
   55, 75
   See also divine love
divine unity
   eschatological concept of, 67, 82, 98
   as *perichoresis*, 97–99
   social concept of, as unitedness, 90
   tritheism and, 90, 98
   union of God with creation, 67, 82
   volitional vs. ontological reality, 98
Dostoyevsky, Fyodor, 39, 53
doxological theology, 19–20
doxological Trinity, 12–13, 91–99
doxology, 21–22, 64

Eastern Orthodox theology, 12, 63–64, 89
ecclesiology, 60–61
   See also exodus church
economic Trinity
   relationship of immanent Trinity to,
     46, 65, 71, 91–92
ecstasis, 73–74, 155
   See also divine love
epistemology, theological, 44–45
eros, 143–144
   See also divine love
eschatology
   concept of future in, 35–36, 49
   creation and, 111–113
   cross-event and, 48–49, 64–65
   divine unity and, 67, 98–99
   freedom as future and, 133
   hope and, 31–37
   nature and task of theology and, 23–
     25, 37
   resurrection-event and, 33–34, 56, 63
   Spirit of new creation and, 62–67
   trinitarian history of God and, 64–67
   See also adventus; *futurum*; kingdom of
     God
exodus church, 17

fellowship, trinitarian. *See* trinitarian
   fellowship
fellowship with Christ, 130
filioque debate, 94–95
freedom, divine. *See* divine freedom
freedom, human. *See* human freedom
friendship, 140–144, 146
   See also divine freedom; human
     freedom; trinitarian fellowship
futurum, 35–36, 49
   See also adventus; eschatology

German Idealism, 35, 50, 88–90
Gestalt, 118
Geyer, Hans-Georg, 53
Gogarten, Friedrich, 31
Grace
   analogy of relation as gift of, 115, 137,
     160
   criticisms of Moltmann's theology of,
     8, 136–137, 160–161
   as gift of life, 134
   sanctification and, 136
   See also Holy Spirit
Grey, Mary, 150

Horkheimer, Max, 39
Harnack, Adolf von, 79
Hegel, G.W.F., 47, 49–50, 95–96
   See also German Idealism
Heschel, Abraham, 51–52
Hodgson, Leonard, 3
Holy Spirit
   as bond of love (*vinculum caritatis*), 47–
     48, 56, 61–62, 89
   consummation of creation and, 81, 86–
     87
   as creative love, 47–48
   Eastern and Western models of, 94
   fellowship with human beings and,
     62, 131–132
   gifts of, in the Christian life, 132–134
   human experience of, 86, 131, 135–
     136
   messianic doctrine of creation and, 110–
     113

Holy Spirit (*continued*)
in Moltmann's mature theology, 86–
87, 95, 108–109, 148–150
as Spirit of creation (*ruach*), 108, 131–
132, 148
as Spirit of life, 131–134, 148
See also grace; pneumatology; re-birth
in the Spirit
human freedom
as freedom for and with another
person, 162
as liberating faith, love, and hope, 132–
134
open friendship and, 145–147
See also trinitarian fellowship

imago Christi, 26, 124, 136
human being's messianic destiny as,
102, 113–119, 121–122, 129–130, 161
See also imago Dei; *imago Trinitatis*
imago Dei
as analogy of domination, 105
as analogy of relations, 26, 102, 121
Jesus Christ as consummation of, 85,
129–130
as messianic (eschatological) destiny,
102, 114
Moltmann's model of, 26, 113–119, 140–
141, 160–161
psychological analogy for the Trinity
and, 104–106
rational soul as, 105, 140
See also anthropology, theological;
imago Christi; *imago Trinitatis*
imago Trinitatis
Augustine's psychological analogy and,
105
as messianic destiny, 101–102, 150–151,
160–161
Moltmann's social model of, 26, 113–
119, 121, 141, 161
in political sphere, 139
See also imago Dei
immanent Trinity
doxological theology and knowledge of,
19–20
Moltmann's model of, 8, 15, 91–99

relationship of economic Trinity to, 46,
65, 71, 91–92
incarnation, 83, 85–87
Iwand, Hans Joachim, 11

Jeanrond, Werner, 8, 146
Joachim of Fiore, 70
John the Damascene, 97
Johnson, Elisabeth A., 6
Jüngel, Eberhard, 53
justification, doctrine of, 126–130, 134–
135

Käsemann, Ernst, 11
Kasper, Walter, 50
kenosis
creation and inward act of, 85–86
as delivering up, 47
trinitarian model of, 46–48, 56, 87,
126
See also divine passion; divine
suffering
Kilby, Karen, 9, 146, 188 n.47
King, Martin Luther, 38
kingdom of God, 56, 79, 125, 127
creation and, 110–113
divine rule and, 81–82, 98
freedom in, 68, 138
nature and task of theology and, 23–
24, 163–164
trinitarian fellowship and the, 7, 81,
156, 162
See also eschatology
koinonia. See trinitarian fellowship

LaCugna, Catherine Mowry, 5–6
Lash, Nicholas, 3
love, divine. *See* divine love
love, human, 143–146
See also divine love; trinitarian
fellowship
Luria, Isaac, 84
Luther, Martin, 43, 58

Marxist-Christian dialogue, 39
Maximus the Confessor, 143
McFague, Sallie, 4–5, 8, 109–110

Meeks, Douglas, 30
Messianic Praxis of Trinitarian
    Fellowship, 137–151
Metz, Johann-Baptist, 17
Miskotte, Hermannus, 49–50, 61
modalism, 4, 70, 89, 96, 158
Moltmann-Wendel, Elisabeth, 17
monarchial monotheism
    Western doctrine of the Trinity and, 6,
        68, 70, 87–90, 158, 181 n.110
    Western theological anthropology and,
        102–107
monarchianism, monotheistic. See
    monarchial monotheism
Müller-Fahrenholz, Geiko, 137–138

narrative theology, 169 n.46
natural theology, 43–44
nature and task of theology, 20–22, 23–
    25, 163–164
    as theologia viae vs. theologia patriae, 37
Niebuhr, Reinhold, 165–166 n.6

oikonomia, 14–15, 45
open friendship, 142–143, 145–146, 162
Origen, 70–72

panentheism, eschatological, 64, 159
panentheism, trinitarian, 84, 110
pantheism, 84
pathos, divine, 51, 52, 72
    See also divine passion; Shekinah
perichoresis
    divine life and, 123, 156
    Moltmann's use of term, 97–98, 109–
        110, 162–163, 188 n.47
    relationship of body and soul, 118
    Spirit's fellowship with the world, 108–
        109, 131
    See also divine unity
persons, divine, 83, 92–95, 95–97
philia, 44, 146
philosophy of hope, Bloch's, 34–36
pilgrimage of love, 22, 25–26, 78
Placher, William, 110
Plantinga Pauw, Amy, 147

pneumatology, trinitarian, xiii, 60–62, 65–
    66, 86, 107–110
    See also Holy Spirit
political monotheism, 103
    See also monarchial monotheism
political theology, 17
praxis, 16–22, 167 n.18
    See also Christian life; Messianic
        Praxis of Trinitarian Fellowship
process philosophy, 35
protest atheism, 6, 39, 53–55
public theology, 23

Rad, Gerhard von, 32–33
Rahner, Karl, 4, 46, 70, 88–91
re-birth (regeneration) in the Spirit, 134–
    136
    See also sanctification; Holy Spirit
relational ontology, 8, 96–97
resurrection-event, 14, 33–34, 55–56, 63,
    127–129
    as inseparable from cross-event, 33, 38,
        41–42, 127
revelation, biblical, 32–33, 36–37, 56
Richard of St. Victor, 70, 95–96
Ricouer, Paul, 22
Rolt, Richard, 72
Rosenzweig, Franz, 67

Sabbath, as feast of creation, 111
salvation
    as consummation of creation, 129
    as deification, 63–64, 123, 130
    foundation of, in Christ, 125–130
    as personal representation vs. penal
        sacrifice, 127
    Protestant order of, 134–137
    trinitarian pattern of, 26, 122–137, 142,
        147
    See also cross-event
sanctification, 136
    See also grace
Schelling, Friedrich, 44
Schleiermacher, Friedrich, 15, 70
scriptures, trinitarian hermeneutics of,

xiii, 11–13, 59, 69–70, 157–158, 191–
192 n.1
See also biblical narrative approach to
the Trinity
Shekinah, 51–52, 67, 72, 84, 108, 125
See also divine love
sin, doctrine of, 43, 123–124, 128, 135,
148
critique of Moltmann's doctrine of, xiv,
147–151, 163
social trinitarian analogy of fellowship,
10, 101, 113, 118–119, 121–122, 159–
164
See also analogy of relations
Soteriology. See salvation
Staniloae, Dimitru, 63

Tanner, Kathryn, 110
Tertullian, 88
theism, 4–5, 53–55, 107, 166 n.14, 177
n.108
theodicy, question of, 39, 53–55
theologia, 14–15, 45
theology after Auschwitz, 39, 52
theology of glory, 44
theology of hope, 31–37
theology of play, 18
theology of the Cross, 17–18, 37–58, 61,
68
theology, doxological, 19, 21
Torrance, Alan, 8, 109–110, 136–137, 149
transfiguration, 86–87
trinitarian fellowship (koinonia)
Christian life and, 7, 16, 18, 133, 138–
144, 147
as communal attribute of Father, Son,
and Spirit, 81, 97, 158
and divine love, 155–157, 159
and divine rule (kingdom), 79–82, 93,
158
as essence of the triune God, 77–78,
99
and experiences of friendship and love,
140–144
nature of, 97–98, 123, 142, 156–157
relationship of God and creation as,
82, 107, 109

as rule of faith, 27, 138, 144–147, 160–
161
salvation as participation in, 15, 122–125
sin as distortion of, 149–151
as structuring theological principle in
Messianic Theology, 10, 156
as theological doctrine of freedom, 9
See also Messianic Praxis of Trinitarian
Fellowship; social trinitarian analogy
of fellowship
trinitarian history of God, 12, 56, 62, 65–
71, 78, 87, 97–99
divine love and, 13
divine sovereignty over creation and,
49
eschatological goal of, 64, 73
relationship to Hegel's concept of, 49–
50
trinitarian praxis, 6, 16–22
See also Messianic Praxis of Trinitarian
Fellowship
Trinity
Augustine's model of, 48, 61
biblical root of, 11–13, 69–70, 77, 79,
155
and the Christian life, 6, 10, 147, 162
christological root for the doctrine of,
78–82
christomonism and, 4
contemporary revival of doctrine, 5–10,
153–164
divine love and, 3–5
as eschatological process, 48–49
forms of the, 12–13, 69
modalism and, 4, 70, 89, 96, 158
Moltmann's doctrine of, 7, 9, 10, 19,
21, 22, 68, 78–82, 87–99 (esp. 95–
99)
as political and doxological doctrine,
16–22
practical relevance of doctrine, 6–7,
48, 146–147, 161–162
soteriological approach to the doctrine,
6, 13–16, 46, 50, 57, 61, 65, 154–155
See also cross-event; social trinitarian
analogy of fellowship; trinitarian
fellowship

Trinity in the glorification, 62–67, 85
  See also trinitarian history of God
Trinity in the origin, 62, 71
  See also divine passion
Trinity in the sending, 62, 64, 66, 69,
  71, 87
  See also trinitarian history of God
tritheism, xii, 90–91, 98–99, 158

Unamuno, Miguel, 72–73

Volf, Miroslav, 161

Weber, Otto, 11, 135
Welker, Michael, 50
Williams, Daniel Day, 25
Wolf, Ernst, 11

Zimmerli, Ernst, 11, 32
zimsum theory, 84–85

CPSIA information can be obtained at www.ICGtesting.com
Printed in the USA
BVOW011030311212

309304BV00005B/90/A